Teaching STEM

by Andrew Zimmerman Jones

Teaching STEM For Dummies®

Published by: **John Wiley & Sons, Inc.**, 111 River Street, Hoboken, NJ 07030-5774, www.wiley.com

For general information on our other products and services, please contact our Customer Care Department within the U.S. at 877-762-2974, outside the U.S. at 317-572-3993, or fax 317-572-4002. For technical support, please visit https://hub.wiley.com/community/support/dummies.

Wiley publishes in a variety of print and electronic formats and by print-on-demand. Some material included with standard print versions of this book may not be included in e-books or in print-on-demand. If this book refers to media that is not included in the version you purchased, you may download this material at http://booksupport.wiley.com. For more information about Wiley products, visit www.wiley.com.

Library of Congress Control Number: 2025934644

ISBN 978-1-394-31346-4 (pbk); ISBN 978-1-394-31348-8 (ePDF); ISBN 978-1-394-31347-1 (epub)

SKY10100824_032425

Table of Contents

Introduction

What would the world look like without global shipping logistics, telecommunications, world financial markets, the pharmaceutical industry, and streaming videos of unlikely pet friendships set to upbeat music? Some might argue that it would be a better world, but it wouldn't be *our* world. The modern world relies on scientific discoveries applied through technological feats of engineering implemented with immense levels of numerical precision. In other words, it relies on science, technology, engineering, and mathematics, otherwise known as STEM, working together.

A world that hangs together on those disciplines should also prioritize educational approaches and policies that teach them. Around the world, educators are discovering that their students are far more advanced than they are in some of these STEM areas, and woefully behind in others. Students who bypass the school's internet security with ease may go on to fail tests that cover basic math skills.

Engaging students with STEM lessons that motivate deep learning is an imperative to bridge these gaps. Teachers must meet the students where they are and lead them to where they need to be. Giving teachers the tools they need to accomplish this mission is the goal of this book. And so, *Teaching STEM For Dummies* takes on the mission of informing you about teaching STEM disciplines.

About This Book

This book serves as an accessible guide for teaching STEM subjects, primarily through classrooms or formal lessons. Here are a couple of things to watch out for in the book:

>> **Source material is summarized.** Though the solutions offered throughout this book are based on the latest scholarship in the science of STEM learning, I focus on clearly summarizing research results and implications rather than quoting researchers directly or citing numerous individual sources. In cases where a single, definitive text on a subject exists, I provide information on that source and, if possible, a link to access it for free.

>> **Web addresses appear in monofont.** If you're reading a digital version of this book on a device connected to the internet, note that you can click the web address — like this one: `www.dummies.com` — to visit that website.

To make the content of this book more accessible, I've divided it into five parts.

>> **Part 1: Getting Started with Teaching STEM.** This part of the book gives a broad overview of STEM education and teaching, including definitions, overviews of the content, and key concepts. I also cover the reason why teaching STEM is so important and the history of STEM education in the United States.

>> **Part 2: Gathering the Building Blocks of STEM.** Throughout this part, I explore the four areas of STEM (science, technology, engineering, and mathematics), including many of the relevant national academic standards. I also discuss ways to integrate STEM subjects with each other and combine them with other subjects, such as English, social studies, and the arts.

>> **Part 3: Employing Approaches to STEM Education.** In this part, I dive into the key elements of creating a STEM lesson and a STEM curriculum, including how to assess STEM education to figure out student progress. I also cover additional ways to enhance the STEM program for your students.

>> **Part 4: Troubleshooting STEM Education.** This part focuses on a variety of cases that dive into the particular aspects of teaching STEM, including planning for classroom needs, finding opportunities for STEM instruction at home, and working with diverse student populations.

>> **Part 5: The Part of Tens.** A classic feature of the *For Dummies* series is the Part of Tens chapters. In this part, you can get some ideas for quick and easy STEM lessons that you can do with little prep and resources that should be available to you free or for a low cost.

Foolish Assumptions

This book is for anyone who teaches STEM subjects to a younger or less experienced person. Though I often reference *teachers*, *students*, *classrooms*, and *schools* throughout this book, most of the information is also useful for homeschooling, tutoring, and non-traditional STEM teaching environments and situations.

I do make the following assumptions about you, the people who are reading this book:

>> **You know the content that you're teaching** (though you need not be an expert). I don't spend much time explaining the actual STEM concepts, except for a bit in Part 2 at a high level. You can find other resources (including many in the *For Dummies* series) if you need a deeper understanding of a specific subject such as physics, biology, or 3D printing.

>> **You have some background experience with the fundamentals of teaching,** such as classroom management strategies and preparing lesson plans, either through formal training or that you picked up along the way. If you need those fundamentals, then two great resources are *Instructional Design for Dummies* and *First Year Teaching For Dummies*.

>> **Your goal is to teach STEM content broadly,** rather than to focus on teaching a specific skill within STEM. Someone teaching a STEM-related career certification course can benefit from this book, but I didn't write it specifically for those situations.

Guidance throughout this book is useful for educators at a range of levels, from administrators to individual teachers and even parents wanting to give more STEM opportunities to their kids.

Icons Used in This Book

Throughout this book, icons in the margins highlight certain types of valuable information that they call out for your attention. Here are the icons you encounter and a brief description of each.

TIP

The Tip icon marks tips and shortcuts that you can use to make planning lessons and teaching STEM easier.

REMEMBER

The Remember icon marks information that's especially important to know. To siphon off the most important information in each chapter, you can just skim through these icons.

TECHNICAL STUFF

The Technical Stuff icon marks information of a highly technical nature that you can normally skip over. (This one isn't often used in this book.)

WARNING

The Warning icon tells you to watch out! It marks important information that may save you headaches, particularly content that can easily cause problems when presented poorly.

Beyond the Book

In addition to the abundance of information and guidance related to teaching STEM that I provide in this book, you get access to even more help and information online at dummies.com. To check out this book's online Cheat Sheet, just go to www.dummies.com and search for *Teaching STEM For Dummies Cheat Sheet*.

Where to Go from Here

If you're looking to get a feel for STEM in general, then start at the beginning (Chapter 1) and work your way through from there. The *For Dummies* style is modular, so feel free to jump around in the book as needed. References within the text give an idea of where you might find useful information in another chapter.

If you are an experienced teacher looking to focus on understanding STEM content, you may want to dive straight into Part 2. If you are knowledgeable about STEM content but want tips on forming lessons, you might find that Part 3 is a good place to start. Of course, the Table of Contents and the Index are good places for finding specific topic.

1

Getting Started with Teaching STEM

Chapter **1**

The Nuts and Bolts of STEM Education

One of the most important jobs that anyone can have involves effectively educating the next generation. Although students need great teaching in all areas, this book emphasizes the teaching of *STEM*, the areas of science, technology, engineering, and mathematics. These four areas represent some of the more complex subjects that students encounter in K-12 (kindergarten through 12th grade in the U.S.) education. And teaching STEM has unique challenges, but the rewards that students receive — for example, satisfaction from accomplishing a worthwhile task and solving a real-world problem — from quality STEM instruction are tremendous.

STEM education is more than just a bundle of subjects, though. When done right, this education is also a student-centered approach to learning that emphasizes authentic, real-world problem-solving tasks that deeply engage the students.

In this chapter, I start by diving into the meaning of STEM education and then explore why teaching STEM enables teachers to get at important skills that traditional approaches often overlook. You find out how STEM lessons can help to motivate learning among students. Also, you discover how STEM approaches redefine the traditional classroom experience.

Thinking about the Meaning of STEM

What do you think of when you think of a STEM class? Do you picture a classroom with math equations written neatly on a dry-erase whiteboard? A clean and orderly science lab with beakers and test tubes? Students building a bridge out of craft sticks, straws, pipe cleaners, and cardboard? A cluttered workshop with a half-built robot? High-tech drones flying through an obstacle course?

TIP

Depending on their backgrounds, any two people can have starkly different images of what it means to teach STEM. Any time you discuss STEM with others, take some time to make sure that they are aware of their preconceptions. You want to be talking about the same thing.

Core STEM subjects

At the heart of STEM are four core subject areas that make up the acronym. Here are definitions that I use as a jumping-off point.

>> **Science:** Systemic approach to studying the structure and behavior of the natural and physical world, through a mix of observation and experimentation.

>> **Technology:** Study of making modifications to objects or structures in the natural world toward a human-driven goal.

>> **Engineering:** Systemic and iterative approach to designing objects, processes, and systems toward a human-driven goal, emphasizing design under given constraints.

>> **Mathematics:** Study of numbers, shapes, and patterns, as well as the abstract and concrete relationships between these concepts and their quantities.

Though schools have included mathematics and science for as long as anyone can remember, only in more recent years have schools demonstrated an explicit drive to loop in engineering and technology, even starting in early elementary school grades.

REMEMBER

Within the STEM paradigm, these four subject areas are not independent silos, isolated from each other and united only by a clever acronym. The point of using the acronym *STEM* is to highlight the underlying connections between these four areas. Some of the connections are obvious — such as the key role mathematics plays in both engineering and science — but some connections are far more subtle (for example, structural similarities between scientific experimentation and engineering design processes).

ACRONYM ORIGINS

The acronym STEM came from those rascals at the U.S. National Science Foundation (NSF), but when they began referring to the concept in the 1990s, they actually used the acronym SMET. In a way, this acronym made more sense because science and mathematics were more well-established as educational subjects, and the goal was to point out the need for greater emphasis on engineering and technology.

Around 2001, American biologist Judith A. Ramaley, assistant director of education and human resources of the NSF, decided to reorder the words to form the acronym STEM. This acronym caught on more broadly and took hold in the ensuing movement to expand teaching in these areas.

Is it a coincidence that a biologist changed the acronym to match the part of a plant? Probably. Regardless, everyone should be very grateful, because talking about STEM just feels better than talking about SMET.

I unpack each of these areas a bit more in Chapter 2 and dive into the related academic standards in Chapter 3. A far more intensive look within each category, and how they integrate together, comes in Part 2.

What different people mean when they say STEM

The four core areas of STEM cover a wide range of human activity, so when people apply the term *STEM*, they might be using it in different ways. Some people have an expansive definition of STEM (encompassing everything that includes any hint of these subjects), while others have a more restricted one (referring to only hands-on projects in a standalone STEM class that is designed to touch on *all* of these domains). In general, throughout this book, I take a pretty expansive definition of STEM. In other words, a mathematics class is a STEM class and benefits from incorporating recognized STEM educational practices into it — including finding ways to incorporate other STEM elements.

To be a little more specific, some people use related terms that may help to clarify or expand on the traditional (and potentially vague) acronym of STEM and related educational areas.

These related terms include the following:

>> **STEM subject:** A subject or class such as science, mathematics, algebra, biology, or computer science, which falls squarely within one of the four categories.

>> **Integrated STEM:** At least two STEM areas combined together, possibly in combination with another area such as art, literature, or social studies.

>> **STEAM:** Acronym for Science, Technology, Engineering, Art, and Mathematics, with an emphasis on highlighting the role of creativity.

>> **STEAMM:** Acronym for Science, Technology, Engineering, Art, Mathematics, and Music, which is like STEAM but also highlights the musical arts.

>> **STEMM:** Acronym for Science, Technology, Engineering, Mathematics, and Medicine, focusing on the medical sciences and service fields as a separate discipline.

>> **Career and Technical Education (CTE):** Related to teaching skilled trades and career preparation, particularly those areas with specific technical requirements. At one time, schools referred to these areas as *vocational arts* or *shop class*.

>> **The Maker Movement:** Cultural and educational movement that emphasizes construction, design, and invention, with a large overlap with the Do-It-Yourself (DIY) culture.

People can feel passionate about their particular acronym or phrasing, and since the goal with all of this is to make sure that students are engaged and learning, I generally find that getting into an argument over exactly what wording you're using isn't worthwhile. See the sidebar, "STEM, STEAM, and Creativity," for more thoughts about the use of various acronyms.

REMEMBER

I mainly use the STEM acronym throughout this book. And I don't intend to exclude the importance of artistic and other aspects to the problem-solving and critical-thinking processes.

Helping Students Acquire Necessary Skills

One way to think about education involves wanting kids, by the time they get out of high school (or college, if that's their path), to be the kind of people that you'd be happy to have as a neighbor or coworker. . .or both! Heck, you might even have them as an in-law!

Toward this goal, society evolved an educational system in which students participate in a little over a decade of education. During this time, teachers (and parents) strive to impart the civic and intellectual skills that will achieve this end — that of producing people who are well-adapted to both the job market and civic life.

But which skills do educators actually focus on? And how does STEM help impart those skills?

Academic skills

Most people naturally think of classes as focusing on teaching academic skills. Classes in school are named for the academic subjects, after all. STEM education is firmly rooted in teaching the academic disciplines, and teaching them with a high level of rigor, so nothing about teaching STEM means moving away from that. However, it may mean thinking about those academic disciplines and assessing those academic skills in less-traditional ways.

Sometimes, very bright kids just don't fit the mold of traditional students. Some very smart kids who can explain things well in discussions freeze up when taking tests. Or kids may test well but have grades that reflect an inability to turn in homework rather than a lack of knowledge.

Here's how the STEM approach steps in to help out all students.

REMEMBER

>> **It focuses on learning *and* doing:** One of the major goals of a STEM approach to education is to embed crucial academic skills in authentic, real-world problem-solving tasks. The learning and the doing of the task are mixed together, so it's very hard for any student to just coast on through without participating.

>> **It advances skills to a higher level:** The academic skills themselves move beyond just the memorization of facts. *How* you know or do things is just as important as *what* you know or do. More details on this concept in Chapter 2.

>> **It benefits kids across the ability spectrum:** Students who traditionally do well academically are successful in applying their knowledge in the real world. Students who haven't traditionally thrived academically have a new path, with practical activities giving context for previously esoteric knowledge.

Collaboration and employability skills

One other major element of STEM instruction is that it often moves away from a traditional individual approach (in which each student is working on their own task) to a structure that was once the bane of all overachievers — the *group project.*

Most people that I know have a negative view of group projects, and that's largely because the people they work with on the projects (the group) have let them down so many times. Historically, teaching collaboration and teamwork skills haven't been a strong component of classroom instruction.

Early education focuses on basic social skills such as getting along, but actually working productively in a group involves more than just not shoving your partner. These group collaboration skills rarely have been a point of explicit emphasis in traditional classroom instruction once you pass into upper elementary school.

REMEMBER

This lack of focus on collaborative skills makes sense in an environment in which science education looks primarily at acquiring knowledge and memorizing facts. When you need to know if each kid has memorized the facts, mixing a bunch of them to work together muddies the water, because you don't know for sure who contributed what. But when the process is just as important as the facts (like in the STEM approach), space opens up for different groups to explore different approaches and find those that work.

STEM, STEAM, AND CREATIVITY

The STEAM acronym has become increasingly popular in recent years. Solving a problem or designing something is inherently a creative act. When given an open-ended problem, groups of people approach it from wildly divergent paths.

As a result, I don't think the "Art" needs to be added in to STEM for you to know that designing and artistic creativity are part of the process. Creativity should be a natural part of the engineering design process (see Chapter 6). So, calling the educational approach STEAM is mostly about messaging.

Could a problem arise when using the STEAM acronym? My only reservation to this term stems from seeing a "STEAM project" that is little more than an art project about a vaguely science-adjacent concept. You could do a dozen such projects and feel like you've accomplished a lot of STEAM, even if you have perhaps touched only slightly on the deep learning of STEM concepts.

For more about integrating the arts and STEM together, see Chapter 8.

You can find out more about these skills in Chapter 2, and then about how to teach (and assess) them throughout Part 3.

Embracing the Challenge (and Promise) of STEM Education

In addition to teaching skills, STEM education meets students where they are and reinforces certain core educational values that will benefit them throughout their lifetimes. I cover these and more benefits of STEM education in greater depth in Chapter 2.

Establish a culture of learning

One sign of a successful, STEM-centered classroom is that students are continually looking for questions to ask, ideas to explore, and things to learn about. You don't want them to passively receive information but instead recognize knowledge as something that they can actively seek out.

Throughout the book, I return to this idea of creating a culture of learning (particularly in Chapters 9 and 13), but here are three key elements you can think about incorporating into your teaching approach immediately:

>> **Encourage intellectual risk-taking.** You might reward students who go out of their way to present an idea that seems out-of-the-box in some way. Instead of quickly dismissing such thinking to get on with the required lesson, validate such unorthodox ideas. You can maybe even spend some time discussing their implications and how you might be able to test or explore them (before returning to the lesson).

>> **Always create a central focus on student questions.** For example, maintain a physical space, such as a guiding questions board, where students can pose questions. Some questions will be resolved quickly, but others might linger and provide motivation for future lessons.

>> **Empower students to look for multiple answers.** Give them an opportunity to brainstorm and come up with as many possible answers before moving on to the stage of resolving whether any specific answer works.

WARNING

Often, teachers find themselves unintentionally thwarting these key elements through applying too much emphasis on getting the facts into the students' brains as quickly and efficiently as possible. And it's understandable, largely due to structural elements of the school day. Teachers have a lot of material to get through, often moving along at a set pace to meet defined learning objectives throughout the year. The neuroscience of learning (see Chapter 9) tells us that taking more time on the initial learning actually helps solidify the information more firmly in the learner's mind.

Encouraging questions is worth the risk

Though I love the saying, "There's no such thing as a stupid question," the reason it gets used so often is that people — both kids and adults — are constantly terrified that they're asking stupid questions. It can be incredibly difficult to ask a question in front of a group of people, especially when you sort of suspect that most of them actually know the answer and that you're revealing your ignorance.

TIP

One goal of a classroom should absolutely be that students feel intellectually safe. It is crucial that students not only feel comfortable displaying their knowledge, but also (and perhaps more importantly) demonstrating, acknowledging, and explaining their ignorance.

WARNING

Of course, this doesn't mean that a student should get by with being rude in the guise of asking questions. You don't have to tolerate an inherently offensive question like "Why is Andrew such an idiot?" just because you're trying to establish a question-asking culture.

Helping kids become question machines

I once heard a famous cosmologist (and also a parent) make the joke that, at some point, the answer to the question of "Why?" is "Go to bed." Kids, by nature, ask questions as a means of engaging with the unknown parts of the world — that is, until they are taught that asking those questions isn't acceptable.

As a teacher, you have no control over the messages kids are getting from their families, their friends, or the media they consume . . . but you can control how you're presenting things in your classroom.

Make sure that questions aren't just allowed but *encouraged*. Almost any lesson that you're doing can contain a couple of minutes in which you solicit a list of questions related to the subject. I cover some specifics on how to approach encouraging questions in Chapter 9.

Students who discover that asking questions is valuable don't just stop asking questions when the bell rings. After you establish that culture of learning, it increases student engagement in all areas. Students will also be inclined to ask questions about world and historical events, or about literature they're reading.

Turning students into answer seekers

It might seem like all of these new student-generated questions can only compound the frustration. How are you going to get through all the material you need to cover? But wait! Though they are comfortable asking you those questions, they aren't actually dependent upon you to give them the answers. In fact, answering all the questions is no longer your job! Your job has now become giving them the tools, resources, and space to figure out the answers on their own.

Being the source of answers to all student questions short-circuits the goal. You don't want to teach them that they can easily get answers to questions from an authority figure. You want to teach them how to figure out strategies to find the answers. Asking the question sets the student's mind on high alert to look for a path to the answers. If the student is mentally alert when engaging with the subject to ask questions, then that means they're also going to be looking for the answers to those questions.

Motivate students with engaging lessons

When you put the students' hands to work, you get their brains for free! And STEM lessons are great at giving students something to do with their hands, and then dragging the brain along for the ride.

Developing STEM lessons, particularly on the first try, might take some extra preparation compared to other types of lessons. For one thing, you often have to gather materials, or plan for the availability of necessary technology. But after you get the project (lesson) going, the students should really begin diving into it and taking ownership. This student engagement gives you the freedom to focus on the students who need help while other groups are able to progress on their own.

Throwing Out the Old Rulebook

You likely have a memory of a fairly traditional classroom experience, and one of my goals throughout this book is to challenge the assumption that the way you learned was the best way to learn. Or, at the very least, to challenge the idea that it was the *only* way to learn.

Despite all the changes that have taken place in classrooms over the years, if you walk into a traditional classroom in most of America today, you won't recognize a huge number of fundamental differences from fifty years ago. Yes, there are a few. Kids have computers and fewer books. Teachers are more likely to arrange desks in groups than orderly rows. Dry-erase whiteboards have replaced chalkboards, and overhead projectors are now digital.

But it's often still a teacher at the front of the class lecturing students. The big change in delivery comes from the occasional video.

Some of the changes noted are improvements, to be sure, but they also don't inherently transform education. A student half-listening to a lecture isn't significantly worse than a student half-listening to a video.

As you read through this book, I challenge you to think about what a classroom learning environment would be like if the students were actively engaged in the lessons. Is there a way to modify the approach to education that centers on the student, by elevating them as the owner of their learning?

My hope is that, by reading this book, you see that STEM provides a foundation for throwing out the old rulebook and building exactly the sort of engaging classroom that we need to educate future generations of lifelong learners.

Chapter **2**

What STEM Is (and Why It Matters)

Shortly after I became a district STEM coordinator, one of the teachers said to me, "I really love STEM, but I hate math." To her, STEM clearly meant something that didn't include mathematics (or, at the least, didn't include a traditional math class). Similarly, I've heard people ask questions like, "Is this lesson science or STEM?" So, some people draw distinctions that I wouldn't, because (as I say in Chapter 1) I use the term *STEM* expansively, and to me, every single science lesson and math lesson could be a STEM lesson, even in a stand-alone science or math class.

In this chapter, you find a broad overview of the meaning of STEM from a variety of perspectives. You find out about the core principles of STEM education that differentiate it from more traditional academic approaches. And you discover the most significant benefits that students can gain from engaging directly with STEM education.

Describing Core STEM Concepts

If you spend any time talking with people about STEM education, you may realize that different people use this acronym in different ways. Suppose you talk to three people; each could be thinking about just one of the following aspects of STEM:

>> A collection of separate, individual math and science classes

>> A standalone integrated STEM class

>> A certification program for a STEM-related profession

From my perspective (and I'm the one writing the book), none of these three hypothetical people are wrong in their use of STEM to name the aspect that they're describing. But they could become confused if they're engaged in conversation with each other because they're thinking of slightly different interpretations (of the term *STEM*) and will certainly face different challenges when dealing with the various aspects of STEM.

TIP

The easiest thing to recognize about STEM is that it's an acronym standing for Science, Technology, Engineering, and Mathematics. Some of these component subjects have always been included in a school curriculum, and others may seem a bit more exotic — and intimidating to teach.

As intimidating as each area is to teach on its own, you also encounter the complication that the boundaries between the component subjects of STEM can be fuzzy. Doesn't engineering depend in part on understanding scientific principles? Doesn't mathematics play a key role in computer programming and scientific experiments? Isn't technology used heavily in science? If you're asking these questions, you're right to do so!

REMEMBER

No clear dividing lines exist between these four subject areas. They constantly touch upon and influence each other. One of the major goals of this book — and the STEM movement in general — is to try to increasingly think of how to teach these concepts together as one single unified whole, without introducing artificial barriers between them.

In the following sections, I explore each component STEM subject in turn and set a foundation for the deeper dive into each of them that you can find in Part 2 of this book.

Science: How the world works

At its core, *science* is the systematic study of the structure and behavior of the natural and physical world, through a careful mix of observation and experimentation. The initial placement of *science* in the STEM acronym helps to highlight its importance in education (although, realistically, an acronym like TEMS probably wouldn't have caught on well).

REMEMBER

Teaching is always a balancing act between teaching the *facts* about a subject (referred to as *content knowledge*) and teaching the *thinking* or *methodology* of that subject (which is called *conceptual knowledge*). Perhaps in no other subject (except maybe mathematics) is the difference between these two types of knowledge more apparent than in science.

>> **The conceptual knowledge of science,** thinking and methodology, involves asking careful questions around the functions of the natural world. When thinking scientifically, you formulate a hypothesis about how some aspect of the world works, then use a mix of experimentation and observation to gather evidence to support or refute your hypothesis.

>> **The content knowledge of science,** facts, involves discovering the answers to the questions used to create hypotheses for experimentation and observation.

Of course, traditional science education has always included the goal of building up habits of thought, reasoning, and ability to engage in an inquiry within a scientific context (the conceptual knowledge). But through much of its history, the main way that science education did so was by transforming the methodology of science into something that could easily be taught and evaluated as a form of content knowledge.

A classic approach to science education uses a scientific demonstration, or lab, where a student receives an ordered list of steps to perform to conduct an experiment. The student knows that following the steps correctly will produce the desired outcome. This approach is great for the teacher, who can then ask questions on a worksheet or test about those steps, and easily identify whether the student remembers and understands the process they carried out. This would seem to provide a clear way to teach (and assess) students regarding the methodology of this scientific idea.

WARNING

The problem with this traditional approach is that you haven't actually taught the students how to ask the questions or come up with a way of resolving the questions (formulate a hypothesis). Instead, you walk them through an example of how someone else has done so. Certainly, examples can be incredibly helpful in showing students how the conceptual process works. But if working through these guided experiments is the culmination of students' scientific engagement in the classroom, then the classroom never gives them practice at struggling authentically with the actual questions.

TIP

A major goal of modern science education is letting the students struggle with the actual questions and figure out how to solve them. The teacher is there to provide support — including direct instruction, review, and *scaffolding* (gradually reducing direct support as a student gains ability and confidence) as needed. But in an *authentic* STEM approach, teachers aren't there to hand out the solutions.

Technology: Tools of the trade

Although teachers and students have always used technology in the classroom, that technology has usually been in service to other educational goals. Students over the last century learned to use slide rules and calculators to help them with math, or learned to use pencils, typewriters, or word processors so that they could write essays. And all of those technologies, at this point, have largely been supplanted by personal computers or the tiny supercomputers (smartphones) that most people carry around in their pockets!

If you pay close attention to the evolution of technologies used in education, you will realize that the definition of technology must be immensely broad. And indeed it is! The National Assessment Governing Board, in their 2014 document *Technology and Engineering Literacy Framework* (found at `https://files.eric.ed.gov/fulltext/ED563941.pdf`), defines technology this way:

> *Technology* is any modification of the natural world done to fulfill human needs or desires.

This view of technology includes everything from the invention of paper to the creation of the internet, or from the wheeled cart to the electronic, self-flying drones that deliver packages to your home (if you're lucky enough to live in the right places).

TIP

If this description of technology feels somewhat like engineering to you, you're not wrong. The *T* in STEM focuses on the actual use of technology, the "modification of the natural world." The process of designing the modification is the *E* in STEM, or engineering. These component subject areas of STEM aren't disconnected silos of knowledge; the concepts touch and overlap with each other all over the place. In this case, every technology was, at some point, engineered!

Because a student has no idea which forms of technology may someday become relevant to their life, having a solid foundation in understanding and using technology is incredibly important. They don't have to become a computer programmer, an engineer, or an astronaut to have a job in which they'll engage regularly with technology.

Engineering: Make it so

Possibly the area of STEM that is least traditional in the classroom is the emphasis on engineering. When I was in middle school, a handful of quarterly classes focused on metalworking and woodworking (generally called "shop class" at the time). These classes covered some elements of design and engineering, but outside of them, engineering concepts were rarely taught.

STEM looks to put the process of design at the extreme front and center in the curriculum. The National Assessment Governing board's 2014 report (found at `https://files.eric.ed.gov/fulltext/ED563941.pdf`) defines engineering in this way:

> *Engineering* is a systematic and often iterative approach to designing objects, processes, and systems to meet human needs and wants.

REMEMBER

Combining the definitions of technology (see the previous section) and engineering is the way someone goes about making changes to create the technology that produces the outcome they want. Engineering is inherently process-driven and gives students an amazing opportunity to engage in hands-on work that is often minimized in favor of more academic (or theoretical) approaches to learning.

TIP

I return to this significant aspect of emphasizing engineering in STEM throughout this book: the idea that STEM work is iterative work. Engineering, more than any other element in STEM, does not expect something to work (be completely understood or successful) the first time. Engineering instruction often explicitly emphasizes the iterative engineering design process (or something similar), as covered in Chapter 6.

In science, technology, or mathematics, if you really understand the concepts at work, you should (at least in theory) be able to conduct an experiment, get a piece of technology to work, or solve a problem on the first attempt. But, despite what you see in comic books (or comic book movies), even the most brilliant engineer won't likely build a fully functional, complex prototype on their first attempt.

Mathematics: By the numbers

Of the subjects related to STEM, the one that paradoxically gets both the most and least interest is mathematics. It gets the most interest because states test mathematics frequently and those tests come with high stakes. Schools and all other stakeholders care about how kids do on mathematics tests. They care that their kids can do the math.

But mathematics is often not the favorite part of a STEM lesson, by either students or teachers (as the STEM teacher at the start of the chapter indicates). If you walk into a room where robots are hurling ping-pong balls at flying drones, you don't immediately think, "There's a lot of math happening in this classroom." (I've never actually walked into a STEM classroom with that sort of activity, although now that I've written the previous sentence, it's on my bucket list.)

As someone who started out in math education, I can tell you that no one says, "Oh, that's exciting!" when you introduce yourself as a math teacher. The reaction is frequently, "I hate math." But you generally get a pretty positive reaction when you tell someone that you teach STEM — assuming they know what the acronym stands for. (I've often wondered whether language arts teachers have educated adults candidly tell them, "I hate books," during small talk at dinner parties.)

But the mathematics associated with STEM projects is crucial, for a variety of reasons. Mathematics

>> **Enables you to be precise in constraints** in a way that gets you closer to the results you need on your initial experimental attempts.

   The old adage in construction — *measure twice, cut once* — holds here. If you're guessing that something looks close enough, you're likely going to need multiple attempts to make exactly what you're aiming for.

>> **Gives you a way of thinking that focuses on breaking down problems** into discrete, well-defined steps.

Sadly, mathematics education doesn't always do a great job of teaching mathematical thinking. In the earlier section, "Science: How the world works," I compare content knowledge and conceptual knowledge, both of which also apply to mathematics. Knowing that the interior angles of a triangle add up to 180 degrees is content knowledge. Knowing what to do with that fact to solve a problem is a type of conceptual knowledge.

REMEMBER

Throughout this book, I push teachers to incorporate mathematics explicitly and thoroughly throughout their STEM instruction. As someone who's taught advanced mathematics to some of the most disadvantaged students in the country, I have developed high expectations about what young people can accomplish mathematically with the right instruction. STEM lays the groundwork for that sort of instruction.

Adopting the Major Principles of STEM Education

A variety of principles in education often seem to find a fairly natural home in STEM education. Built on recent research in neuroscience and the psychology of learning, STEM approaches leverage some basic elements of the best traditional teaching practices in a way that can be hard to match in other content areas.

Inquiry and project-based learning

A central aspect of a STEM-based approach to learning emphasizes the importance of authentic work that ties into the real world. This focus largely comes about through lessons that teachers structure in two ways:

>> **Inquiry-based learning,** in which students work to formulate and answer specific questions; and

>> **Project-based learning,** in which students work to accomplish a productive task.

STEM lends itself particularly well to both of these educational approaches because they are foundational for how progress happens in STEM fields. And because these approaches are fundamental, people often equate STEM primarily with them and may not consider a traditional science or math lesson to really be STEM. (I mention this question from a teacher — "Is this lesson science or STEM?" — in the chapter introduction.)

TIP

In order for STEM teaching approaches to work, the problems around which students are asking and answering questions or completing projects must be relevant to them. The problems must resonate with their interests and their lives.

A teacher's personal enthusiasm for gardening, rock collecting, or aviation history may carry through to the students and provide a rich foundation for a variety of STEM projects — or it might not. Experienced teachers often have stories about a lesson plan that worked great for one school year but fell flat with the next group of students. The second group just had no interest in the lesson material, even though the teacher didn't change anything when presenting it.

WARNING

Structuring lessons by using inquiry-based learning and project-based learning isn't a magic bullet that automatically converts otherwise unsuccessful learning experiences into successes. As with many situations in life, *implementation* (the execution of the structured lesson) matters. I focus on implementation in Chapter 9, but later in this chapter, I cover benefits of (in the section, "Reaping the Benefits of STEM") and concerns with these learning approaches.

Mistakes as cornerstones of learning

Many view the goal of a lesson as having the students understand things quickly and do a task without making mistakes. Not only is this perspective frustrating — because it's often unrealistic — but it's also not desirable. Authentic learning generally comes from failing at something and then correcting your thoughts or behavior to try again and remedy that failure.

TIP

Mistakes are fundamental to the learning process, not an impediment to it. Everyone makes mistakes, but the key to learning is figuring out how to avoid making the *same* mistakes in the future. An intelligent person should move on to making entirely different mistakes!

Integrating concepts across content

Not to sound like a broken record, but subjects in education are often siloed in artificial ways because that's how the schools schedule class time and hand out grades. But in reality, there's always a huge overlap between content areas.

This structural issue isn't isolated to STEM, of course. If you're studying history by referencing historical essays or primary sources, you're also practicing and demonstrating your reading comprehension ability.

REMEMBER

The fuzzy borders between the different STEM subjects help highlight that traditional silos are artificial, and that knowledge and skills have a flexible quality to them that can cross boundaries. Although you will certainly find differences between analyzing a chemical compound and debugging a computer program, you will also discover some significant similarities between those mental processes.

Step-by-step reasoning

The STEM fields, perhaps more than any other subjects (except philosophy), help focus the mind on clearly defining and walking through steps of reasoning to arrive at a conclusion. And in STEM, if your reasoning has a flaw, you're likely to recognize it when you put your hypothesis to the test (as opposed to much of philosophy, where tests often don't exist).

Learning to *reason* (think logically) has benefits well outside of STEM, of course. For example, I don't know whether you know this, but I'm currently writing a book. (*Hint:* You're currently reading it.) To the degree that I am able to frame and communicate a clearly written line of reasoning (and you can be the judge of that), I attribute much of that ability to my training in the sciences.

Centering the student

Centering the student in STEM education involves making the student's active participation, enthusiasm, and sense of ownership in the learning process the driving priority. Teachers accomplish this connection with the students in various ways, including

>> **Encouraging creativity and self-expression:** The goal of many well-constructed STEM lessons involves having the teacher define the parameters of a problem without specifically defining every element of the strategy that the students must use to solve it.

   The emphasis, particularly in younger grades, is on clearly demonstrating that lessons have room for the students' creativity and self-expression in both science and engineering. (Perhaps less self-expression in math, although looking at the work of M.C. Escher or Jessica Hagy can show an awful lot of room for self-expression and creativity.) Check out Figure 2-1 for a look at Hagy's deceptively simply way to draw connections between diverse topics.

>> **Offering opportunities for successful participation:** Of course, some other lessons may be narrowly defined. These types of lessons are essentially demonstrations in which the students perform the demonstration for themselves by following a pre-set recipe.

   Chemistry and physics students traditionally complete lab assignments where they follow well-defined instructions. For these assignments, if the students make mistakes, the result can show an unexpected outcome. Even in this case, though, students derive a benefit from walking through the process, rather than merely watching the teacher provide a demonstration in front of the class.

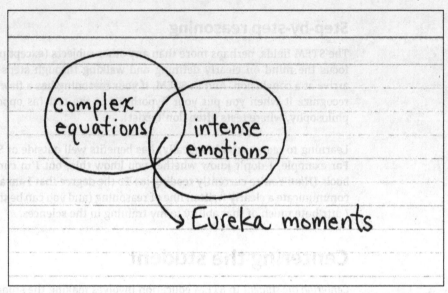

FIGURE 2-1:
Connecting ideas simply but impactfully.

Courtesy of Jessica Hagy

Equity and access in STEM

When I talk about centering the student in STEM (see the preceding section), keep in mind that I mean centering *every* student in STEM. Too often, when schools incorporate STEM as an elective subject or enrichment activity — perhaps even an afterschool club — certain groups of students are potentially excluded. This exclusion can happen because they are deemed to not have the background knowledge or inherent skill to succeed at the STEM activity.

As students advance through school, STEM instruction becomes more specialized and can focus more on college-preparation or job-preparation skills (see the sidebar, "Speaking of STEM Careers," later in this chapter). These varying focuses may cause disparities between the instruction received (and the skills obtained) by groups that end up in different types of courses.

Some of the issues with equity and access to STEM are structural and involve both school organization and society in general. You find these barriers to equity and access in these following areas.

>> **Economic status:** Is it surprising to think that affluent students are more likely to register for high school dual courses in computer programming than students who live in poverty? This tendency seems like the default expectation, which, to me, means that if you want to fight against the economic factor, you have to plan years in advance to make sure that more students in poverty have the opportunity to think of themselves as computer programmers.

» **Timing of access to STEM education:** If you wait until middle school or high school to offer students access to STEM, then you're already fighting against certain well-established patterns of self-thought. For this reason, among others, making sure that all students have access to rigorous STEM instruction from early ages is important.

» **Differing student capabilities:** For students with disabilities, creating equitable and accessible STEM education includes giving proper consideration to any accommodations or modifications required for the students to engage with the lessons.

These are not all of the areas in which equity and access are issues, and schools in different areas run into different sorts of challenges. A school in a wealthy suburban area has different challenges than a school in a poor rural area — and both of those will have different challenges than a school in a poor urban area. Chapter 15 focuses more on this range of issues, to make sure that STEM education is available for all students.

Iterations and reflection

One other area where STEM has a particular advantage is in learning through iteration and reflection. A prototype, whether an experimental set-up, a design challenge, or a computer problem, rarely works exactly as intended on the first try.

Being part of a STEM culture of learning, of course, students are expecting these initial failures to come along and they know to learn from them. They look at the designs that work better than theirs and collaborate on changes with their teammates. STEM encourages learning insights and innovations from both successful and unsuccessful attempts!

I'm not intending to say that STEM is the only place where iteration and reflection is taught or matters. In writing, of course, a major component of the process involves revising and improving the text. (Or so I'm told; my first drafts are flawless.)

But while a student may say (and believe) that their essay is fully completed (even though it contains major flaws), saying (and believing) that they've successfully built their robot when it refuses to move along the intended track is much harder. If your bridge-building project collapses as soon as you put weight on it, it's hard to deny that you need some design changes.

Reaping the Benefits of STEM

Learning always has benefits, but learning through STEM can have particular advantages that go above and beyond learning in a traditional classroom.

Mirroring natural learning

No matter where it takes place, *learning* is a process of building on known facts and using that developed knowledge to get to unknown facts. That process is a pretty good description of what STEM education does, and it mirrors what scientists know about how humans learn.

Research indicates that young children begin learning things through an experimentation-like process, often modeled in their modes of play at an early age. Children investigate the world and the way things work, drawing inferences and conclusions from the data they gain.

REMEMBER

STEM education at early ages leverages and nurtures the natural scientist that resides in all young children. And if you can keep those natural scientists alive and growing long enough, eventually they may become grown-up scientists (even if their job doesn't end up being in the sciences).

Engaging hands and minds

Being physically engaged with a new task also causes you to be mentally engaged with it. By getting students to take part in a STEM activity physically, you also encourage them to understand it. If they don't know what they're supposed to do with the materials provided for the STEM activity, at some point they almost *have* to ask questions about it.

TIP

Students' disengagement and confusion are easier to identify in a hands-on activity than in a more passive one. You can tell at a glance whether a group is behind on building a prototype, in a way that you cannot tell when the class is supposed to be reading a book or writing an essay. This gives you an ability to more easily identify the groups of students that may need some additional focus from the teacher. Maybe the student has questions they aren't comfortable asking. Maybe something is happening in their personal life that makes it hard to focus. But hopefully you have some bandwidth during the project to deal with disengaged students and help get them back on track.

TECHNICAL STUFF

MAKING LEARNING VISIBLE

Dr. John Hattie performed detailed analyses of over 1,000 meta-analyses (studies of research studies) to identify the educational impact of factors related to student achievement, whether it involves student life choices, home situation, teacher, curricula, or teaching and learning approaches. He calls this research *visible learning,* and the title of his original book on the topic is *Visible Learning for Teachers* (Routledge).

The visible learning analysis assigns a numeric value (called *Cohen's d*) to each factor involved in learning. The *average effect size* (the influence on student learning) for all of the factors is 0.40, so a value of *d* = 0.40 serves as a *hinge point* (a natural pause in which teachers can assess student understanding). Factors that rate *d* higher than 0.40 are more positively effective than average, while factors that rate *d* lower than 0.40 are less effective than average.

The Visible Learning website (at `https://visible-learning.org/` — the source for this sidebar's information) has 252 factors that the research tracks. Here is a handful, to give you a hint of the effect sizes related to different educational factors:

Lack of sleep: –0.05	Scaffolding: 0.82	Collective teacher efficacy: 1.57 (highest)
Suspension/expelled students: –0.20	Summarization: 0.79	Self-reported grades: 1.33
Corporal punishment in home: –0.33	Problem-solving teaching: 0.68	Cognitive task analysis: 1.29
Moving between schools: –0.34	Direct instruction: 0.60	Jigsaw method: 1.20
Depression: –0.36	Engagement: 0.56	Prior ability: 0.94
Boredom: –0.49	Science programs: 0.48	Strategy to integrate prior knowledge: 0.93
Deafness: –0.61	Positive self-concept: 0.41	Classroom discussion: 0.82
ADHD: –0.90 (lowest)	Inquiry-based teaching: 0.40	Summarization: 0.79

TIP

The overall goal of visual learning is to transition the use of low-effectiveness strategies into the use of high-effectiveness strategies. Obviously, teachers have no control over many of these factors (deafness, for example), but for the factors that they can influence, knowing the size of the *d* effect impact is important.

Negative effect sizes are particularly problematic and indicate the loss of ground (for learning) over time. Negative effect sizes don't necessarily mean that students forget things they once learned (although that might be part of it), but that they learn and retain so slowly that, over time, they fall behind their previous level of learning.

Engagement versus boredom

It doesn't take an expert in education to tell you that an active and engaged student will learn more than a bored and disengaged student. STEM has the benefit of engaging students by getting them involved in interesting hands-on activities. Both inquiry-based and project-based learning excel at that.

To try to solidify exactly the effect on learning of engagement versus boredom, I cite some numbers based on Dr. John Hattie's *visible learning* research (see the nearby sidebar, "Making Learning Visible"). But don't worry; even though this book is about teaching STEM, I stay fairly light on the numbers.

Here are some points to consider about engagement and boredom as learning factors:

>> **The positive effect size of engagement is 0.56,** which is higher than the average effect of 0.40 (as noted in the sidebar). In other words, just getting the student to pay attention to the lesson, by itself, is making progress toward improving the student's learning situation. (That's probably not a big surprise to anyone who has ever tried to teach anything to anyone.)

>> **The negative effect size of boredom is –0.49,** which puts the other end of the spectrum at a pretty strong negative effect size. This factor's negative effect is even worse than the effects of moving between schools, depression, corporal punishment at home, suspension/expulsion, and lack of sleep. In fact, only two factors in the visible learning research came up worse for learning than boredom: deafness and ADHD!

But if you consider that engagement is essentially the opposite of boredom, then you may begin to see the significance of this learning strategy. If you take a student who is normally bored in a class and can apply a strategy that creates an engaged student, then you're converting a –0.49 effect size directly into a 0.56 effect size, which equals a total positive gain of 1.05 on the learning effectiveness scale!

TIP

Setting up a classroom in which a student is engaged instead of bored can not only be done, but is also (I contend) one of the most important responsibilities of the teacher. And you can reference the visual learning research to find the numbers to back up this statement! Take time to examine the factors in the visual learning list that have a higher effectiveness size to get a sense of the impact that applying related strategies could potentially have. Many of the factors that have the highest (prior ability at 0.94) and lowest (ADHD at –0.90) effectiveness values are outside of a teacher's control, but in the case of student engagement, a teacher can *absolutely* have some degree of control.

Questions versus confusion

Unfortunately, Hattie's research into learning strategies is not quite as supportive of the inquiry-based teaching method, which gets only a 0.40 — right at the hinge point (a natural break where teachers can assess student understanding). However, you need to recognize that this research takes into account the effect of inquiry-based teaching across all studies, not only when it is properly implemented but also when it's implemented improperly.

WARNING

The evidence does suggest that inquiry-based approaches can fall flat if students don't have the background knowledge or vocabulary they need to frame their questions.

TIP

When an inquiry-based teaching approach is used at the right time — after students have the foundation upon which to ask questions — it can have a positive effect. And, even when used improperly (without this foundation), the overall effect is average (0.40), so don't be too concerned about incorporating more inquiry-based strategies just because you may be unsure of the students' foundation. You can always reclaim the reins to help out if the students aren't ready to pose questions on their own.

In Chapter 9, I talk about ways to be sure that students are prepared to move on to the inquiry- or project-based lesson and when they're ready to get the most benefit from it.

Learning through play

In recent years, research (such as that published by LEGO Education) demonstrates the important role of play in learning. In addition to being inherently engaging, play inherently destigmatizes mistakes and failure. In video games, and in most other games, the process of repeated play trains kids to recognize they aren't going to always succeed. That's what they're signing up for when they choose to play the game and also part of the mindset they adopt.

Unfortunately, parents and teachers don't always train young learners well to adopt that same mindset for academic work, despite the fact that significant research suggests learning is more effective when it takes the form of play.

WARNING

The trend toward *gamification* of educational concepts can result in a concept that game designer Justin Gary calls *chocolate-covered broccoli* (although I don't think he coined the term). This gamification approach takes an inherently unfun task and tries to wrap it up in something fun. In the process, you may think that you've now made the unfun task into a fun experience. Kids don't fall for this. If you are going to make learning into play, you must structure the play so that it actually *is* a fun experience. I cover this concept further in Chapter 9.

Empowering through problem-solving and creativity

At its most basic level, an ideal structure of a STEM lesson follows this process:

1. **Students begin with a problem for which they don't know the solution or even how to reach the solution.**

2. **Students then come up with a strategy that they apply to solve the problem.**

Regularly working through this process can give students a profound sense of empowerment to tackle the challenges they encounter in life. (You can find a more comprehensive structure for STEM lessons, the 5E instructional model, in Chapter 9.)

In addition, because students can witness other groups work through the lesson, they also get a sense of how everyone is tackling the problem in different ways. Their problem-solving is not purely a product of their intellect, but also springs from their unique approach and creativity.

Risk-taking and resilience: Building a *can try* spirit

I, for one, have rarely felt quite as ready to give up on something as I have when working on home Do-It-Yourself (DIY) projects. I'm not good at them. They always involve *way* too many return trips to the home improvement store. But, when I actually get to the end of the project, I feel an incredible sense of accomplishment.

TIP

This situation applies to kids, as well, and the sense of accomplishment at the end of a project is useful for teaching them how to stick with something that is challenging. Students may not be successful at every project they try, but as a teacher, you can help instill the sense that they can at least try for success on every project.

Global impact of STEM

Violence. Weather disturbances. Natural disasters. Disease. Famine. Civilization has developed entire institutions and fields of knowledge — ranging from governments and cities to medicine and agriculture — to deal with the crises caused by these societal problems. In a sense, human civilization can be seen as the means humans employ to deal with problems that affect them.

But even with all human efforts, these problems continue to exist. Some of the problems that humans face are handled better than they were in the past, but sometimes solving one problem can tend to create new ones (for example, building a dam to supply power to one area can create environmental problems). And that, in turn, requires a new solution.

The problem-solving process inherent in STEM education mimics how humans go about dealing with these societal problems, and I will confidently state (and not overstate) that the degree of success with which humanity deals with problems in the future will be directly related to how well people teach future generations to handle problem-solving in these areas.

Developing collaboration and employability skills

At a workshop of local industry leaders, I listened to a vice president from a major industrial electricity company say that he worried more about employability skills among his new hires than he did about academic or even technical skills. He described firing some of his smartest engineers because they just didn't know how to work with other people. He expressed confidence that he could teach the necessary technical skills, but found that teaching employees how to work with others was a lot harder.

This concern was the consensus among the industry leaders who attended that workshop. In fact, one of them explicitly identified the three abilities that they look for most when hiring in their technical fields.

>> Collaboration: the ability to work together with others to complete a task

>> Communication: the ability to provide and/or receive information from others

>> Innovation: the ability to develop new ideas and solutions

You probably won't be surprised to know that I contend that STEM is uniquely situated to prepare students with all three of these crucial abilities, starting at fairly early ages. See the sidebar, "Speaking of STEM Careers," for more on this idea.

Instilling digital and technological literacy

One last benefit of STEM education is how it provides a means to really focus on digital and technological literacy — which rarely gets a direct emphasis in elementary education. Even though more schools are equipping students with individual devices (such as an iPad) throughout their educational careers, they are largely left to figure out how to use these devices on their own.

REMEMBER

STEM lessons provide an opportunity for incorporating more robust digital and technological literacy into instruction throughout K–12 education, which benefits students in ways that go beyond the STEM class content. Students also learn about the tools that can assist them with learning and applying the STEM content.

Chapter **3**

Teaching STEM, Then and Now

Teaching kids how to do things can often be a difficult task. Because you're reading this book, I assume that I'm not telling you anything that you don't already know. Looking back at the history of education — particularly in relation to STEM fields and concepts — can help you to establish where STEM development is right now in the realm of education.

In this chapter, I explore the history of STEM education, to reflect on the endeavors that have worked (or not worked) in the past and to recall changes that have transpired over the years — especially in science education. I offer a fairly detailed look at the national science standards that largely guide science instruction in the United States today. I also look into other related sets of instructional standards, such as those for mathematics, computer science, and engineering.

Casting a Brief Look Back at U.S. STEM Education

You might think that science has always been taught a certain way, but it definitely hasn't. Modern thinking about science education evolved significantly from the context of the post-World War II era, in which modern American education thrived.

Teaching apprenticeships and early education

These days, the talk about educating children tends to focus on formal schooling, either public or private, but that hasn't always been education's primary form. Throughout most of human history, young people learned many skills and concepts through a sort of practical, on-the-job training — usually through helping around the house and farm with chores.

Even the more academic training, such as learning to read, largely came from within the home. At that point, only the economic and social elites had the luxury of sending off their youth to private tutors or schools that specialized in education.

Changes in society also brought about changes in educational systems. The transition from an agrarian to an industrial society created the need for more specialized industrial work, and educational systems developed to provide specialized training. One example of this type of system involved *apprenticeships,* in which a professional skilled laborer would take on a younger, unskilled laborer, and teach them the ins and outs of the trade. And the apprentice usually received an extremely low amount of pay. (If you've ever been told that a job, perhaps an internship, offered pay in "experience," then you can relate.)

Here are some less-than-stellar characteristics of historic apprenticeships:

>> **They were contractual obligations** in an era before labor rights laws existed. I don't know that too many of us would wish the associated working conditions (long hours and no benefits, for example) upon ourselves or others.

>> **They tended to be one-on-one relationships** that reflected the teaching styles and knowledge of the individual tradesperson doing the training. And so, apprenticeships didn't provide a systematic way to teach people their skills. But that would change with the true rise of industrialization.

Looking at the rise of public education

Throughout the 19th century, public education transformed learning into a full public enterprise. And with that transformation came an attempt to specialize education, just like what happened with specialization in other industries. Many great education innovators and reformers (see the sidebar, "Founders of STEM Education") worked to lay the foundations for cognitive development, which supports much of the push for enhanced STEM education today.

REMEMBER

One educational philosophy to come out of the early 20th century is *constructivism*, the idea that students construct their knowledge out of experiences. Through experimenting, building, revising, explaining, and debating, young people construct their own knowledge framework. The teacher simply facilitates and cultivates the natural learning process.

Focusing on U.S. science education

The transformation in scientific knowledge at the start of the 20th century led to a new emphasis on science education, particularly in the wake of World War II. The U.S. had defined its power on the world stage through technological might, which culminated in the dropping of atomic bombs on Japan. Because of its growing rivalry with the communist Soviet Union (U.S.S.R.), the U.S. doubled down on education as the means of bolstering their superpower status.

The Soviet Union launched the satellite *Sputnik 1* in 1957, and Soviet cosmonaut Yuri Gagarin successfully completed the first manned spaceflight in 1961. As a result, U.S. President John F. Kennedy put the full force of the American government behind beating the Soviet Union to the moon. (He made his famed speech on the race to the moon at Rice University in 1962.)

FOUNDERS OF STEM EDUCATION

Many key education philosophers, innovators, and reformers have laid the foundation for modern STEM education. If you want to dig deeper into their work on the philosophy of education, here are some names to look for:

Jean-Jacques Rousseau (1712–1778)	Maria Montessori (1870–1952)
Johann Heinrich Pestalozzi (1746–1827)	Jean Piaget (1896–1980)
Friedrich Fröbel (1782–1852)	Alfred Carlton Gilbert (1884–1961)
John Dewey (1859–1952)	Seymour Aubrey Papert (1928–2016)

Lacking a nationwide policy

Between the invention of the atomic bomb and the race to space, the U.S. rivalry with the Soviet Union led to a strong emphasis not only on education in general, but also on math and science education in particular. The U.S. sought to out-science and out-engineer their Soviet adversary.

REMEMBER

Every state and locality had a system of public education, and their governments also had almost absolute local control over the content and structure of education. Educational funding came from state and local sources, and little in the way of national educational policy existed. The Department of Health, Education, and Welfare (formed in 1953) did include an Office of Education, but this office had little authority (or inclination) to become directly involved in local education decisions. But that changed in the 1960s.

Understanding the modern education policy

The role of the U.S. federal government in local education transformed when they began offering federal funding for local education through the 1965 Elementary and Secondary Education Act (ESEA). The federal government is generally wary about state and local officials misusing federal funds, so New York's junior senator Robert F. Kennedy led a group of his colleagues to put some key evaluation requirements into the bill, with these results:

>> **To qualify for funding in future years,** a state would have to evaluate the program they funded in the current year.

>> **To have a standard form of assessment,** the first federal law tied into what would eventually become known as *high-stakes testing*. And thus, from the best of intentions, this assessment began with the first administration of the National Assessment of Educational Progress (NAEP) in 1969.

With federal funding going into local education and nationwide data that could be used to look at educational outcomes, it wasn't long before the federal government began to focus on developing a strong federal education policy.

TECHNICAL STUFF

The Department of Health, Education, and Welfare split into the Department of Health and Human Services and the Department of Education with the passage of the Department of Education Organization Act, signed into law by President Jimmy Carter on October 17, 1979. This created a Cabinet-level position reporting to the president that was directly and exclusively responsible for educational policy issues.

Recognizing recommendations and reforms

Under President Ronald Reagan, the U.S. Department of Education formed a National Commission on Excellence in Education, which published a seminal report, *A Nation at Risk: The Imperative for Educational Reform*, in April of 1983. The report expressed concern about perceived drops in performance from 1963 to 1980, with a strong emphasis on science and mathematics performance. The report also issued a number of recommendations for reforming education. One particularly astounding and far-sighted recommendation suggested a required half-year of computer science for high school students!

Despite some criticisms of its analysis, the report's results and recommendations continued to be cited by those seeking educational reform. One key realization about education — in the wake of *A Nation at Risk* — was that the curriculum being taught varied widely among states and even within each state.

REMEMBER

Probably one of the most wide-scale reforms in the wake of *A Nation at Risk* (although it wasn't one of their explicit recommendations) was the adoption of a standards-based approach to education in most states.

Adopting academic standards

Academic standards are learning expectations — set by grade level and subject area — which define what a student should be learning throughout each grade. The general goal for adopting an academic standard is to have the students be proficient according to the standard by the end of that school year. In a well-defined structure, the standards in upper grades build on the knowledge and skills established in lower grades.

Academic standards are set by the individual states because, despite the existence, influence, and authority of the U.S. Department of Education, the implementation of education is still primarily a state responsibility. For this reason, the standards had a wide range of variability among states. One state might have very high, ambitious standards as a goal of what students should attain, while another state might have decided to establish lower, pragmatic standards as a baseline for what all students should know.

Increasing investment and accountability in education

In 2001, President George W. Bush signed into law the No Child Left Behind Act (NCLB), which increased not only investment in education, but also accountability related to education — with an even greater emphasis on getting data from testing of academic standards. Each state needed to procure data about student performance that aligned to their standards. Specifically, they had to determine what percentage of their students were below, approaching, or at proficiency in relation to those standards.

Here are some points regarding the resulting attempts to comply with NCLB.

>> **Increased cost for compliance:** Because each state had their own sets of standards, they each had to create their own tests to assess those standards. This situation led to huge expenses for both the states and federal government that stemmed from designing and delivering custom tests as opposed to using established tests.

>> **An imbalance in testing by subject matter:** NCLB mandated annual testing in mathematics and English language arts (ELA) from grades 3 through 8, but the requirement for science (and social studies) was significantly lower. In science, NCLB required states to test only three times: once in grades 3 through 5, once in middle school, and once in high school.

WHY COMMON STANDARDS?

The movement toward a common set of standards is largely driven by two major points, one largely philosophical and one practical:

- Grade-appropriate concepts shouldn't differ from state to state (philosophical).
- Publishers can produce (and sell) curricula, textbooks, and assessments more cheaply if they can create the same materials for multiple states (practical).

When philosophical and practical goals line up, there's a solid basis for change.

Though groups like the National Council for the Social Studies have published proposed nationwide standards and curricula over the years, adoption has proven difficult. For example, identifying grade-appropriate content concepts for social studies causes more political and cultural tension than does identifying the same concepts for math, reading, or even science.

After the required NCLB testing began, some issues became clear:

>> **Two states might have wildly different proficiency rates,** but this didn't necessarily correspond to the states' relative performance on the National Assessment of Educational Progress, or NAEP (begun in 1969).

>> **A state with a low proficiency rate** might be a state that had very ambitious standards, but perhaps neglected to give the schools and teachers within the state the necessary guidance or resources to reach those standards.

>> **A state might attain a very high proficiency rate** because it tested against very low standards, so the proficiency rate didn't correspond to high content knowledge among that state's students.

Responding to inconsistencies in standards and testing

State education leaders began an initiative to create and administer common tests across multiple states, which lifted the burden off of each individual state to develop their own test. In order to do this, each state needed to adopt a common set of academic standards, which led to the publication of the *Common Core State Standards* for mathematics and ELA in June of 2010 after approximately two years of development. (See the sidebar, "Why Common Standards?")

After common standards for mathematics and ELA were in place, discussions about developing similar common standards for science began. And outlining those standards — the ones most relevant to this book — is where I focus my attention.

Digging into National Science and Engineering Standards

The National Research Council (NRC) of the National Academies formed a committee of key thinkers in science and engineering education to pull together the crucial elements of past research in this area to develop a set of recommendations to guide the formation of new K-12 science education standards. These were published in 2012 in *A Framework for K-12 Science Education: Practices, Crosscutting Concepts, and Core Ideas* (https://nap.nationalacademies.org/read/13165/chapter/1).

In 2013, a multi-state effort created an organization and some common standards that you can find at www.nextgenscience.org. The name of the standards and their full text is copyrighted and trademarked by WestEd and National Academies Press, but I will refer to these standards, called NGSS, throughout this book. Not all states have adopted the full NGSS, but many are using it as a foundation for their own sets of science academic standards.

Throughout this book, I will reference the NGSS, as it is the most prominent example of science standards built on the NRC frameworks. Chapter 4 will provide some additional guidance on how the NGSS breaks down science understanding across the grade levels.

Describing desired outcomes

The point of having a set of standards or a framework for education is to reach a desired outcome, so spelling out the goals you're aiming toward is quite beneficial. Here are the central science goals for *all* students to achieve by the completion of 12th grade (paraphrased from the *Framework*'s summary):

>> Some appreciation of the beauty and wonder of science

>> Sufficient knowledge of science to engage in public discussions on related issues

>> Careful consumption of scientific and technological information related to their everyday lives

>> Ability to continue to learn about science outside school

>> Skills necessary to enter careers of their choice, including (but not limited to) careers in science, engineering, and technology

The NRC recognized that science education in the United States has largely been a hodgepodge without any overarching systemic organization for the subject content. Despite making every American elementary student memorize the *scientific method* (the systematic approach to making observations, forming hypotheses, experimenting, analyzing, and drawing conclusions which tries to capture the spirit of science), science education has historically focused on individual, discrete facts, rather than a more holistic understanding of science as an activity that finds connections between the known and the unknown. (See Chapter 4 for a discussion of why teachers need to be looking well beyond the scientific method to teach realistic science.)

Despite a narrow factual approach to science, schools have done a pretty good job of teaching science to the select handful of students who survive the grind of elementary school and continue their love of math and science into the middle- and high-school years. For students who have become turned off by the math and science subjects, though, high schools have little choice but to try to pass those students through with just enough science and math credits to earn a diploma. At that point, teaching a genuine appreciation of science (as outlined in the bullets earlier in this section) is generally a lost cause.

REMEMBER

The goal, then, is to teach these science concepts in a coherent way throughout the grades that is more likely to engage and maintain a student's appreciation of science. Take heart in the NRC's framework for science education, which uses a three-dimensional structure to highlight three distinct — but related — aspects of understanding science that teachers want to impart to students in K-12 science and engineering education. The three areas (or dimensions) of the framework are as follows.

Dimension 1: Scientific and engineering practices

Dimension 2: Crosscutting concepts

Dimension 3: Disciplinary core ideas (DCIs)

REMEMBER

As you review these dimensions — which I outline in the following sections — consider that the explicit goal of this structure isn't to aim at just the high-achieving kids. Instead, the goal is to address the science-related skills and knowledge that *all* students need to have by the time they complete their high school education. I introduce the concepts in this chapter and offer more detail on the individual practices, concepts, and core ideas of teaching science in Part 2.

Process and practices: Discerning how you know

Rather than starting out with the facts involved in science, Dimension 1 in the three-dimensional science education framework presents a list of eight science and engineering practices.

REMEMBER

Science isn't about the facts you know; it's about the process that you implement to explore the world.

Here's a list of the practices for K-12 science classrooms (explained in more detail in Chapter 4):

>> Asking questions and defining problems

>> Developing and using models

>> Planning and carrying out investigations

>> Analyzing and interpreting data

>> Using mathematics and computational thinking

>> Constructing explanations and designing solutions

>> Engaging in argument from evidence

>> Obtaining, evaluating, and communicating information

Looking at this list, a major commonality is viewing STEM as a way of approaching questions, information, problems, and evidence. Different problems require different practices, of course. The computational thinking applied to a task may vary considerably in the amount of precision required. That is, the measurement methods used depend on whether you're looking for an exact mathematical answer or a general estimate to start engineering a solution to a large-scale problem.

But, despite the differences in how they manifest, this list is a fairly comprehensive outline that forms the foundation of scientific and engineering practices used in diverse contexts.

Connections and crosscutting concepts: Understanding how you think

Dimension 2 of the science education framework focuses on seven concepts that show up repeatedly in different areas of STEM. These crosscutting concepts provide threads that connect seemingly different scientific ideas. And they relate these ideas in a way that helps teachers and students better understand the commonalities among various ideas in science.

The seven crosscutting concepts are

>> Patterns

>> Cause and effect

>> Scale, proportion, and quantity

>> Systems and system models

>> Energy and matter: Flows, cycles, and conservation

>> Structure and function

>> Stability and change

By just looking at this list, you can probably see the connections between different ideas. The first couple of crosscutting concepts are fundamental and really get to the heart of what it means to *explore scientifically*. Others relate more to *methodology* — the way people conduct explorations in science — but not necessarily to what science itself is doing. In both cases, these concepts provide useful ways to connect and move among scientific ideas. These crosscutting concepts are described in more detail in Chapter 4.

Content and core ideas: Figuring out what you know

Finally, you get to Dimension 3 of the science education framework, the disciplinary core ideas (or DCIs). This dimension involves what people traditionally think of as the goal of science: determining the actual scientific facts about how the world works. These DCIs are core ideas of the discipline because they are high level ideas that explain a range of different phenomena within that area of science, encompassing a range of individual content standards students will encounter across the grades.

Here are a few key criteria that help identify disciplinary core ideas, with each core idea meeting two or more of these criteria:

>> Broadly important across multiple science/engineering disciplines

>> Key organizing principle of a single science/engineering discipline

>> Crucial tool for understanding/investigating more complex ideas and solving problems

>> Relevant to student interests and life experiences

>> Connected to societal or personal concerns that require scientific or technical knowledge

>> Both accessible at introductory levels to young students and also able to be investigated, at greater depths, over the years

TIP

The full standards break down each disciplinary core idea into standards at each grade level, so you'll want to become familiar with the specific skills that are tied to the grade level that you're working with.

In the sections that follow, I take a high-level look at the categories of disciplinary core ideas laid out in the framework and the standards, as well as their narrower component ideas. See Chapter 4 for a more detailed analysis of these core ideas, component ideas, and the related science skills.

Physical Sciences

In the science framework, the category for physical sciences is the set of disciplinary core ideas that focus most directly on matter and energy. Specifically, several of the core ideas of physical sciences have to do with the motion and behavior of matter and energy, as well as the resulting interactions. See Table 3-1 for the full list of physical science core and component ideas.

TABLE 3-1

Physical Sciences Core and Component Ideas

Core Idea	Component Idea
PS1: Matter and Its Interactions	PS1.A: Structure and Properties of Matter
	PS1.B: Chemical Reactions
	PS1.C: Nuclear Processes
PS2: Motion and Stability: Forces and Interactions	PS2.A: Forces and Motion
	PS2.B: Types of Interactions
	PS2.C: Stability and Instability in Physical Systems
PS3: Energy	PS3.A: Definitions of Energy
	PS3.B: Conservation of Energy and Energy Transfer
	PS3.C: Relationship Between Energy and Forces
	PS3.D: Energy in Chemical Processes and Everyday Life
PS4: Waves and Their Applications in Technologies for Information Transfer	PS4.A: Wave Properties
	PS4.B: Electromagnetic Radiation
	PS4.C: Information Technologies and Instrumentation

These core ideas come in at an extremely high level, which is intentional. Table 3-1 doesn't show a set of grade-level standards, but instead identifies core ideas that span the teaching of physical science in the K–12 grade levels. But the group that wrote the standards also broke down these core ideas into individual standards that are appropriate to each grade level.

In other words, the facts and concepts that students learn about the structure and properties of matter in lower grade levels are different from the facts and concepts that they learn about in the upper grades. The standards provide a coherent flow of growing knowledge across the grades that builds on earlier understandings.

Recognize that STEM-related ideas don't want to stay neatly in human-created buckets. You might believe that the physical sciences category of core ideas covers physics and chemistry, and you'd be pretty close to accurate on that. But the nuclear processes of the physical sciences also make stars, which fall under earth and space sciences. And after all, these connections are part of the reason that the framework has a dimension of crosscutting concepts.

The inherent messiness of the actual universe is a great place to start kids making connections and asking questions. But it can also create problems if you try to stick rigidly to your categories of ideas. Remember that the standards and categories exist to help you organize ideas and learning content, not to get in the way of your teaching about what actually happens!

Life Sciences

The life sciences, as the name implies, are a set of disciplinary core ideas that focus on living organisms. This category covers a wide range of systems, relationships, and patterns associated with living organisms — from viruses and bacteria to the largest creatures alive (a blue whale, for example). This category spans the full range of biodiversity manifested in Earth's ecosystem. You can find the full list of life sciences core and component ideas in Table 3-2.

By examining the arrangement of the ideas in Table 3-2, you can see how students of various grade levels find different entry points to engage with the concepts. You can teach Structure and Function (LS1.A) of organisms early on (in lower grades) by identifying features such as wings, legs, and fins, and describing how they function differently. You can then progress to more elaborate structures and functions (such as cellular structures and homeostasis) in higher grades.

After having the groundwork laid in lower grade levels, students can then progress from studying the commonalities and differences among Structure and Function (LS1.A) to providing the Evidence of Common Ancestry and Diversity (LS4.A). It's the circle of life!

TABLE 3-2

Life Sciences Core and Component Ideas

Core Ideas	Component Ideas
LS1: From Molecules to Organisms — Structures and Processes	LS1.A: Structure and Function
	LS1.B: Growth and Development of Organisms
	LS1.C: Organization of Matter and Energy Flow in Organisms
	LS1.D: Information Processing
LS2: Ecosystems — Interactions, Energy, and Dynamics	LS2.A: Interdependent Relationships in Ecosystems
	LS2.B: Cycles of Matter and Energy Transfer in Ecosystems
	LS2.C: Ecosystem Dynamics, Functioning, and Resilience
	LS2.D: Social Interactions and Group Behavior
LS3: Heredity — Inheritance and Variation of Traits	LS3.A: Inheritance of Traits
	LS3.B: Variation of Traits
LS4: Biological Evolution — Unity and Diversity	LS4.A: Evidence of Common Ancestry and Diversity
	LS4.B: Natural Selection
	LS4.C: Adaptation
	LS4.D: Biodiversity and Humans

Earth and Space Sciences

The earth and space sciences disciplinary core ideas center first around understanding Earth's place in the universe — which also means understanding other objects in the universe — but then narrows in on looking at systems at a planetary scale on the Earth. Table 3-3 contains the full list of core and component ideas outlined for Earth and space sciences.

An interesting trait of the Earth and Space Sciences category is that it takes ideas from other scientific disciplines but organizes them based on a common scale. In a sense then, Earth and space sciences are inherently more interdisciplinary than even the previous two sets of disciplinary core ideas (physical sciences and life sciences).

TABLE 3-3

Earth and Space Sciences Core and Component Ideas

Core Ideas	Component Ideas
ESS1: Earth's Place in the Universe	ESS1.A: The Universe and Its Stars
	ESS1.B: Earth and the Solar System
	ESS1.C: The History of Planet Earth
ESS2: Earth's Systems	ESS2.A: Earth Materials and Systems
	ESS2.B: Plate Tectonics and Large-Scale System Interactions
	ESS2.C: The Roles of Water in Earth's Surface Processes
	ESS2.D: Weather and Climate
	ESS2.E: Biogeology
ESS3: Earth and Human Activity	ESS3.A: Natural Resources
	ESS3.B: Natural Hazards
	ESS3.C: Human Impacts on Earth Systems
	ESS3.D: Global Climate Change

Engineering, technology, and application of science

The final set of disciplinary core ideas outlined in the science education frameworks and the standards are those related to engineering, technology, and the application of science. This category reflects the fundamental idea that understanding the operating principles of engineering is crucial to understanding applied science. Centering the first set of core ideas in this section around engineering design principles highlights this connection. I cover the core and component ideas listed in Table 3-4 more thoroughly in Chapters 6 and 8.

TIP

You should embrace the engineering, technology, and application of science core ideas. They not only bring the engineering design process explicitly into K–12 instruction for the first time, but also help to highlight the integrated nature of STEM instruction. Among these disciplinary core ideas, the science and engineering practices, and the crosscutting concepts, you can see clearly that integrating STEM concepts is built into the educational objectives outlined for science education. Science and engineering not only support each other topically, but also support each other's mutual instruction.

TABLE 3-4 **Engineering, Technology, and Application of Science Core and Component Ideas**

Core Ideas	Component Ideas
ETS1: Engineering Design	ETS1.A: Defining and Delimiting an Engineering Problem
	ETS1.B: Developing Possible Solutions
	ETS1.C: Optimizing the Design Solution
ETS2: Links Among Engineering, Technology, Science, and Society	ETS2.A: Interdependence of Science, Engineering, and Technology
	ETS2.B: Influence of Engineering, Technology, and Science on Society and the Natural World

Bringing together the three dimensions

One explicit goal of the NGSS is to integrate the three dimensions that form the framework for science and engineering education. Each grade-level standard not only identifies the explicit skill or knowledge for that grade level, but also outlines the related practice, crosscutting concept, and disciplinary core idea that supports the identified skill or knowledge.

Throughout Part 2 (and particularly in Chapter 4), I delve more deeply into how to apply the grade level standards of the NGSS. Figure 3-1 gives you an initial look at the structure of an NGSS standard for a disciplinary core idea and its key elements:

>> **Performance expectations** in the form of an explicit (and assessable) statement about what students should be able to do and know

>> **Three dimensions** that make up the base framework of the NGSS — science and engineering practices, disciplinary core ideas, and crosscutting concepts

>> **Connections** to other science disciplines in this grade and others, as well as mathematics and ELA

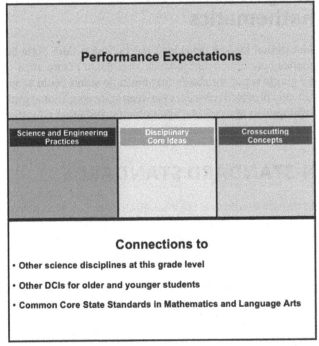

Disciplinary Core Idea

Performance Expectations

| Science and Engineering Practices | Disciplinary Core Ideas | Crosscutting Concepts |

Connections to

• Other science disciplines at this grade level

• Other DCIs for older and younger students

• Common Core State Standards in Mathematics and Language Arts

FIGURE 3-1:
The structure of a standard in the NGSS, focusing on a performance expectation.

NGSS Lead States. (2013)/with permission Next Generation Science Standards/Achieve, Inc./https://www.nextgenscience.org/sites/default/files/resource/ files/How%20to%20Read%20NGSS%20-%20Final%2008.19.13_0.pdf, last accessed on 6 March 2025.

Exploring Math and Computer Science Standards

Though the science standards are incredibly detailed in the realm of science and engineering, teaching STEM also incorporates mathematics and technology. The mathematics standards focus exclusively on what mathematical operations and concepts should be offered at each grade level. When bringing a concept or operation from mathematics into one of the other STEM areas, you will want to know whether you can expect the students to be familiar with it.

Looking at Common Core standards in mathematics

State educational leaders developed the Common Core State Standards (CCSS) in mathematics (www.thecorestandards.org/Math/) from 2008 to 2010 in an effort to have a single set of standards that multiple states could adopt. This set of standards not only provided coherence between state educational goals, but also streamlined development of curricula, assessments, and other educational resources.

NON-STANDARD STANDARDS

The CCSS for mathematics and ELA involved an ambitious effort to create national cohesion around the academic goals of the country. Various states immediately pushed back, and their motivation often reflected political tensions instead of strong educational policy considerations (though both came into play).

The states that didn't adopt the Common Core State Standards needed to develop competitive standards. And they found a two-fold problem with writing entirely new standards from scratch:

- The CCSS represented some of the best thinking from researchers around the country about what students should be learning and when they should be learning it.

- New curricula, textbooks, educational resources, and assessments that aligned with the CCSS became significantly less useful to any state whose standards deviated too far from the CCSS. This situation resulted in increased costs for those states.

Between these two problems, a lot of states that adopted non-CCSS standards ended up with ones that looked remarkably similar to the CCSS. For example, compare two eighth grade standards about the Pythagorean Theorem. The standard CCSS 8.G.B.6 directs students to "Explain a proof" of the theorem, but an Indiana standard 8.GM.7 instead says to "Use inductive reasoning to explain the Pythagorean relationship." Because of these two standards' similarity about proving the Pythagorean Theorem, most of the resources and assessment items that are written for the CCSS 8.G.B.6 standard can also apply to the Indiana 8.GM.7 standard.

When I worked at the Indiana Department of Education helping to develop their new assessment, ILEARN, it licensed banks of items aligned to the CCSS. The development process required an extra step in which a committee of educators from around the state confirmed that the CCSS items also aligned to the Indiana Academic Standards (IAS). The vast similarities between the CCSS and IAS helped to make the confirmation an easy process for most of the standards.

REMEMBER

As an overall strategy, the developers of the CCSS in mathematics made the decision to break apart the "what" of mathematics (the concepts) from the "how" of mathematics (the operations) — to the degree that they could. I take the opportunity in this chapter to introduce the CCSS for mathematics, but if you're wanting an in-depth analysis, you can jump to Chapter 7.

Mathematics practice standards

Just like with science, mathematics isn't only about individual, discrete skills but is also about a way of thinking about numerical and other relationships. The Standards for Mathematical Practice represent eight core skills that teachers should be seeking to develop in their students across all of the grade levels. With these skills, students can do the following:

>> Make sense of problems and persevere in solving them.

>> Reason abstractly and quantitatively.

>> Construct viable arguments and critique the reasoning of others.

>> Model with mathematics.

>> Use appropriate tools strategically.

>> Attend to precision.

>> Look for and make use of structure.

>> Look for and express regularity in repeated reasoning.

If you look at the earlier section, "Digging into the National Science and Engineering Standards," and compare the preceding list of practices to the ideas outlined in Dimension 1: Science and engineering practices and Dimension 2: Crosscutting concepts in the science education framework, you can find some natural conceptual overlap.

TIP

When you emphasize reasoning, constructing arguments, modeling, patterns, and structure in the mathematics core skills, these practices all resonate with the related concepts defined for the sciences. The key is that these are solid, logical thinking practices — regardless of the discipline that you're working with — and your goal is to impart these practices to your students.

Mathematics content standards

The grade-level content standards for mathematics are categorized into groups called *domains*, which center on similar mathematical concepts. Table 3-5 shows these domains and the grade levels they apply to.

TABLE 3-5 **Mathematics Domains for Kindergarten through 8th Grade**

Domain	K	1	2	3	4	5	6	7	8
Counting and Cardinality	✓								
Operations and Algebraic Thinking	✓	✓	✓	✓	✓	✓			
Number and Operations in Base 10	✓	✓	✓	✓	✓	✓			
Measurement and Data	✓	✓	✓	✓	✓	✓			
Geometry	✓	✓	✓	✓	✓	✓	✓	✓	✓
Numbers and Operations — Fractions				✓	✓	✓			
Ratios and Proportional Relationships							✓	✓	
The Number System							✓	✓	✓
Expressions and Equations							✓	✓	✓
Statistics and Probability							✓	✓	✓
Functions									✓

As you can likely tell from Table 3-5, the emphasis through grade 5 is on establishing a basic understanding of how numbers behave, including how to do operations with them.

Here are some notable progressions in the math content standards through the grade levels.

TIP

>> **Working with fractions:** One major increase in complexity comes from grades 3 to 5, when students begin working with fractions. In essence, fractions blur the previously clear dividing lines between a number and an operation. A fraction represents both an operation between two integer values (division) and a new number in its own right. Representing a fraction as an operation or a number depends largely on the context.

>> **Focusing on the relationship of mathematical entities:** Moving from grade 5 to grade 6 demonstrates another significant shift. What students understand moves away from defining individual mathematical entities (values, operators, and so on) and focuses more on how those entities relate to each other through number systems and equations. Starting in sixth grade, being able to interpret different types of mathematical relationships becomes more important than knowing discrete mathematical facts.

>> **Changing domains across high-school grades:** Once students move into high school, the following domains are the focus of instruction:

Algebra	Modeling
Functions	Number and Quantity
Geometry	Statistics and Probability

In several of these high school domains, you can easily see how they connect to the mathematics content that students experienced in earlier grades. The standards in high school aren't broken down by individual grades (9 to 11), but they do have recommendations for how they apply by course or subject area. The group that formed the CCSS presented both a classic Algebra 1–Geometry–Algebra II sequence of courses as well as a sequence that used three Integrated Mathematics courses to teach the same content in a different sequence.

Looking at national standards for computer science

Another academic area that is particularly relevant to any discussion of STEM is computer science, and educators from around the country have also tried to develop a coherent educational framework for instruction in that field.

In 2016, the K-12 Computer Science Framework (https://k12cs.org/) laid out a variety of practices, core concepts, and crosscutting concepts that they deemed to be central to computer science education. Then, building on this work in 2017, the Computer Science Teachers Association (CSTA) created a full set of standards for computer science education (https://csteachers.org/k12standards) across grades K through 12.

Computer science practices

Like both mathematics and the science standards, the computer science standards break out a set of skills that are fundamental to the discipline, and also crucial to teach throughout the grade levels. The Seven Core Practices of Computer Science are as follows:

1. Fostering an inclusive computing culture

2. Collaborating around computing

3. Recognizing and defining computational problems

4. Developing and using abstractions

5. Creating computational artifacts

6. Testing and refining computational artifacts

7. Communicating about computing

REMEMBER

Practices 3 through 6 in the preceding list focus on the skill of computational thinking, which involves breaking down problems into the sort of algorithms or steps that you need to express to a computer. The goal of these practices is to instill into students a way of thinking about problems, and this way of thinking resonates with both the science and engineering practices and the mathematics processes described earlier in this chapter.

Though not specifically tied to coding skills, the first, second, and seventh practices represent social skills that are essential in computer science work. These skills of building respectful relationships with others, collaboration, and communication are crucial to develop for future success in the workforce and in life more broadly.

Computer science core concepts and subconcepts

In addition to the practices, the computer science standards frameworks identify both core concepts and cross-cutting concepts.

The core concepts are similar to what the math standards call domains, which represent broad categories within which different computer science standards will fall. You can find five core concepts and related subconcepts that help organize skills and knowledge across the grades in Table 3-6.

TABLE 3-6

Computer Science Core Concepts and Subconcepts

Computer Science Core Concept	Computer Science Subconcept
Computing Systems	Devices
	Hardware and Software
	Troubleshooting
Networks and the Internet	Network Communication and Organizations
	Cybersecurity
Data and Analysis	Collection
	Storage
	Visualization and Transformation
	Inference and Models

Computer Science Core Concept	Computer Science Subconcept
Algorithms and Programming	Algorithms
	Variables
	Control
	Modularity
	Program Development
Impacts of Computing	Culture
	Social Interactions
	Safety, Law, and Ethics

Computer science crosscutting concepts

The crosscutting concepts, as in the science frameworks, represent connections among various concepts and standards. The idea of crosscutting identifies that these concepts integrate throughout the other elements of the framework, rather than existing as a standalone entity in the framework.

The crosscutting concepts for computer science are as follows:

>> Abstraction

>> System relationships

>> Human-computer interactions

>> Privacy and security

>> Communication and coordination

Hopefully, you can see how these crosscutting concepts have the potential to interact not only with the individual subconcepts and skills taught in an individual standard or lesson, but also with some of the broader practices in computer science. The communication and coordination crosscutting concept, for example, has a natural affinity with core practices such as fostering an inclusive computer culture.

If you're looking to dive more deeply into the frameworks and related standards for computer science, jump ahead to Chapter 5.

2

Gathering the Building Blocks of STEM

Look deeper into a view of the world through science, and discover key learning objectives for the STEM discipline that comes first in the acronym.

Find out how technology tools inform the standards and practices of STEM education.

Get advice on integrating engineering design principles into STEM education, with a focus on solving problems in the real world.

Tackle the challenges of teaching math, and discover how thinking mathematically impacts all the other STEM disciplines.

Explore a more robust, integrated STEM approach to education that involves not only combining the four core areas, but also incorporating STEM knowledge with other educational areas such as reading, writing, social studies, and the arts.

Chapter **4**

Understanding the World with Science

Science involves coming up with questions about how and why the natural world works the way it does and then figuring out systematic, structured ways of resolving those questions. That statement may seem straightforward, but scientists (and philosophers) debate about what exactly constitutes science and how it works all the time, so pinning down the definition of science can get a little confusing for both students and teachers.

Though science is a crucial subject to teach at all grade levels, the teachers' comfort level with the subject varies widely. In general, someone teaches high school biology or physics because they chose that subject as an area of high interest — probably dating back to their own positive high school (and certainly college) courses. In my experience, the average elementary school teacher has different passions that drive them to teach and may never have had much direct exposure to high levels of science.

Teachers don't need to be an expert in every single idea they explore with their students, but they should have a general sense of how the ideas they're teaching link together. They need to be able to highlight the connections between ideas. Most education programs for elementary grade levels don't focus enough on robust scientific experience to provide that framework to teachers. Instead, teachers at the lower grade levels often have to pick up the framework after they're confronted with teaching science.

In this chapter, I explore the broad range of content that science education covers from kindergarten through twelfth grade, as presented through the disciplinary core ideas (DCIs) of the science education framework (introduced in Chapter 3). Then, I discuss how science education teaches the methods used in science — both the traditional scientific method and the modern lens of the science and engineering practices from the science education framework. I also look at ways to combine science content areas by focusing on all dimensions of the science education framework.

Splitting Science into Buckets

The science education framework breaks the content of science down across four sets of disciplinary core ideas. I introduce these ideas broadly in Chapter 3, but in the following sections, I cover the first three: physical sciences, life sciences, and Earth and space sciences.

The fourth disciplinary core idea focuses on the engineering and technology end of things, as well as science applications. I cover the core idea of Engineering Design in Chapter 6, and the core idea of Links Among Engineering, Technology, Science, and Society in Chapter 8.

TIP

You should check the standards outlined on your state's education department website to identify precisely what standards should be taught in which grade in your state. Though not all states utilize the NGSS as their formal standards, most of the resources you can find for K-12 science education align to NGSS, so familiarity with the structure of those standards helps in understanding the resources. I encourage you to view the full standards text — along with the extensive supplemental materials — at the NGSS website (www.nextgenscience.org/).

REMEMBER

Keep in mind that the science standards are not a science curriculum. A *curriculum* is a set of lessons, usually in a planned sequence, that are aligned to the standards.

This chapter doesn't contain the explicit standards, lessons, or curriculum. The goal here is to give you a sense of where science concepts fit in with science education framework, but this chapter doesn't specifically prepare you to teach any single concept. For that goal, you should have curriculum materials that offer an in-depth look at how to administer your lessons. You can find guidance for planning your own lessons and curricula in Part 3.

Studying Matter and Energy

The first disciplinary core idea in the NGSS involves the physical sciences category, which breaks down into the science related to physics and chemistry.

REMEMBER

The strict dividing line between physics and chemistry is a historical artifact from earlier times (thank Robert Boyle for that). It still persists at times today, but scientists broadly see these disciplines as different approaches to the same underlying effort to understand and manipulate matter and energy — at both large and small scales. The NGSS unites physics and chemistry in an attempt to maintain a strong cohesion between these related ideas.

Four disciplinary core ideas comprise the standards in the physical sciences portion of NGSS. These are

PS1: Matter and Its Interactions

PS2: Motion and Stability: Forces and Interactions

PS3: Energy

PS4: Waves and Their Applications in Technologies for Information Transfer

TIP

The first three of these disciplinary core ideas (PS1–PS3) drill down to fundamental concepts about how the physical world operates. Even at very young ages, kids instinctively ask questions such as "What is that made of?" and "Why did that happen?" and these questions provide a very convenient, inquiry-based pathway into exploring the related scientific concepts.

That fourth disciplinary core idea (PS4) may seem intimidating, particularly to any teacher who doesn't have a strong background in physics or technology. But don't worry; I break it down in this chapter so that you can understand why it's an important part of the physical sciences core ideas.

In the following sections, I focus in greater depth on each of the core ideas and their related component ideas.

Getting to the heart of matter

The first steps in scientific understanding come from trying to get a clear sense of what objects are and what they're made of. These steps constitute the definition stage of science. If you look back at the earliest proto-scientific thinking of the ancient Greek or Chinese cultures, you find thinkers (for example, Aristotle and Wang Chong) who attempted to figure out the components of the universe.

Modern views of matter differ greatly from the ancient views, but the central importance of understanding matter's basic material structure remains.

The renowned 20th-century theoretical physicist Richard Feynman speculated about how you could pass along the most information about science in the fewest words, and he concluded that you would use the *atomic hypothesis*, which he stated as follows:

[A]ll things are made of atoms — little particles that move around in perpetual motion, attracting each other when they are a little distance apart, but repelling upon being squeezed into one another.

Explaining that statement is what the first core disciplinary idea of physical sciences aims for. PS1: Matter and Its Interactions is divided into three component ideas.

PS1.A: Structure and Properties of Matter

PS1.B: Chemical Reactions

PS1.C: Nuclear Processes

REMEMBER

The standard associated with this core idea (PS1) says that a student should understand (by the time they graduate high school) that matter is determined by the types of atoms present in an object and how they interact with each other. In particular, students need to have a general sense of the two main interaction types: chemical reactions and nuclear processes.

This ultimate goal doesn't mean you're teaching atomic fusion to kindergartners. The NGSS standards take these core and component ideas and establish individual standards at each grade. These standards are appropriate for the content accessible to students at that grade level and create a progression of content across the grades. With each grade level, teachers prepare students for full understanding of the core concept (often referred to as *proficiency* or *mastery*) by the time they graduate. Here are some of the high points.

Early elementary science:

>> **Classify matter:** Describe different material properties (such as color, weight, and texture) and classify materials by common properties. Explain why some materials make more sense for specific purposes, such as why cars are made of metal instead of paper. (Second grade)

>> **Understand complex objects:** Use experiment and observation to explain how complex objects made of smaller pieces can be disassembled and then reconstructed into new objects, often modeling with materials like cardboard, LEGO pieces, or other building materials. (Second grade)

>> **Thermal properties:** Explain changes that happen when heating and cooling objects, including why some changes can be reversed while others cannot. (Second grade)

Upper elementary science:

>> **Atomic basis of matter:** Understand that matter is made up of particles too small to be seen. Build and describe models of that understanding. (Fifth grade)

>> **Material properties:** Move beyond the basic understanding of properties of different materials to begin exploring more complicated properties such as conductivity. (Fifth grade)

>> **Conservation of mass:** Understand that physical processes conserve mass, and support this with measurement and data. (Fifth grade)

>> **Physical combinations:** Perform experiments that identify whether combining two substances results in a new substance. (Fifth grade)

Middle school science:

>> **Atoms and molecules:** Understand physical composition in terms of atomic structures and how atoms compose simple molecules.

>> **Natural versus synthetic materials:** Explore the structure and purpose of different natural and synthetic materials, including their properties, how they impact society, and how the materials behave and change during different types of physical interactions, including chemical reactions.

>> **Matter transitions and reactions:** Explicitly understand and justify principles of conservation of mass during physical processes, including chemical reactions and changes of physical state.

High school science:

>> **Chemical properties and reactions:** Understand basic chemical reactions and their consequences, including how they relate to the properties of the elements and their position on the periodic table.

>> **What holds matter together:** Investigate how the physical structure of matter in atoms, molecules, and ions affect properties like melting point, physical strength, conductivity, and reaction speed.

>> **Energetic reactions:** Model the absorption and release of energy in chemical reactions.

>> **Understand nuclear processes:** Understand and create basic models of nuclear fission, nuclear fusion, and radioactive decay, including how those relate to the physical structure of the atom.

PLANNING AHEAD FOR SUCCESS

Sets of standards, whether NGSS, state standards, or an individual curriculum, plan out specific skills for mastery at certain grades. Since teachers have to get through their grade-level standards, they tend to laser focus on the standards assigned to their grade. It is worthwhile for the students, however, if they have some preparation in advance for the concepts that they'll see in upcoming grades.

Consider the following sort of lesson, which is intended to establish some base understanding of the PS1 core ideas, but in a way that is perfectly age-appropriate in either kindergarten or first grade, even though the NGSS doesn't explicitly include these standards until second grade. In the lesson, students follow these basic steps:

1. Build a house with building blocks.

2. Build a house with modeling clay.

3. Compare the properties of the two materials.

Coming up with a lesson like this in kindergarten or grade 1, however, would require

- Looking ahead at the vertical progression of standards across the grades, to see what skills are coming up

- Thinking of activities that can prepare students for gaining these skills

No one is going to test kids on the concepts yet, but these basic lessons lay the foundation that will make meeting the standards easier for them (and their teachers) in later grades!

Be sure to ask your students not only what properties are *different* between building blocks and modeling clay, but also what properties are *similar* between them!

REMEMBER

The NGSS lists no PS1 standards prior to grade 2. This means that teachers in earlier grade levels have no explicit requirements to teach material related to these standards, and no related assessment occurs in kindergarten or grade 1. This doesn't mean, however, that a concept cannot or should not be introduced prior to grade 2. See the sidebar, "Planning ahead for success."

Interacting with forces

The universe would be a pretty boring place if matter didn't interact with other matter. The next disciplinary core idea, PS2: Motion and Stability: Forces and Interactions, focuses on the types of motions and interactions that take place within physical systems.

PS2: Motion and Stability: Forces and Interactions is divided into three component ideas.

PS2.A Forces and Motion

PS2.B Types of Interactions

PS2.C Stability and Instability in Physical Systems

The motions introduced in kindergarten are related to simple pushes and pulls (prompting the question from one teacher, "So can our swing set count as a science lab now?"). The ideas then progress into a greater understanding of underlying principles such as the laws of motion and forces related to electricity, magnetism, and gravitation.

Early elementary science:

>> **Strength and direction of motion:** Explore how pushes and pulls can change the motion (both speed and direction) of an object. (Kindergarten)

Upper elementary science:

>> **Balancing forces:** Investigate ways that balanced and unbalanced forces can affect the motion of an object. (Third grade)

>> **Predict future motion:** Use data about an object's current motion to make predictions about its future motion. (Third grade)

» **Magnetic attraction:** Explore understanding of electricity and magnetism to identify how objects can push and pull each other at a distance, and use this understanding to solve problems. (Third grade)

» **Orient gravity:** Understand the concept of gravity, but explicitly that gravity from Earth is a force exerted downward toward the Earth. (Fifth grade)

Middle school science:

» **Forces and motion:** An object's motion depends on the force acting on it and the object's mass.

» **Colliding and falling objects:** Use Newton's Third Law to understand, model, and solve problems involving collisions of objects, including falling objects.

» **Electricity and magnetism:** Explore the intensity of electricity and magnetism and find ways to make them stronger and weaker.

» **No defying gravity:** Understand that gravity is an attractive force between objects, based on their mass, and that it holds planets together in relation to each other at great distances.

» **Invisible forces:** Consolidate understanding of gravity, electricity, and magnetism into an understanding of fields between objects that exert forces between them without the need for direct physical contact.

High school science:

» **Obey Newton's laws:** Use Newton's laws to explain and understand relationships between mass and force, concepts of inertia, and other elements of motions and collisions, along with other related concepts like conservation of momentum.

» **Obey invisible force laws:** Expand understanding of gravitation and electrostatics to a more formal ability to work with the laws governing them to both calculate and describe interactions with these forces. This includes a basic understanding of the deep relationship between electricity and magnetism.

» **Engineer safety devices:** Apply understandings of collisions to understand and design objects like helmets, parachutes, seat belts, or air bags that are designed to minimize damage during a collision.

TIP

Throughout the grade levels, core idea PS2 provides a solid set of concepts that you can apply in related projects. Anytime students are doing an activity where things are moving, they can connect their clear observations of these projects in the real world with their theoretical understanding of science — and quantify those understandings of speed and forces with solid mathematics. Integrating

STEM disciplines is a way to keep skills sharp in grades where no explicit standards are provided.

For example, in third grade students are introduced to both the scientific concept that forces must balance out, but also the mathematical concept of fractions. You can use the physical balancing concept to reinforce the comparison of fractions, by having a see-saw that is balanced when one-half pound is on each side but becomes unbalanced when you have one-half pound on one side and one-third pound on the other side. This similar model could be continued in fourth grade. Even without an explicit need to teach the balanced forces skill, by using it in the comparison of more complex fractions (like three-fourths versus two-thirds) you reinforce both the mathematical and the scientific concepts that the student needs to solidify moving forward.

Getting an energy boost

According to the DCI of PS3, energy takes on a more underlying concept related to interactions of objects and the remarkable feature of physical systems that ensures they always conserve the *total energy* of the system. But to understand these concepts, the student really needs to understand all the various types of energy that can go into a system to be part of the total energy.

PS3: Energy is divided into four component ideas.

> PS3.A Definitions of Energy
>
> PS3.B Conservation of Energy and Energy Transfer
>
> PS3.C Relationship between Energy and Forces
>
> PS3.D Energy in Chemical Processes and Everyday Life

The lower grades don't do much with PS3 — aside from understanding in kindergarten that the Sun provides energy— but related education ramps up with motion and collision interactions in grade 4.

REMEMBER

Though the science education frameworks split up PS3 ideas into large buckets of concepts, they regularly overlap. The progression between motion, forces, and energy is a great example of this. Teachers teach the grade 4 science skills because they build on the grade 3 skills shown in the preceding section. To capture this progression of ideas, you need to look not only vertically at what the student has learned and will learn within a single DCI, but also across concepts such as matter, forces, and energy. One of the crosscutting concepts is even titled *Energy and Matter*. (See the section, "Crosscutting concepts," later in this chapter.)

Early elementary science:

>> **Sunlight:** Understand and use the benefits of sunlight. (Kindergarten)

Upper elementary science:

>> **Speed and energy:** Describe relationships between the speed of an object and its energy, including when collisions occur. (Fourth grade)

>> **Types of energy:** Understand that energy can be transferred by sound, light, heat, and electricity across distances. Identify and design ways to turn one form of energy into another. (Fourth grade)

>> **Bioenergy:** Understand and model how energy from the sun makes it into animals' food to provide energy to sustain life. (Fifth grade)

Middle school science:

>> **Mass and speed matter:** Explain and graph the relationships between speed, mass, and kinetic energy.

>> **Stored energy:** Understand that not all energy takes the form of motion, and that potential energy can be stored in a system to be released later.

>> **Thermal insulation:** Design and refine solutions to minimize or maximize the movement of heat (thermal energy) between different parts of a system.

>> **Conservation of energy:** Recognize that energy changes form through interactions, but that the total energy of a system remains the same, even when it changes form.

High school science:

>> **Energy flows:** Track how energy moves between objects in a system, either by flowing between them or kinetic energy transferring in a collision.

>> **Thermodynamics:** Explore principles of heat transfer to identify that heat travels with the goal of reaching thermal equilibrium.

>> **Engineering energy conversion:** Understand and design ways that energy can be converted from one form to another toward useful purposes.

>> **Electromagnetic interactions:** Understand how the energy of a system changes due to the electromagnetic fields that interact within the system.

Catching the waves

Even someone who never studied physics probably has no problem understanding why learning about matter, motion, forces, and energy is important. But the concept of *waves* may seem oddly specific. Not only are waves a crucial concept in physics, but our modern society functions on technology that exists because of the underlying physics of waves, such as electricity and cellphones.

PS4: Waves and Their Applications in Technologies for Information Transfer is divided into three component ideas.

PS4.A Wave Properties

PS4.B Electromagnetic Radiation

PS4.C Information Technologies and Instrumentation

Lessons related to this area begin in first grade with simple physical waves, but the material evolves over time into a deeper understanding of wave structure that is more abstract (for example, electromagnetic radiation).

Early elementary science:

>> **Sound and light:** Explore basic behaviors of both sound and light, including how they can be used for communication. (First grade)

>> **Light properties of objects:** Investigate what happens when light shines on different objects, identifying differences between transparent and opaque objects. (First grade)

Upper elementary science:

>> **Wave patterns:** Identify mathematical patterns and properties of different types of waves, including wavelength and amplitude. (Fourth grade)

>> **Light reflections:** Model reflection of light and how the change in light motion relates to being able to see reflected objects on the light that enters the eye. (Fourth grade)

>> **Information transfer:** Generate ways to use sound and light to send messages, including encoded information. (Fourth grade)

Middle school science:

>> **Amplitude and energy:** Represent waves mathematically and relate the amplitude of a wave to its energy.

>> **Wave-material interactions:** Model how mechanical and light waves interact with different types of materials to be reflected, absorbed, and transmitted through them.

>> **Digitized wave signals:** Expand understanding of communication with waves by identifying that digital wave signals are more reliable for encoding information than analog waves.

High school science:

>> **Wave theory:** Expand previous understanding of the mathematics of waves to include frequency and the speed of waves.

>> **Waves in technology:** Understand how different types of waves interact with technology, ranging from the design of solar cells to digital information transmission and storage, and the effects of waves on users.

>> **Wave-particle duality:** Evaluate the idea that light and other forms of electromagnetic radiation can be modeled in both wave models and particle models, based on the appropriate situation.

REMEMBER

In physics, the deep commonality among waves represented in various phenomena shows that they follow a similar mathematical structure. Students really don't have the grounding necessary to appreciate these similarities between the mathematical forms until high school (or beyond). Even in fourth grade, though, the standards for PS4 provide a good foundation for tying in mathematical patterns and models that can hint toward the more robust models students encounter in later grades.

Getting to Know Living Things

Because humans are living things, the fact that they (and the society they've created) have a strong interest in understanding living things is not surprising. The formal study of living things is life sciences, or biology.

My background lies in both mathematics education and the physical sciences. Because I haven't taken a course in the life sciences since sometime in high school, I have the least academic street cred to throw around in the next few sections. My claim to fame in the life sciences is that I've met zoologist and best-selling author Richard Dawkins, who wrote *The Selfish Gene* (Oxford Landmark Science), which takes a look at the role of genes in evolutionary biology. Be that as it may, I still lay out the life sciences standards in the following sections.

REMEMBER

The life sciences study not only individual living things, but also the systems in which they exist and the relationship of the living things to those systems and to each other. A living thing exists in the context of an *ecosystem* (a biological community of interacting organisms and their physical environments), which in turn exists in the context of energy flowing from the Sun into those living things and their environments. The life sciences standards are connected on a deep level with standards in both the physical sciences and the Earth and space sciences. When you're teaching the PS3 science of using energy from sunlight in kindergarten, you're not just setting the student up to understand later physical science skills, but also to understand life science. Knowledge doesn't care about the labels we put on it.

Processing the structure of life

One amazing thing about living things is that they represent fascinating complex systems, even at the smallest unit of life, the cell. Living organisms of larger size are composed of cells, which are themselves composed of smaller pieces that exist in a careful hierarchy. Life, be it individual cells or organisms, goes through similar cycles: growth, reproduction, and death.

LS1: From Molecules to Organisms: Structures and Processes is divided into four component ideas.

LS1.A Structure and Function

LS1.B Growth and Development of Organisms

LS1.C Organization for Matter and Energy Flow in Organisms

LS1.D Information Processing

At the lower grades, students begin to recognize observable physical features of organisms, identifying how those features help an organism survive. Progressing through the grades, the students begin to develop a deeper understanding of the cycles and processes that influence life. By middle and high school, students explore the complex underlying mechanisms that drive these life processes, such as photosynthesis and genetics.

Early elementary science:

>> **Survival traits:** Describe what different plants and animals need to survive. (Kindergarten)

>> **Survival behaviors:** Understand that certain behaviors from offspring and the responses of their parents help offspring survive. (First grade)

>> **Mimic nature:** Design solutions to human problems by mimicking external features and body parts of plants and animals. (First grade)

Upper elementary science:

>> **Life cycles:** Compare life cycles among different organisms, including common and distinct features. (Third grade)

>> **Survival structures:** Identify examples of physical structures in plants and animals that support their survival. (Fourth grade)

>> **Animal senses:** Describe how animals are able to receive sensory signals from their environment. (Fourth grade)

>> **Plant nutrition:** Understand that plants matter comes mostly from air and water, rather than from the soil. (Fifth grade)

Middle school science:

>> **Cells build life:** Understand that living things are made of cells, and how cells work together to form larger living systems, structures, and organisms.

>> **Reproduction strategies:** Make evidence-based arguments on why plants and animals have properties based on their usefulness in reproduction.

>> **Growth and development:** Explore how environmental and genetic factors contribute to the growth and development of living things, including the availability of food and energy.

>> **Sensory systems:** Recognize that sensory information received by the body is transmitted to the brain for processing and storage.

High school science:

>> **DNA and proteins:** Explain that the essential functions of a cell are carried out through proteins, and that the protein structure is determined by the genetic information within a cell's DNA.

>> **Cells, mitosis, and homeostasis:** Understand that cells work together to create larger structures, including multicellular organisms, and explain the major roles played by both mitosis and homeostasis within these larger systems.

>> **Fuel and energy:** Explore different methods by which plants and other organisms gain food and energy from their environment, such as photosynthesis, sugar molecules, and other related chemical processes.

Exploring the ecosystems

When studies move from individual living organisms to complex networks of organisms, the student finds out about the hierarchical structures of the environment and how it affects those living organisms.

LS2: Ecosystems: Interactions, Energy, and Dynamics is broken down into four component ideas.

LS2.A Interdependent Relationships in Ecosystems

LS2.B Cycles of Matter and Energy Transfer in Ecosystems

LS2.C Ecosystem Dynamics, Functioning, and Resilience

LS2.D Social Interactions and Group Behavior

These concepts evolve from understanding (in grade 2) what makes plants grow, spread, and thrive, to ultimately recognizing (in high school) patterns that exist in the behaviors of large systems of interconnected organisms — such as food chains.

Early elementary science:

>> **Plant growth:** Investigate the needs of plants in growth and reproduction, including pollination and dispersal of seeds and the roles of animals in this process. (Second grade)

Upper elementary science:

>> **Animal groupings:** Understand that animals often form groups (flocks, herds, packs, etc.) for purposes of survival. (Third grade)

>> **Matter movement:** Model how matter transitions among plants, animals, and decomposers within the environment. (Fifth grade)

Middle school science:

>> **Resources shape ecosystems:** Understand that an ecosystem is strongly influenced by the resources available within that ecosystem, and that changes in the resources available have impacts upon the ecosystem.

>> **Ecosystem behaviors:** Explain different sorts of behaviors between organisms, such as predator/prey relationships, competition, and mutual benefit, that are predictably part of virtually all ecosystems.

>> **Maintain ecosystems:** Evaluate and design solutions for maintaining an ecosystem and the biodiversity within it.

High school science:

>> **Circle of life:** Understand the energy and matter flows through an ecosystem, and how different components of the ecosystem interact with each other to maintain that system.

>> **Ecological equilibrium:** Recognize that changes to an ecosystem can cause a stable state to change, and use evidence and data to model changes that could result.

>> **Environmental design:** Design and evaluate evidence related to ways to mitigate impact of human activity on ecosystems.

Passing along knowledge of heredity

Living things have a vast majority of their traits in common with their parents, but they aren't identical to their parents. Children can get a glimpse of this idea of inherited traits from their own lives (by looking at their parents), but exploring heredity across all living creatures is the goal of this disciplinary core idea.

LS3: Heredity: Inheritance and Variation of Traits is divided into two component ideas.

LS3.A Inheritance of Traits

LS3.B Variation of Traits

This core idea has relatively fewer specific concepts compared to other core ideas, but it does lay the groundwork for the next core idea that addresses evolution. (See the sidebar, "Don't Teach the Controversy.")

Early elementary science:

>> **Basic heredity:** Use observations to justify that young plants and animals are often like, but not identical to, their parents. (First grade)

Upper elementary science:

>> **Basic variation:** Explain that within groups of similar and related organisms, there will be variation among observed traits. (Third grade)

>> **Environmental influence:** Recognize that environmental influences can affect traits in plants and animals. (Third grade)

Middle school science:

>> **Genetic variation:** Model and explain how changes in genes can result in offspring with genetic variation, even among organisms that reproduce asexually.

>> **Protein's role:** Understand that genetic mutations can cause the creation of variant proteins, and it's the different proteins that can create changes in the structure of the organism.

High school science:

>> **DNA and chromosomes:** Develop a more complete understanding of how chromosomes can produce replication errors during the process of creating new cells, including identifying the likely causes for these errors based on specific evidence.

>> **Probability analysis:** Use probability and statistics to determine how different types of expressed traits are distributed throughout a population.

Evolving an understanding of unity and diversity

One of the central conceptual ideas in biology is the idea of evolution, which is that biological changes between generations are selected by a process of *natural selection*. Just as a breeder selects consciously for traits that they want in a plant or animal, natural selection selects for creatures that are able to survive in the environment — or at least survive long enough to have viable offspring.

REMEMBER

DON'T TEACH THE CONTROVERSY

Some scientific ideas can trigger negative reactions from certain parents or students. Higher risks of negative reactions come in conjunction with discussions of evolution (LS4), the age of the universe (ESS1), the age of the Earth (ESS1), or global climate change (ESS3). But these scientific concepts are crucial to the ESS core, so how do you — as a teacher — approach them?

When dealing with delicate and potentially controversial issues like this, focus on a rigorous look at the evidence. Robust discussions that include differing viewpoints are important to a good science class, but you also don't want to turn a scientific inquiry into a debate class.

You can circumvent many problematic discussions by asking for scientific explanations. Asking a simplistic question such as "How old is the Earth?" is arguably asking for a student's overall conclusion from everything they know and believe. It is even better to ask your students what evidence would be needed to figure out the age of the Earth.

Trying a "teach the controversy" approach to potentially touchy topics — wherein you use class time to present the evidence for a topic and also arguments against it — may seem open-minded, but often slips non-scientific arguments into a science class.

Know your school's opt-out policy. If you don't know the policy (or need to stall an irate parent), then tell them that you need to investigate the policy. Reach out to your school administration for guidance on how to handle the situation.

The goal is to teach students the scientific understanding of these concepts. There may be other views and perspectives that aren't supported by science at this time, but that isn't the focus of the class.

REMEMBER

A trait that confers any distinctive sort of survivability benefit is likely to persist through the generations and become more dominant among the plant or animal population — even if it starts out as an extremely rare trait.

LS4: Biological Evolution: Unity and Diversity is broken down into four component ideas.

LS4.A Evidence of Common Ancestry and Diversity

LS4.B Natural Selection

LS4.C Adaptation

LS4.D Biodiversity and Humans

The LS4 standards begin in elementary school with a focus on how individual animal diversity leads to a difference in suitability for distinct environments. This, combined with the LS3 insights on heredity, lays the logical foundation for natural selection, which students begin confronting more directly in middle school and high school science curricula, notably in their high school biology class.

Early elementary science:

>> **Biodiversity:** Observe that a wide range of different plants and animals make homes in different types of habitats. (Second grade)

Upper elementary science:

>> **Survival traits:** Recognize that within a species, a variation of traits can lead to some organisms surviving better than other members of that species within a given environment. (Third grade)

>> **Fossils:** Use evidence from fossils to make claims about organisms and the environments in which they lived. (Third grade)

>> **Ecological problems:** Evaluate solutions to a problem caused by changes to an environment and its organisms. (Third grade)

Middle school science:

>> **The fossil record:** Recognize that patterns among large numbers of fossils can be used to reach conclusions about organisms and ecosystems in the past.

>> **Compare animal structures:** Compare structures of modern and historical animals, and also between embryos of different species, to identify and infer relationships among those creatures.

>> **Population variation:** Understand that populations vary and that the variation may lead to different survival changes, and use mathematics to model how variations could spread widely through a species by natural selection.

>> **Variation and technology:** Explain how different human innovations and technologies have led to the selective breeding of animals and plants for specific genetic traits.

High school science:

>> **Explain and justify evolution:** Understand that multiple lines of scientific evidence lead toward the conclusion of common ancestry and the process of evolution by natural selection, including both direct evidence-based arguments and those derived from statistics and probability.

>> **Model biodiversity changes:** Model to test solutions to reduce possible negative biodiversity effects of human behavior, including simulations and mathematical modeling.

WARNING

One easy-to-take misstep when presenting ideas from LS3 and LS4 happens when you misrepresent the generational aspect of change due to heredity and evolution. I witnessed a third-grade class in which the teacher explained to students that giraffes got long necks from stretching over time to reach fruit in trees. This is actually a pre-Darwinian understanding of evolution, called *Lamarckism*, which suggested that acquired traits of individual animals (such as large muscles or even wounds) could pass on to the next generation. It isn't a valid way to think of heredity as we understand it today.

Exploring the Planets (Including Earth) and Outer Space

The third category of DCIs is Earth and space sciences, which steps back to give a more universal perspective on science. This is a wide-ranging category; it covers content from the cosmic scale of understanding stars and galaxies, and then zooms back to the Earth to understand the systems at work in our world and the ways that human activity affects those systems.

Understanding space stuff

The first DCI within Earth and space sciences consists of the content that most of us probably think of when we think of the subject. In this first core idea, you find out about galaxies, stars, and planets. You also take a narrower look into our solar system in particular and then even closer for the history and development of Earth.

ESS1: Earth's Place in the Universe is divided into three component ideas.

ESS1.A The Universe and Its Stars

ESS1.B Earth and the Solar System

ESS1.C The History of Planet Earth

REMEMBER

This series of ESS1 standards shows an evolving understanding that begins with easily observed patterns and systems and moves on to a deeper understanding of what these patterns reveal about the objects in space around us — particularly the Sun and the moon.

Early elementary science:

>> **Predict space patterns:** Observe the sun, moon, and stars to recognize that there are regular patterns (most notably day/night) that can be predicted, including the amount of daylight at different times of year. (First grade)

>> **Earth event timing:** Recognize that different events on the Earth can happen quickly or slowly, by comparing things like earthquakes to erosion forming rivers. (Second grade)

Upper elementary science:

>> **Geological changes:** Identify from evidence in rocks and fossils that there have been changes to landscapes over time. (Fourth grade)

>> **Sun's brightness:** Recognize that the sun is a star, and the reason that it appears to bright is because of how close it is to the earth. (Fifth grade)

>> **Patterns in stars and light:** Use graphs to depict changes in the light in the sky, stars in the night sky, or length of shadows. (Fifth grade)

Middle school science:

>> **Earth, moon, and sun:** Model the relationships of the Earth, moon, and sun, including cycles of seasons, lunar phases, and eclipses.

>> **Geological time:** Use evidence from rock formations to explain the 4.6-billion-year history of Earth in terms of different geological eras.

>> **The solar system:** Understand the relationships and scales of different objects within the solar system.

>> **Gravity holds us together:** Recognize that gravity is the attractive force that can act between planets, stars, and galaxies at large distances.

High school science:

>> **Giant nuclear furnace:** Understand that stars (including the sun) are giant balls of plasma undergoing nuclear fusion, where the nuclear reaction within the star generates heat, light, and new elements.

>> **Nucleosynthesis:** Explain how the life cycle of stars results in the creation of heavier elements from lighter ones, and distribution of those elements out into the universe.

>> **Origins of the universe:** Use evidence to explain the argument in favor of the Big Bang theory.

>> **Model Earth and solar system:** Use evidence, mathematical models, and computer simulations to explain the motion and age of objects on the Earth (due to plate tectonics) and within the solar system, including interactions like meteor collisions.

Catching up on the Earth

Many people don't think about it too much, but the Earth's surface is a complicated place composed of a number of interconnected, complex, and dynamic systems. The interactions within these systems cover (literally) *geologic timescales*, with energy and matter flowing and transforming over hundreds of millions of years.

During these timescales, continents have formed, broken apart, and moved vast distances from each other. The very flow of water can reshape the surface of the planet! The goal of understanding these systems and their interconnected nature is at the heart of ESS2.

ESS2: Earth's Systems standard is broken down into five component ideas.

ESS2.A Earth Materials and Systems

ESS2.B Plate Tectonics and Large-Scale System Interactions

ESS2.C The Roles of Water in Earth's Surface Processes

ESS2.D Weather and Climate

ESS2.E Biogeology

Four primary Earth systems are emphasized within these standards.

>> **Atmosphere:** The layer of gases that surround the surface of the Earth.

>> **Biosphere:** The parts of the Earth and its ecosystems where life exists.

>> **Geosphere:** The solid parts of the Earth.

>> **Hydrosphere:** The parts of the Earth that include bodies of water, and also liquid water within the atmosphere.

REMEMBER

Understanding Earth's systems means recognizing these different components and how they interact to generate phenomena such as weather and climate.

Early elementary science:

>> **Weather patterns:** Observe local weather and describe how weather changes over time. (Kindergarten)

>> **Environmental adaptation:** Explain how plants and animals (including humans) change the environment to meet their needs. (Kindergarten)

>> **Bodies of water:** Identify where different bodies of water can be found on the Earth, in both solid and liquid forms. (Second grade)

>> **Erosion prevention:** Compare plans to lessen the change of land by wind or water.

Upper elementary science:

>> **Climates and weather:** Use data and information in a variety of forms to describe climates and typical weather conditions in areas. (Third grade)

>> **Changing landforms:** Understand how the Earth's surface is changed by erosion, plate tectonics, earthquakes, and other processes. (Fourth grade)

>> **System interactions:** Model phenomena on the earth as interactions between two of the Earth's systems.

>> **Water distribution:** Explain the distribution of water on the Earth by graphing amounts of fresh and salt water in different locations around the Earth.

Middle school science:

>> **Earth surface changes:** Understand, explain, and model the various processes involved in changing the surface of the earth, including plate tectonics, melting, crystallization, and related phenomena, and use information available to explain past changes to the Earth.

>> **Water cycle:** Model the water cycle on the Earth, including how it is driven by the force of gravity and energy from the sun.

>> **Atmosphere, water, weather, and climate:** Explain how the processes of heat flow within the atmosphere and ocean influence both long term regional climates and changes in weather conditions.

High school science:

>> **Understand interconnected systems:** Model and explain not only the ways that individual systems behave, but how the Earth's systems interact with each other, and how changes in one system can impact the other systems.

>> **Heat and energy models:** Understand that the Earth's systems run on heat and energy that flows through and between the various systems, and be able to use these explanations to model and predict phenomena on the Earth.

>> **Life and Earth's systems:** Describe the evidence that supports the interconnection between the development of Earth's systems and the formation of life on Earth.

Examining humanity's impact

Over the last several decades (especially since the 1980s), a widespread scientific consensus described how humans have had a profound impact on the systems of the Earth. This impact is unfolding at a rate that far exceeds the natural change of the Earth's systems, as observed in ESS2. And so, the ESS standards warrant a separate DCI to specifically investigate how human activity impacts the Earth.

ESS3: Earth and Human Activity is divided into four component ideas.

ESS3.A Natural Resources

ESS3.B Natural Hazards

ESS3.C Human Impacts on Earth Systems

ESS3.D Global Climate Change

These standards begin with young students recognizing the simple fact that living things depend strongly on the resources available in their environment and how humans have to respond to the environmental dangers they face. Eventually, students begin to understand that people use resources from the environment in important ways to power our society, and that the choices about how they use those natural resources have consequences. Students also learn how to understand and evaluate those consequences, and ultimately explore the arguments (sometimes controversial) about how humans need to act based on that evidence.

Early elementary science:

>> **Habitat requirements:** Model how different plants and animals need resources obtained from the places they live. (Kindergarten)

>> **Severe weather preparation:** Use information from the weather to predict and prepare for severe weather, such as by choosing appropriate clothing. (Kindergarten)

>> **Reduce environmental impact:** Explain ways that individuals and groups can act in ways to reduce negative impact on the local environment. (Kindergarten)

Upper elementary science:

>> **Weather protection:** Evaluate a proposed solution to a weather hazard. (Third grade)

>> **Natural resources:** Understand that humans obtain resources from the Earth to provide energy and fuel, and how the use of those resources affect society and the environment. (Fourth grade)

>> **Disaster protection:** Create proposed solutions for protecting humans from natural Earth processes, like earthquakes, floods, or volcanoes. (Fourth grade)

>> **Environmental resources:** Understand different ways that communities act to protect natural resources and the environment. (Fifth grade)

Middle school science:

>> **Resource origins:** Understand that distributions of natural resources on the Earth are a result of historic physical processes on the Earth.

>> **Predict and mitigate events:** Use data on natural hazards and the impact of human activities to predict future trends or events, and ways to lessen their negative impacts.

>> **Temperature increases:** Explore the causes related to global temperature rise over the past century.

High school science:

>> **Influences on humans:** Explain using evidence how various aspects of the natural world have had an impact on human activity, both historically and in the present.

>> **Natural resource usage:** Explore ways that humans can utilize natural resources while mitigating the dangers from that process, including designing solutions to more efficiently gather and utilize those resources.

>> **Influences by humans:** Model the impacts of human activity upon the natural systems of the Earth, including predictions of future implications of that activity.

TIP

Because human activity in various times and places can be so different, the ESS3 standards provide a useful place to begin comparing the activities of modern society in the U.S. to the activities in historical periods and other countries. This comparison allows educators to create projects that include not only these science concepts, but also social studies as well. And, if you incorporate discussion about the technology or engineering principles that humans use or have used to build their societies, you've got the makings of a fully integrated STEM lesson!

Some Brief Thoughts on the Scientific Method

Science education has always involved more than just memorizing scientific discoveries and facts. A full science education must also introduce students to an understanding of and appreciation for the process scientists use to discover those facts. Unfortunately, the underlying process of scientific reasoning is both nuanced and complex. In an effort to cut to the chase, most science education has relied on a shorthand version of the process by teaching something called the scientific method. (Sometimes it's even capitalized as Scientific Method, to make it sound *really* official and important.)

REMEMBER

With the embrace of the NRC science education frameworks, though, the national discussion around science education has moved away from the idea of teaching a rigid scientific method to a more flexible approach that engages with the three dimensions (practices, cross-cutting concepts, and disciplinary core ideas) of the science education frameworks. The more traditional scientific method has been replaced largely by Dimension 1 of the science frameworks, the science and engineering practices.

Reviewing the scientific method steps

Finding a single method of scientific discovery that all students can learn would be difficult; it doesn't exist. But often a science curriculum spells out a scientific method (sometimes with capital S and capital M) that is broken down into a series of steps that cover these general ideas (although hardly any two textbooks will actually be identical):

1. **Make an observation or ask a question.**
2. **Research known facts.**
3. **Formulate a hypothesis.**
4. **Test with experiment.**
5. **Analyze data.**
6. **Report conclusions.**

From an educational standpoint, this scientific method has two main benefits:

>> **It is convenient.** The steps can be taught, learned, memorized, and tested.

>> **It is generally correct.** The process gets across the idea of how science works.

I don't mean to downplay the importance of either of these benefits. For someone just encountering scientific thinking, this method provides a guideline for approaching scientific investigation. And it certainly maps well onto classic historical examples of how scientists made and confirmed scientific discoveries. But it has been given a central role in science for far too long.

Recognizing the shortcomings

Whatever value you can find in the traditional scientific method, you can find a number of problems as well, including the following:

>> **Scientists don't use it.** In my entire time earning a physics degree, I never once referenced the scientific method.

>> **It is too simplistic.** It suggests a single process that will lead to knowledge of all types.

>> **It overemphasizes experimentation.** Much science is confirmed through observation or building models.

>> **It offers no room for theory.** The exclusive grounding in observation misses the importance of theoretical insights as a basis for knowledge and discovery.

>> **Science requires community.** The traditional method doesn't recognize that acquiring scientific knowledge requires a social network of scientists constantly engaging and challenging each other.

What the scientific method gets right is that it acknowledges science as far more than merely a set of isolated facts about nature. The method offers a process for asking questions about those facts and applying general rules and values about how to proceed with acquiring new facts.

REMEMBER

But in trying to prescribe a clear and simple method, the scientific method oversimplifies everything about science. Simplicity might be okay when you initially introduce concepts because you usually introduce scientific ideas simplistically and then develop them over time. For example, when you talk about the Sun to young elementary students, you appropriately discuss it as a giant "ball of burning gas" instead of calling it a giant "gravity-driven nuclear fusion reactor."

Needing more than memorized steps

Instead of a straightforward, linear set of steps, the National Research Council proposes thinking about three main spheres of activity that scientists and engineers engage in, as depicted in Table 4-1. (Also see the sidebar, "Briefer thoughts on the engineering design process," if you're wondering how engineering fits in here.)

TABLE 4-1: **Three Spheres of Activity for Scientists and Engineers**

Investigating	Evaluating	Developing Explanations and Solutions
The Real World		**Theories and Models**
Ask Questions		Imagine
Observe	Argue	Reason
Experiment	Critique	Calculate
Measure	Analyze	Predict
Collect Data		Formulate Hypotheses
Test Solutions		Propose Solutions

Here is a breakdown of how I like to think about Table 4-1:

>> **The far-left "Investigating" column represents the experimentation part of science.** You look at the real world by asking questions, observing, performing experiments, and measuring, including collecting data and testing solutions. The activities described in this column are the focus of the traditional scientific method.

>> **The far-right "Developing Explanations and Solutions" column is the work of the theoretical portion of science,** which is more interested in developing explanations and solutions than in conducting tests. It is focused on exploring theories and models (as opposed to necessarily exploring the real world), and it explores these theories and models by imagining, reasoning, calculating, and predicting. This leads to formulating hypotheses and proposing solutions.

>> **The middle "Evaluating" column is where much of the work of science actually happens.** It isn't independent of the right column and the left column, but instead, it is the place where scientists explore their deep understanding of the natural world. By using an iterative process of argument, critique, and analysis, scientists — both as individuals and in groups — check their own work against the work of others.

REMEMBER

Instead of viewing this as three distinct columns, it's better to think of it as a continuous dialogue between the Investigations in the left column and the Explanations and Solutions developed in the right columns, mediated by the Evaluating taking place in the middle column. To check their work against that of others, scientists attend conferences and listen to each other discuss their theories and experiments, and then try to poke holes in the thinking by using arguments based firmly on evidence. This hole-poking doesn't come from animosity or jealousy, but it represents what the scientific process involves. The only way to derive new knowledge is by poking holes in the understanding of current knowledge.

WARNING

Now, I'm certainly not presenting Table 4-1 as something new to show to your students. In fact, I wouldn't. Students don't need to look under the hood at this level in order to follow STEM lessons, and trying to understand all of this would frankly be a distraction.

And the approach shown in the figure, although superior to the rigid scientific method, is far from a perfect depiction of how scientific discoveries happen. For example, the split between the experimental and theoretical columns (the first and third columns) may suggest that the investigating and developing explanations and solutions segments are completely distinct. In truth, these segments can certainly work in conjunction with each other.

REMEMBER

Regardless of its flaws, though, Table 4-1 is useful for a teacher who thinks that scientific experiments should be straightforward and follow a linear process. A teacher trying to get across the complex and nuanced nature of scientific reasoning *does* need to understand how messy authentic scientific thinking can be. If you really believe that scientific discovery is a straightforward process, then you're not going to teach the richness of the thinking involved.

Behind the method: Science and engineering practices

The Science and Engineering Practices are components of the NGSS that try to get at this complex nature of scientific inquiry. Eight practices are included, and I discuss each one in the following sections.

Practice 1: Asking questions and defining problems

Science rightly focuses on asking questions about the natural world. What exists and why? What happens and why? (Science is a big fan of "and why" at the end of questions.)

REMEMBER

Scientific thinking is rooted in asking questions about what's happening in the world. Young people do this instinctively, so it's a great place to connect their natural thinking to the scientific enterprise.

TIP

As a teacher, you want to encourage questions and not stifle them, but you also have to actually get things done. Create a *parking lot* (a designated space) for questions generated by your students. The simplest way to create a parking lot is with sticky notes that students can use to write a question and post it in the designated space. Perhaps create a bulletin board or designate a section of the whiteboard as your parking lot. If you don't have much wall space, you could create a decorated question box, an online discussion board, or whatever fits your situation. Be sure the questions aren't just posted and then ignored. I return to this idea in more detail in Chapter 9.

Practice 2: Developing and using models

In their 2010 book *The Grand Design*, theoretical physicists Leonard Mlodinow and Stephen Hawking coined the term *model-dependent realism* to describe the central role of models in science. To them, science isn't concerned with identifying true reality but, instead, it is concerned about building and refining models that more closely match what people can observe in reality.

The idea may be controversial, but what isn't controversial is that models are vitally important to science. Some models are more accurate than others — and some apply more universally — but scientists spend most of their time working with models of a physical system.

REMEMBER

Models may contain not only physical elements — like a model of an atom or a *food web* (a system of interdependent food chains) — but also conceptual elements. The periodic table of the elements includes not only the physical information about the elements, but also conceptual information about how those elements relate to each other. Sophisticated models may also include mathematical representations, such as equations or even computer simulations (see more in Practice 5).

Practice 3: Planning and carrying out investigations

This practice really encompasses two types of investigations:

>> Observing and describing the world

>> Developing and testing theories and explanations about the world

With Practice 3, you may begin to see an important difference from the Scientific Method approach. Carrying out an investigation in either of the two types involves not only engaging with Practice 3, but also jumping back into Practices 1 and 2. The sorts of questions that a student asks (Practice 1) will drive these investigations as they build their models (Practice 2).

Students are no longer thought to be diligently moving from one step to another. Instead, they now engage in a creative dance in which they uncover what they already know, think about the phenomena they're investigating, and combine ideas to lead to new discoveries.

Practice 4: Analyzing and interpreting data

The currency of scientific inquiry is data. Students need to be proficient not only in gathering data, but also in knowing what to do with it after they have it. The level of data analysis and the display of that data change over time based on the age of the students. However, you can begin processing data as early as possible.

REMEMBER

From an early age, you should have the expectation that part of any investigation includes having students record, present, and explain the data that they obtain. This habit is important for students, even if their first efforts may be in rough form. First efforts are always rough, and that's why you start early to get past them.

Of course, as students move up in grade levels, the methods of analyzing and representing the data become more formalized, but instilling the expectations in early grades helps you build on a firmer foundation.

Practice 5: Using mathematics and computational thinking

One of the most powerful tools in scientific thinking is mathematics. Computational modeling has unlocked amazing innovations. I devote all of Chapter 7 to the importance of mathematics, so you can jump there if you want to dig particularly deeply into how to hone mathematics.

TIP

In both Practices 4 and 5, you have ample opportunity to engage students with strong mathematical thinking in a real-world context. Figure out how you can use the STEM lesson to reinforce the concepts you're teaching in math. Students may not even realize the connection until they're in the middle of doing the mathematics. It's always exciting (for the students and the teacher) when a student realizes that something they're doing in another class is relevant to the current one. This also keeps them on their toes to look for connections.

Practice 6: Constructing explanations and designing solutions

The counterpart to asking questions involves ultimately coming up with explanations that answer those questions. If you don't have an explanation for what you're talking about, you're just guessing (see the sidebar, "Hypothesis, Guess, Theory").

HYPOTHESIS, GUESS, THEORY

In science, a *hypothesis* is a plausible explanation that can predict what will happen in a given situation, usually based on a specific observed phenomenon or series of phenomena, or possibly on a general conceptual understanding of a model.

A *guess*, on the other hand, comes with no underlying plausible explanation. Often students have an underlying explanation that they are unable (or unwilling) to articulate. Take time to see whether you can encourage the student (or another student) to articulate the reasoning. Even in cases where a guess is wildly off and you don't think any plausible reasoning exists, students may surprise you by revealing unstated misconceptions that they have.

A *theory* in scientific terms is a construct built on a diverse set of evidence and investigation and that has stood up to extensive scrutiny from the scientific community, usually over a period of many years. A theory is always open to revision based on new evidence.

And what about a scientific law, like Boyle's Law or the law of gravity? In truth, a scientific law is no more inherently true than a well-supported theory, and is also always open to revision based on new evidence. Scientific laws are generally theories that were named by people who got a little too sure of themselves.

Part of constructing the explanations will be interacting with students who may have other explanations for the questions being asked. Student-to-student discussions can be fruitful and provide a strong basis for Practice 7.

Practice 7: Engaging in argument from evidence

One of the key traits of scientific reasoning is that arguments must be firmly rooted in the available evidence. Much of the work in Practices 1 through 6 orients toward obtaining evidence that everyone agrees has some measure of value and integrity.

REMEMBER

As students formulate and defend explanations of their investigations, they need to understand that their emotions and convictions are not the cornerstone of the argument. They need to consistently refer back to the evidence they've gathered to support their claims.

TIP

The goal of being correct often discourages students from admitting that they were wrong. Encourage students to change their minds if they realize that the evidence no longer supports a previous view. This can be a great learning moment when it happens. Celebrate it!

Practice 8: Obtaining, evaluating, and communicating information

While some earlier practices focused on the analysis and presentation of data and mathematical information, Practice 8 has to do more with being able to absorb and generate written work about science. At young ages, this practice ties in strongly with literacy initiatives and reading books that introduce basic science concepts. In higher grades, the practice may mean presenting students with articles from peer-reviewed science journals.

Mixing the Buckets Together

The Disciplinary Core Ideas (DCIs) split up the scientific content into a variety of buckets, but these ideas still connect together in many ways. The historical distribution of these concepts into completely separate categories was an artifact of how scientists stumbled into different discoveries without realizing the deep connections between them.

For the remainder of this chapter, I focus on how the NGSS works to draw together the scientific core ideas.

Crosscutting concepts

In addition to the practices, the NGSS has the crosscutting concepts dimension that provides another level of connection between the scientific ideas that students study across the grades.

REMEMBER

The crosscutting concepts are the second dimension of the framework, which highlights their importance relative to the specific DCI (the third dimension). In a very significant sense, it is more important that a graduating student understand these crosscutting concepts than that they understand any particular science standard.

Crosscutting concept 1: Patterns

Just like asking questions is a natural starting point for the practices of science, identifying patterns is a natural starting point for concepts that cut across scientific disciplines. Even young children recognize commonalities among things. Classifying things by common attributes is a great entry-point into scientific activities.

It's not by accident that so many brilliant insights in the biological sciences were made by men like Charles Darwin, who were obsessive collectors that recognized patterns and similarities between biological specimens.

Crosscutting concept 2: Cause and effect

As part of their pattern-seeking behavior, children also look for patterns where two things consistently happen near to each other in time. In this way, they recognize their first cause-and-effect relationships.

REMEMBER

As children grow, they begin to understand that these relationships may be much more complex and not always as obvious as the ones they first noticed. They hopefully develop a greater understanding of the difference between *causation* (where one phenomenon directly causes another) and mere *correlation* (where two things may or may not have a relationship, but one doesn't cause the other), and they retain the understanding that identifying correlation can often provide useful insights into causation relationships.

Crosscutting concept 3: Scale, proportion, and quantity

Many concepts that are extremely useful in one scientific situation don't apply particularly well in another, often because the scale of the situation is different. Scientists spend a significant amount of time carefully defining the context of their explanations and experiments to focus on a particular well-defined situation and are hesitant to apply those results more broadly.

Consider these points:

>> **If a scientist explores nuclear reactions,** then the specific internal structure of the atomic nucleus is extremely important.

>> **After the scientist moves on to studying chemical interactions,** though, the specific structure of the atomic nucleus is less important. To illustrate this point, Antoine Lavoisier discovered and studied chemical reactions well over a century before anyone knew the nucleus *had* an internal structure!

>> **When science experiments and explanations scale up to talking about Earth's ecosystem or food webs,** the nuclear structural details become even less important.

Humans perform scientific studies on three scales of phenomena that are

» Directly observable with the naked eye

» Extremely small or fast, requiring microscopes or other tools

» Extremely large or slow, requiring telescopes or other tools

REMEMBER

Not surprisingly, scientists usually study the directly observable category first, while the latter couple of scales require technological advances or the gathering of large data sets to begin to explore.

Crosscutting concept 4: Systems and system models

The real world is large and complex, and part of what scientists do is narrow their focus to a specific system — or a specific aspect of a specific system — and try to understand that as clearly as possible. For example, some biologists devote their whole careers primarily to the study of one specific type of insect, and some physicists spend the bulk of their time exploring one question about the cosmological history of the universe.

REMEMBER

Students should understand the idea of taking a narrow focus and, over time, be able to analyze and create models for more complex systems. By breaking a complex scientific problem into simpler systems that they can model, it will help them gain a better understanding of scientific questions and solutions in their learning process.

Crosscutting concept 5: Energy and matter — flows, cycles, and conservation

Conservation of energy and matter are key concepts in physics, and one of the major discoveries of science as a whole is how matter and energy flow and cycle through physical systems, including living systems. In fact, often the key thing that you use to define a system model is the flow of energy and matter within the system. For example, understanding many weather processes involves understanding the heat flow within the atmosphere.

In earlier grades (namely 3 through 5), these concepts generally focus on the flow of matter through a system and establish that matter is conserved. The concept of conversion of matter into energy within systems begins to develop during middle school and gets refined in high school. At the high school level, students can really begin to understand the relationship between matter and energy.

Teachers should take care to distinguish between matter and energy when presenting these concepts in a STEM lesson. Food is matter, not energy, even though food is necessary for the body to produce energy. You can easily establish and reinforce misconceptions about the distinction between matter and energy (or other related concepts) if you don't present the concepts carefully.

Crosscutting concept 6: Structure and function

A recurring theme of structure and function exists throughout the sciences (and engineering) and ties into the understanding of other concepts such as scale, proportion, and models. Students realize that if they're going to change the structure of something, that change could result in a change of function. A balloon filled with ordinary air functions differently from one filled with helium.

Students begin exploring the relationship of structure and function in macroscopic ways by looking at engineering designs, or by studying the design of things such as wings in living creatures. As this understanding grows, students realize that one of the first steps toward understanding a new phenomenon is to carefully examine the related materials in detail, including their shape. Many students get insights into how to make something fly by observing bird wings (which was also how the Wright brothers figured it out).

Crosscutting concept 7: Stability and change

Change is a constant in the universe, but the universe has been running a long time, so a lot of the changes that we observe are conditions that have already attained a level of equilibrium and stability. The cycles of the moon and the planets represent not only change over the month and year, but also stability over longer timeframes.

Though little in the universe is static, students benefit from understanding *dynamic equilibrium* (a balance between changing processes, which can exist long-term) as well as more rapid change. When mixed with concepts such as models and time scales, seeing different types of changes allows for a deep understanding of how short-term changes such as genetic variability between generations can lead to the evolution of new species.

Integrating science into the real world

The real world has little care for the nice, neat categories that academics use to categorize their thinking. Thinking scientifically means connecting diverse scientific concepts in real time while engaging with authentic problems in the real world.

REMEMBER

Science is only one element of STEM, but integrating it together authentically with technology, engineering, and mathematics can still be a challenge. Natural connections exist between many STEM concepts (for example, designing environmental protections and mechanical engineering), but they're frequently taught in fragmented ways that fail to highlight those connections for the average student. How do you teach STEM in a way that negates that fragmentation?

The three dimensions working together

One key insight of the National Research Council (NRC) science education frameworks is the understanding that the old way of teaching science — by lecturing on a concept and then running a lab — wasn't cutting it. Students can develop scientific understanding (as well as proficiency or mastery) only if they engage with real questions and have discourse with each other in a process of inquiry and discovery.

REMEMBER

And so, each standard in the NGSS lays out not only the disciplinary core idea, but also related practices and crosscutting concepts that apply. I go over how to read and interpret these standards in Chapter 3, but you must think about how the three dimensions relate to each other when dealing with the standards.

In Part 3 of this book, I focus on how to apply these three dimensions together in practical ways to provide STEM instruction that can engage students.

Making a final case for applied science

This chapter focuses on the core ideas that science needs to get across to students before they graduate from high school. If you take away anything from the chapter, please recognize that

>> Scientific concepts must come across to students in authentic ways — through applied science experiences.

>> You can't reduce the presentation to the lecture method that many readers probably remember from their own introduction to science. Even though those lectures likely had the occasional positive outcome, STEM offers better ways to get this material across.

If you are reading this book, there's a good chance that you're motivated to teach STEM. But now think back. Despite all the great teachers that you likely had, what were the things that really made you love science? Was there a single science lecture or unit that resonated with you and motivated you to pursue science?

REMEMBER

In almost every case, a passion for pursuing scientific knowledge comes about because of an *experience* that the person has with scientific discovery. That experience may have come during a class lecture, of course, but it more likely occurred in a lab experiment or demonstration. Students classified as *gifted* or *high ability* early on get more of those authentic experiences, which in turn helps give them more opportunities to develop a passion for science, in a self-reinforcing cycle.

TIP

Making authentic, applied science the cornerstone of scientific instruction for all students means that you grant every student the chance to have more authentic interactions. You're giving them the chance to think of themselves as people who discover things scientifically. And whether their career involves STEM directly or not, that's a worthwhile mode of thinking to develop.

IN THIS CHAPTER

» **Examining different technologies**

» **Exploring the digital world**

» **Diving into computer science**

» **Using technology in the real world**

» **Looking ahead at future technologies**

Chapter **5**

Leveraging Computing and Technology Tools

The *technology* part of STEM is simultaneously one of the most pervasive and least emphasized portions of STEM education. On a daily basis, teachers and students utilize technology as a regular part of education, but they rarely spend time teaching about the technology itself. The lesson goal is always some other content, and the technology is just along for the ride. Often, technology instruction takes place as a required obstacle. At worst, students are left to figure out the technology on their own.

As I mention in Chapter 2, for the purposes of STEM, *technology* is defined broadly as "any modification of the natural world done to fulfill human needs or desires."

Although this chapter covers information about technology and computer science, its goal is to speak to teachers who are not already experts in these technological areas. A high school computer science teacher hopefully already knows the content in this chapter. For those teachers, I suggest jumping ahead to Chapter 8, where I discuss how to integrate computer science with other areas.

In this chapter, I explore what the next generation needs to know about technology. I talk about the internet and how online access can be a springboard for a wider discussion about the role of technology in our lives. Then, I help you explore computer science in more depth, including (but not limited to) coding and computational thinking. I also cover technologies that are more practical, and how you can leverage a student's experiences to give a deeper appreciation of the role of technology in their lives. And I discuss how to make sure students are looking at technology in a way that prepares them for the transformations that they can expect in the future — and the ones that none of us see coming — yet.

Exploring Technology in the Classroom

As students grow up, they confront an increasingly technological world. Those not prepared to thrive with technology may find themselves left behind. I'm not saying that every student needs to be ready to dive into professional coding, but hardly a single job in the working world hasn't been transformed by technology.

Doubt it? Keep in mind that one of the first major mass-market successful robots was designed to vacuum the floor. The current rise in artificial intelligence (AI) application is displacing people as the creators of written and graphic content. If you had asked (30 or so years ago) about jobs that would be safest from takeover by technology, there's a good chance that artists, authors, and custodians would have made it onto the list of safest occupations.

Students should be familiar with various types of technologies. In general, you can think of them falling into these five buckets:

>> **Building, construction, and manufacturing:** Building tools, ranging from saws, screwdrivers, and other traditional tools, to 3D printers and associated software.

>> **Information and communications:** Computers, smartphones, tablets, and other computing devices that connect to the internet for information purposes.

>> **Programming and coding:** The procedures necessary to program within computing environments, and familiarity with basic programming languages. This technology area includes physical computing applications such as robots, drones, and other devices.

>> **Audio and visual technologies:** Creating and engaging with everything from a slideshow presentation to infographics, web pages, videos, podcasts, and animations. These technologies include virtual reality and augmented reality, and potentially many types of video games.

>> **Functional office technologies:** Word processors, spreadsheets, data displays and graphing, e-mail clients, and so on.

Looking through this list, you no doubt recognize certain types of technology that your students engage with all the time in the classroom or in their daily lives. You may also recognize certain types of technology that they rarely (if ever) engage with.

Embracing the overlap

Although I define these technologies as occupying different buckets, they will often overlap. For example, while creating a slideshow presentation (audio and visual technology), students may need to generate an appropriate data display (functional office technology). Lessons about how to use e-mail fall into both the *information and communication* bucket and the *functional office technologies* bucket. Rather than buckets, it might be better to think of these technologies as enclosed in mesh bags.

REMEMBER

I say this earlier in the book (at least once, see Chapter 1, for example), but it's worth repeating: STEM areas of study are not independent silos. An underlying paradigm of STEM education is that knowledge silos don't exist. STEM is an integrated, holistic approach to knowledge and understanding. But the embrace of knowledge silos is so ingrained in the fundamental structure of modern education that you really must work hard to get out of that mode of thinking.

As an example of this, I fell into following this misleading myth in structuring Part 2 of the book you're reading. As an example, the line between physical making and digital making has become particularly flexible in recent years. I hold off most of the discussion regarding the building, construction, and manufacturing technology category until I discuss their application to the STEM area of engineering in Chapter 6, in which I present robotics and other forms of physical computing. And the engineering design process ideas from Chapter 6 also become useful in designing purely digital computing artifacts, just as they facilitate engineering of physical build projects.

Focusing on computer-related technology

Throughout most of this chapter, the technology I talk about relates mostly to computers. And, specifically, I emphasize the need to teach computer science to students as a core part of their STEM education.

In 2006, the Association for Computing Machinery (ACM) defined *computer science* as "the study of computers and algorithmic processes, including their principles, their hardware and software designs, their implementation, and their impact on society." This is the definition used in the development of the Computer Science frameworks and subsequent standards of the Computer Science Teachers Association (CSTA). See the sidebar "Standards for Computer Science" for more about those standards, which I provide in this chapter for easy reference in your planning.

As I mention in Chapter 3, as far back as the 1983, the *A Nation at Risk* report recommended a required semester-long computer science course for all American high school students. The 2015 STEM Education Act explicitly included computer science as part of STEM (in case there was any confusion about that) and then later that year the Every Student Succeeds Act (ESSA) classified computer science as part of a well-rounded education. Much of this chapter focuses on computer science, because it is an essential technology that you can weave into a wide variety of STEM lessons.

STANDARDS FOR COMPUTER SCIENCE

Much of this chapter focuses on computer science, so I suggest reviewing the related portion of Chapter 3. The chapter lists the concepts and subconcepts of the computer science standards developed by the Computer Science Teachers Association (CSTA), and the full set of standards can be found at https://csteachers.org/k12standards.

As I discuss the teaching of technology concepts throughout this chapter, I reference the related subconcepts. As with the science standards in Chapter 4, teachers should know what students have covered in previous grades and where they need to focus next to get the students to understand the science concepts and know why they need to understand them. Also, recognize that standards are not a curriculum. See Chapters 9 and 10 for more about implementing the content in the classroom.

The high school standards, particularly those designated for grades 11-12, are not intended for all students. Those standards are oriented towards students who are preparing for a career in a technical field, or even explicitly in computer technology and programming. If a student graduates from high school proficient in — or even just familiar with — the computer science standards through grade 8, they'll be in a good position to engage with technology in their daily lives after high school.

In addition to the standards for students, CSTA has a set of standards for computer science teachers (https://csteachers.org/teacherstandards/) of key approaches and professional skills that CS teachers should meet.

Living and Learning in a Digital World

Growing up in the 1980s, I knew from movies such as *WarGames* and *Tron* that society was moving toward a digital world. But when I logged into my first bulletin-board system (BBS) in the early 1990s, I had little understanding about how comprehensive the integration of technology would become in our world.

REMEMBER

Students today aren't just interacting with technology; they are living lives fully integrated with technology from their earliest memories. For this reason, young people today are often called *digital natives*, and they have been for nearly a generation.

I first realized that a gap (between digital natives and the older crowd) was forming as a college junior in the late 1990s. Almost all of my classmates and older students could remember the day that we got our first game system (usually Atari, but in some cases Nintendo), our first classroom computer (generally a Commodore 64 or Apple Macintosh), and our first home computer. But many of the students just a couple of years younger than I (who would qualify as millennials today) had no real memory of a time when they didn't have at least some sort of video game system or computer close at hand at either home or school, and usually in both places.

The growth of and familiarity with digital technology at home and in the classroom expanded even more throughout the 1990s with the development of the World Wide Web. Advancements that led to smartphones ensure everyone has instant access to more information and computing power than ever before. As teachers, it's our job to help students learn how to handle that responsibly.

This crazy little thing called the internet

For over a generation at the time of this writing, the internet has been one of the most dominant forces in the technological world. It has revolutionized every aspect of our lives in countless ways, for both good and ill.

A few years ago, a politician famously said that the internet was a series of tubes. This observation pokes at a core truth about the internet. The internet is fundamentally a network of connections, and the information we access on the internet is the data that passes between those connections. (Whether the wires and cables and wireless signals that carry the information are appropriately classified as "tubes" is another matter — and a valid topic for a robust STEM classroom debate!)

TIP

As modern digital natives, kids today don't realize how the world transformed because of technology. This is just the way the world is. For you as a teacher, a key aspects of providing a STEM education is making students consciously aware of the role of technology in their lives. They shouldn't just plug into the latest app because it exists, but instead, they should understand how to take charge and make that app (or any technology) serve them.

Students begin engaging with the internet from an early age, but they don't understand the essence of what they're interacting with at first. Just as I didn't understand how the images appeared on the television, kids don't understand how the text, images, and video they see online get there. And they don't explicitly need to know that as soon as they begin using the internet.

But by the time students are in the 3-5 grade band, they should be learning in class about how the internet transfers data as part of the Network Communication & Organization subconcept.

As students progress into middle school — and then into high school — their understanding of these network elements is intended to grow. This progression represents the growing sophistication of how they understand this series of tubes.

Communicating and working through technology

Most people can function pretty well in the digital world without actually knowing the details and technical protocols of sending information around the internet. If you know how to type in a web address or even web search terms, you can usually find the sort of information you're looking for. What is far more important for most people is knowing how to behave online.

Safety and cybersecurity

While they can find no shortage of benign uses of the internet, students should be aware of potential nefarious uses. They need to be taught about scams and cyber-crime, and that certain people on the internet may want to gain access to their private information.

In short, students need to be familiar from an early age about appropriate types of online threats and the measures everyone can and should take to avoid those threats. This element of computer science is covered under the Cybersecurity subconcept.

REMEMBER

Starting with early grades, students must understand the importance of strong passwords and of keeping those passwords private. Teachers should explicitly teach them not to write down their passwords.

As you progress in cybersecurity, of course, these lessons turn into discussions rather than hard-and-fast rules. For example, I personally experienced opposing advice regarding password security, as follows:

>> **On a podcast, the chief security officer of Google** said that they recommend writing your complex passwords down in a physical notebook. The reason, he said, is that the far greater danger is using non-complex passwords, repeating passwords, or having your passwords hacked because they are stored in an online password manager (or, even worse, in a Google Doc).

The Google security officer was worried about some random cybercriminal getting access to your passwords and posting them onto the dark web.

>> **During a corporate cybersecurity training,** the facilitator advised the audience not to write down passwords, but instead, to save them within Google Password Manager — one of the tools that Google's own chief security officer had specifically said that Google employees don't rely on because of security concerns!

The local security officer was worried about someone grabbing your notebook of passwords out of your cubicle.

Both people were experts on computer security, and certainly both were far more knowledgeable than I am, but they came to opposite conclusions about the best way to move forward regarding personal password security. Both have valid concerns, and people must decide for themselves which to weigh more heavily when thinking about their personal information. (For your work information, of course, you should follow workplace policies.)

Impacts of technology and computing

One of the more intriguing core concepts of the CSTA standards is "Impacts of Computing," which focus on the ways that *computing artifacts* (products created by a human using a computer) have had an impact on human society. This element of computer science can be easily overlooked because the impact may at first seem pretty disconnected from the science end of things.

But computer science is about more than just the technical aspects of creating programming artifacts; it's about how humans use those artifacts and the related impacts on the world, including on human society. Just as the science standards include the interaction of humans with the natural world (see Chapter 4), computer science involves teaching about the human component of the computing world.

TIP

This approach is useful for a variety of technologies, not just computing. When teaching anything related to technology, take time to consider how technology has changed human life. Whether you consider the steam engine, the home washing machine, or the cellphone, technology has demonstrated the amazing power to transform the world — often in unexpected ways.

Science fiction author Neal Stephenson has an excellent example about the unpredictability of technology's impact on society. He points out that when Thomas Edison turned electricity into a consumer product by developing the light bulb, he certainly never thought that one of the consequences of that would be the electric guitar, let alone the advent of rock and roll.

As a STEM educator, I automatically go to the next step: How many students would be engaged in a lesson where they tried to figure out the ways that electricity has transformed musical performance? (And I cover designing lessons like this in Chapter 9.)

Technology changes that affect culture

Looking at the way technology has changed society is the entry point to the Culture subconcept of the CSTA computer science standards, but it progresses to consider traits like accessibility and usability. Ultimately, this subconcept is about realizing that most technological advances will have positive and negative impacts on society. And figuring out how to weigh those impacts against each other becomes a factor when determining how to responsibly use the technology.

Another part of using technology responsibly involves making sure that the creators and users of technology are considering other people in their activities.

REMEMBER

The impact of technology on culture provides a great opportunity to explore both social-emotional learning concepts and mindfulness regarding our own emotional states. My wife is often able to tell when I've had an unpleasant online interaction, because she sees something on my face while I'm reading my laptop and then I respond to her "What's wrong?" by snapping "Nothing." We all need to learn how to regulate our emotions online, and it's never too early to begin.

Just like educators must teach the soft skills of collaboration and respect for others during their in-person interactions, they must also make it clear that those skills apply online. The importance of interpersonal skills online comes through the Social Interactions subconcept.

Schools and adult authorities teach students that laws are important and should be obeyed. Just like you teach a student not to steal someone's physical property, you need to help them understand the more abstract notion that stealing digital property is also a form of theft. These are spelled out in the CSTA standards for the Safety, Law, & Ethics subconcept.

TECHNOLOGY OF EDUCATION

Students need to learn some technology just because they use it in schools. While engaging with technology does help foster a general sense of digital literacy and comfort, I don't spend a lot of time on EdTech throughout this chapter.

In the interest of teachers being familiar with technological tools, here are a handful of examples of digital tools that many find useful in education:

- **Kahoot!:** A game-based learning platform that enables teachers to create quizzes, surveys, and interactive lessons. (kahoot.com)

- **Nearpod:** A platform on which teachers can create multimedia presentations and build quizzes around them. (nearpod.com)

- **Padlet:** A visual platform on which teachers can build virtual *walls* that students can interact with, either by adding graphics or providing feedback. (padlet.com)

- **Edpuzzle:** A platform that helps teachers create video lessons for students to watch and then associate quizzes for the students based on the lessons. (edpuzzle.com)

In addition to the above, teachers can and should make use of the systems (such as their learning management system, or LMS) and other collaboration tools in their school districts, including Google Classroom (and related apps), Seesaw, Canvas, or Microsoft Teams.

Like I cover in Chapter 9, you want to make choices about technology carefully as part of the lesson-planning process. You may find that a more authentic task is to ask students to record a video or create a slide presentation rather than to fill in feedback on a Padlet.

Coding and Computer Science

Though the definition and standards for computer science do deal with understanding the impact of computer science in society, and using them ethically and responsibly, the core of computer science is knowing how computers work and having the skills to make them do the things you want them to do. Students should come away from their schooling with a solid understanding of the basic physical and computational concepts that explain how and why computers work.

Understanding computer hardware and software

Before delving deeply into how to create programs to run on computers, students need a basic understanding of what computers are and how they function. The more familiar students are with these concepts early on, the easier they'll be able to grasp the deeper and more sophisticated concepts (such as programming and networking) that accompany their later work with computers.

Identifying the pieces and parts

From early grades (through grade –5), you can focus on having students identify and recognize different parts of a computer, as well as explain how different software is useful for different applications. These are the standards laid out in the Devices and Hardware and Software subconcepts of the computer science standards.

TIP

This is a good place to consider my earlier claim that there are no knowledge silos, because these computer-related learning standards provide excellent ways to build vocabulary in young students. Here's an example of how you can build vocabulary by using computer terms:

>> Students have tablets or laptops, which have screens. A desktop's computer's screen, however, is called a monitor. Have students use the appropriate terms and learn to spell them.

>> Windows (like those in the students' homes) also have screens, so you can discuss the idea that the word *screen* applies to both their laptop and the windows at home, even though these objects are quite different.

You can do the same vocabulary-building activities with many other computer terms, such as *mouse* or *drive*. This promotes deep engagement with language that is tied to an authentic and relevant context: understanding computers.

Tackling data-related functions

While the students are learning the basics of the devices and their components, they are also learning about what they do. As early as kindergarten, students should be learning how to save, organize, and retrieve files on computers. The Storage subconcept focuses on understanding the ways in which computers store and translate the information within their systems.

Troubleshooting computer operation

When your students begin using computers, particularly in non-trivial ways, they will inevitably (and probably quickly) run into a problem with the operation of the computer. The Troubleshooting subconcept has standards that focus on being able to identify and explain these operational issues, and take reasonable steps to resolve them.

REMEMBER

Initially, of course, students aren't expected to necessarily solve an operational problem, and the learning emphasis is on identifying the problem. Students need to know that just saying "the computer doesn't work" isn't particularly helpful. They must learn to identify the exact nature of the steps that triggered the issue, as well as any error messages spawned by the issue. For example, if there's a pop-up screen, the student should read what it says and possibly even write down the message before closing it out, in case it includes useful information to resolve the issue.

Efforts to fix computer problems will no doubt begin with trial and error because students haven't developed any experience with resolving the operational problems that they run into. In middle school and beyond, they should have gained enough experience to really internalize a systematic approach to dealing with computer operations issues. By that point, among other things, they have hopefully learned the power of unplugging and restarting the computer.

Skills at troubleshooting computer problems also prove particularly useful as students move from being users of computers to creators who generate (and eventually test and correct) their own computer programs.

Algorithms as the basis of coding

The part of teaching technology that really makes you and the students feel like you're delving into computer science happens when the student is actually using some computer coding language to create computer code. This activity requires not only understanding the various aspects of the computer language, but also applying it through careful use of reason and logic to achieve a specific outcome. Coding is not just the heart of computer science, but it brings together other STEM themes, such as logical reasoning, mathematics, and iterative testing.

WARNING

JUMPING STRAIGHT INTO CODING

You will likely want to lay the groundwork of students understanding what a computer is and how to use it before you get into coding, but you could be bold and dive into coding early on as soon as students begin to engage with computers. This may be particularly tempting if you have a handy resource like engaging robotics with extremely user-friendly programming interfaces.

After your students begin coding, feeling like you're doing a great job with computer science is easy (and you likely are). But you do still need to figure out how to work in the less glitzy parts of computer science, like teaching how to store files and learning the names for different computer components. If the entirety of your computer science curriculum involves students learning how to use Scratch Jr. or program a specific type of educational robot, then the computer science curriculum needs diversification.

When you create computer code, you're actually creating an *algorithm*, which is a step-by-step process to complete a task. After you write the code, the computer will then execute the algorithmic steps you wrote, exactly as you told it to (though not always as you intended).

The Algorithms subconcept of the CSTA standards show the steps for building algorithms. From an early age, students meet algorithms in a non-computing context by thinking through and completing step-by-step directions.

TIP

Early lessons for building algorithms can be incredibly engaging and can easily help kids appreciate how difficult giving clear directions can be — especially to someone (or something) that is intent on taking them literally.

Defining clear instruction with low-tech algorithms

Here are two low-tech examples of creating an algorithm with younger students, which gets at these machine learning ideas:

>> **Ask students how to make a peanut butter and jelly sandwich and instruct them to write down the process step-by-step.** Their first step will likely be something like "Put the peanut butter on the bread." When you then grab the jar of peanut butter and sit that closed jar on top of the loaf of bread (still in its bag), they quickly realize they weren't clear enough in outlining their first step. The students will not need prompting to begin refining their instructions.

>> **Have students work in groups to write out rules for looking at features of a picture to identify whether the picture shows a cat.** After each group has their rules completed, go through a prepared slide deck that contains some basic cat pictures, but then also includes some dogs, and maybe a rabbit. But then also include pictures of cats without fur, cats without tails, and a leopard. (You can also probably find a picture of a 3-legged cat online somewhere.)

You can really do this cat example with students of any age. I've seen it done with groups of teachers, and it's still eye-opening how difficult it is to define an accurate sorting process.

REMEMBER

When you assign exercises designed for students to create (and fine-tune) a step-by-step or sorting process, be sure to use computing terminology with wording such as, "Great job on refining our algorithm. Let's write down the steps of the algorithm as we debug it."

Emphasizing the idea of refining algorithms

When students begin to dive into the problem-solving elements of writing an algorithm, you have a great opportunity to highlight for students (and for yourself) that the programs (algorithms) they write will not work correctly the first time. That idea of embracing failure and that mistakes are the cornerstone of learning (see Chapter 1), really comes into play here.

REMEMBER

A mistake in a program is always an opportunity to learn something new about how the elements of the program function and make changes accordingly. If you had realized that the code worked in a certain way (and not the way you intended), you wouldn't have made the mistake when writing the program.

A good analogy for the idea of repetitive cycles of refinement is particularly appropriate to programming: video games. When playing a new video game, you will make mistakes and fail to achieve the objective. In many popular video games — from Super Mario Brothers to Halo — this means that your character dies. But then what happens? You respawn and are able to retry.

In video games, this repetitive cycle of correcting your past mistakes is understood to be part of the process. By dying in a video game, you're learning which procedures do *not* achieve your objective (not dying, presumably). You might not be thrilled that you died, but you know that if you do then you'll have to repeat part of the game. Repeating part of the game is, in itself, just part of learning the game.

TIP

Encourage your students to take a repetitive approach to designing a computer program. For example, suppose that your students are designing a video game, and they define a parameter that, when they run the game, causes objects in the game to go racing off the screen. To fix this problem, they'll have to modify the associated parameter, through either trial and error or planning and calculation, until they define it properly to achieve their desired outcome when they test their game.

Connecting with variables and control structures

One concept that students encounter in computer science well before they reach it in mathematics is the idea of variables. Again, there aren't any knowledge silos (I can't say it enough!), so there's no reason you can't jump between the idea of variables in computers and the idea of variables in math and use them to reinforce each other. My first job out of college involved teaching abstract algebra to elementary students in Detroit public schools, so let me assure you, students can catch onto the concept of variables very quickly if you give them the opportunity.

After students understand the concepts of algorithms and variables, they can progress to more sophisticated programming structures. These sequences, loops, events, and conditionals all fall under the Control subconcept in the CSTA standards.

Now that I'm hitting some of the more programming-intensive elements of the standards, I want to define some of the related terms. The primary source for these definitions is the CSTA K-12 Computer Science Framework, although in certain cases, I have modified to make the definitions clearer or more accessible, or to elaborate.

Loop: A programming structure that repeats a specified sequence of instructions until meeting a specific condition.

Event: An occurrence that has significance for hardware or software, such as mouse clicks, keystrokes, error messages, or loading a program.

Conditional: A decision-making structure in which the program performs different computations or actions based on a specific condition. These are frequently framed as "If X, then Y" in a logic structure.

Nested loop: A programming structure where within one loop, another loop is built, with its repetition often based on a different set of conditions.

Compound conditional: A more elaborate form of a conditional programming component in which multiple conditions determine the different outcomes or actions that may be performed. A structure for this may be something like "If X and Y, then B, otherwise if X and not Y, then C, otherwise if not X and Y, then D, otherwise if not X and not Y, then E." This example provides distinct consequences for every possible combination of truth values for X and Y.

Procedure: A specific piece of code that performs a concrete task. Procedures are referenced by larger body of code any time that concrete task needs to be performed. These pieces of code can also be called a method, function, or even module in some programming languages.

Module: A software component that contains one or more procedures.

TIP

Although *flowcharts* — a series of boxes that help outline the sequence of steps in any process — are not explicitly present in the standards until the middle school grades, you can use them even earlier as another way to organize and compare students' algorithmic thinking. A good trick for introducing a concept earlier than it shows up in the standards is to offer a tantalizing transition such as: "I'm not really supposed to show you this until you're in the sixth grade, but I think you can handle it."

Detailing modularity and program development

The ideas expressed in the Modularity subconcept bring together the ideas of breaking a process down into a discrete sequence of instructions and then also looking at algorithms as combinations of these sequences of steps. These ideas begin in early grades with the exploration of clear instructions, as I discuss in the section "Defining clear instruction with low-tech algorithms" earlier in the chapter.

While students are still in early grades, you can pull many of these concepts together as forms of play. The Program Development subconcept really gives an opportunity for students to think about sequences and work out a plan for finding and fixing problems in the process.

The amusing algorithmic activities — which I discuss earlier in the chapter in the section "Defining clear instruction with low-tech algorithms" — are also perfectly appropriate to use here, even before you're getting into actual coding within a real computer programming language.

Coding with visual blocks and text

You might be surprised that, in a chapter which has focused so heavily on computer science, I haven't shown any actual computer code, or even talked in depth about computer languages. You may notice, however, that the standards aren't that specific about computer code and languages either.

The goal of the standards (and of this chapter) is to provide a broad foundation for what students need to know about technology and computer science — with the understanding that the principles discussed will be useful in a variety of contexts.

If your school has a formal computer science or coding curriculum, then it will likely come with many resources to help you understand the specific programming languages that you'll be working with. (I describe some great free programming resources in Chapter 17 that will be particularly useful.) If you do definitely want some books with programming guidance — including coding projects — go to your favorite online bookstore and search for terms such as *coding for kids* or *scratch for kids.* You will find many options.

Keep in mind, though, that this technology can sometimes evolve rapidly, and sometimes print resources (or digital resources, for that matter) quickly become out of date. That's part of the reason I focus on more timeless principles over specific programming languages and resources.

Starting with block coding platforms

Here are a handful of considerations, though, that you should consider when adopting programming resources, particularly for younger students.

>> **Lack of K-12 school-specific features:** Scratch and ScratchJr are great resources for free coding. Released in 2003 by MIT, Scratch was the first form of *block coding,* in which — rather than typing text to generate code — students can create code by combining different blocks. The shapes of the blocks, and even their colors, helped differentiate elements. (You find some coverage of Scratch and ScratchJr in Chapter 17, but you can find out more about them online at https://scratch.mit.edu/ and https://www.scratchjr.org/, and educational resources at https://scratched.gse.harvard.edu/.)

However, one issue with these platforms is that they were created by a university, and don't really address the specific needs of other school systems. For example, they may lack the protection around student data and accommodations for accessibility that many schools would like. These platforms are extremely useful, but they don't give the full educational functionality that you'd get from a paid platform such as CodeHS (some of which use Scratch as their programming language).

>> **Potential transition issues between coding formats:** Another issue that comes up — not just with Scratch, but also with other block coding languages such as Blockly (from Google) — is that the simplicity of the block coding language sometimes creates a barrier when the students transition to more sophisticated, text-based coding languages.

This situation is something of a paradox because the simplicity

- *Is exactly the benefit of block coding.* Students can create programs without having to worry about the precise text-based syntax. It is easier on the blocks to identify and modify specific parameters, whereas finding the right parameter within a lengthy string of text can be extremely challenging.

- *Engenders incomplete understanding.* The students who use block coding often understand the structure of the blocks, but not necessarily the underlying logical structure of the code. They understand a loop (see Figure 5-1) as repeating the steps contained within a loop block but will later have difficulty translating that into a text-based loop sequence that looks extremely different.

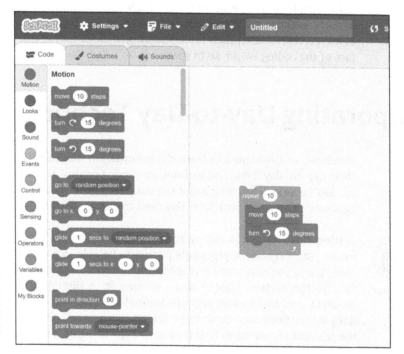

FIGURE 5-1.
A screen capture showing a Repeat block from the Scratch coding language.

REMEMBER

I don't point this out to turn anyone off from block coding. I taught it to both of my kids before they ever explored it in the classroom. You can definitely reap benefits by learning the logic of coding and computational thinking through early block coding. The problem comes from the fact that students can believe that — just because they know block coding — they understand coding. That isn't the case. Not really. Not yet.

Embracing the scope of coding formats

Just like learning multiple spoken languages can lead someone to appreciate features of their own original language and understand language (in general) more deeply, students need to understand multiple programming languages (and not just block coding languages) before they really understand coding.

That analogy extends in the opposite direction, too, and suggests that jumping frequently between many different programming languages wouldn't help students understand coding any more than sampling a dozen different spoken languages would help them understand linguistics. You definitely want to focus on a depth of understanding because the major coding principles are uniform and transcend any individual programming language.

TIP

While block coding is great in the early years, you should encourage your students to begin at least some exploration of simple text-based languages, such as Python, as early as they can. They don't have to become Python experts, but they should at least recognize that their understanding of block coding just scratches the surface of the coding world, so to speak.

Incorporating Day-to-Day Technology

In school, students need to learn the information that they'll need to function in their day-to-day lives, and technology plays a central role in modern lives. And so, don't overlook teaching about the more common technologies and their applications that students will definitely need to engage with as part of their lives.

REMEMBER

Getting kids engaged in coding activities is fantastic, but most professions in the future won't require every single person to be able to write their own computer code. When you cover concepts about the internet and communications (as I discuss in the section "Living and Learning in a Digital World" earlier in this chapter), you also look at areas of technology where students have more direct, daily interactions. And these technologies (such as cell phones or tablets) are also the relevant technologies that they see adults using on a regular basis.

But these communication and computing examples are far from the only technologies that students are familiar with. Consider these other day-to-day technologies and their functions that students should learn something about:

>> **Home convenience items:** You could spend entire lessons listing the technologies available in their kitchen, for example, which would include obvious appliances like the refrigerator, stove, and microwave, but also technologies as diverse as drawers, can openers, and the kitchen sink.

>> **Audio and video media elements:** One common branch of technology, used in both business and personal communications, is related to audio and video. Many students are adept with the basics of editing videos and adding filters and other elements, so you can easily jump from those activities to having your students create more robust video or audio projects — perhaps in place of (or alongside) a written report on the relevant research.

>> **Manipulation and representation of data:** In addition to specific technological devices that adults need to work with, they may often engage with transforming data into useful information.

The final bullet in the list brings me to the last couple of subconcepts in the computer science frameworks, Collection, Visualization, & Transformation and Inference & Models, which are the standards that focus on these skills.

Whether you need to read information in a news story or create a sales presentation, this set of concepts is incredibly important. I also cover the concepts in Chapters 7 and 8, because they are closely tied to the data elements of mathematics — and provide a great way to really bring out some integrated STEM instruction.

Preparing for the Future

Educators must make sure that students are able to utilize the technology in the current world, but the real goal of STEM education is to prepare them to engage with technologies that they've never seen. Someone graduating from high school in 1990 (unless they were specifically going into a technology field) would never have guessed how central computers would be to their daily lives just a decade later, let alone two decades later.

The advent of new technologies doesn't just create a new technology, it creates whole new industries and opportunities. Consider the airline industry as one example:

>> The invention of the airplane originated an entire massive airline industry that includes not just the people who build and operate planes, but also careers as flight attendants, air traffic controllers, and major airports are like tiny cities that have their own mini economies.

>> Mix the airline industry with the creation of the internet, and you have entire groups of companies working together (and in competition) to figure out how to bundle together flight, hotel, car rental, and vacation packages that they can sell online. These packages are driven by massive data analysis engines that update in real time based on seat, room, and rental availabilities.

Contextualizing modern technology

Kids don't know what they don't know (well, I guess that applies to anyone), and one crucial goal of education is to give students a context beyond their narrow world view. This goal is an explicitly part of STEM, through the Culture subconcept in the computer science standards. This idea expands beyond just computer science to encompass a general understanding of modern technology in their lives.

I focus more on this broader context in Chapter 8 when talking about how to incorporate STEM with social studies, but one significant way that you can impact student understanding of the world is to clearly show them how technologies influence society as a whole.

When looking back (isn't hindsight marvelous?), people can see the obvious impact of technologies on society, but that impact is almost never obvious at the time the technology arrives. Here are some examples:

>> **When the internet began,** the consensus among thinkers at the time was that it would basically lead to a new form of television and new ways to distribute television content. Instead, it completely broke the business model of television!

>> **Speaking of television,** here's another unexpected way that television has an impact on human society. In 1960, there was the first ever televised presidential debate between John F. Kennedy and Richard M. Nixon. Those who listened to the debate on radio generally felt that Nixon had clearly won, while those who watched it on television tended to think that Nixon had clearly lost. The technologies involved were largely responsible for this dichotomy.

- Kennedy was a handsome young man and carried himself well, which came across more readily on television than over the radio.

- Nixon had chosen not to have any makeup on for the debate, and under the hot lights of the television studio, he was profusely sweating. The overall impact was that visually Kennedy looked calm and composed while Nixon looked uncomfortable and stressed.

For decades after that 1960 debate, presidential debates were primarily viewed on television, and the expectations from presidential candidates changed as a result. But you also had to be in front of a television if you were going to watch the debate, and there wasn't really any way to watch the debate in full if you had missed it (unless you had a VCR set up to record it starting in the 1980s, of course). So the only people who watched the whole debate were those who had prioritized their schedule to be in front of the television for the debate.

>> **Regarding the internet,** today, presidential debates as well as many other live events are streamed online, and you can view them after the fact. Watching the full debate or athletic event at a later time can be more convenient, meaning there's less incentive to sit and watch it in real time when it's going on. But if you don't watch it in real time, you're likely going to see commentary either from media figures, online personalities, or friends before you get a chance to make up your own mind about the exchange.

These examples are far from the only ones that show how our modern media environment influences the way people engage with culture in a way that's different from the past. Discussions like this can not only help students explore the past through understanding technological revolutions, but also understand some of the reasons why past culture was different. They can even learn some things from the past about how to approach bias in their own world.

Dreading (and anticipating) the artificial intelligence revolution

At the time of writing this book, one of the most controversial elements being discussed in the realm of technology is artificial intelligence (AI). If you are reading this, then it's a good sign that our potential digital overlords have not yet risen up and destroyed us. Hooray!

Recognizing that you'll be reading this at some point in the future and that things are moving fast, I go out on a limb and define a handful of terms that are useful to know. It's possible new types of AIs will come up

Generative AI: A type of AI that creates new content and ideas based on prompts. Common types generate written content, computer code, visual/graphic content, and even video content.

Large Language Models (LLM): A type of AI that can process and generate human language.

Artificial General Intelligence (AGI): The gold standard of artificial intelligence, this would be a type of artificial intelligence that is relatively unconstrained and could replicate roughly the full range of problem-solving capabilities that people expect from a highly intelligent human.

Chatbot: A computer program designed to simulate conversation with human users, especially over the internet.

AI implementations are rolling out across a variety of industries and not without some pushback. For example,

» Serious copyright, privacy, and bias issues can result from how these systems were trained on existing content without compensating the creators and owners or evaluating the content for completeness.

» Legitimate concerns about the amount of energy needed to keep these technologies running are real.

» Some extremely intelligent people even fear that further research into artificial intelligence will result in the end of humanity.

But, aside from humanity's impending annihilation, there appears to be little to stop people from using AI, and it isn't going away. So, get used to it.

One of the first conversations I had with an entrepreneur in our community after taking the job as STEM coordinator for the school system quickly turned to the subject of AI, with the following conversation:

"What are you teaching students about AI?" he asked.

"Nothing, I don't think." I said tentatively.

"Well, they're going to need it. I'm not saying that it's going to take every engineering job, but in ten years I'd guess that it's taken nine out of ten of them." he replied.

REMEMBER

Assuming for the moment that this entrepreneur's prediction is correct, I prefer to think of the possibility with some measure of hope. What I believe he is really saying is that, in the future, a single engineer will have the design capacity of ten current engineers. Instead of losing engineers, I assume that, in the future, we have exactly the same number of engineers as we have today. That would mean our future planet has ten times the engineering capacity that it has now thanks to AI. What sorts of problems can we solve with that increase in design capacity?

After the conversation (and I'd picked my jaw up off the floor), I agreed with the entrepreneur that the teaching of AI was a serious point of concern, and then began thinking of a plan. I began talking to other teachers about it. I shared that anecdote, and my hope for what it could mean. Usually, they looked back at me blankly, with little idea of what to do. I offer these points regarding the teaching of AI in STEM education:

» No one really has a good sense, at this point, of the right way to handle AI in the classroom. People are trying different things, and it's just too soon to tell what works and what doesn't.

» An outright prohibition on AI is probably not a realistic approach, any more than previous generations succeeded at prohibiting the use of calculators, the internet, or Wikipedia.

» Recognizing that you will be reading this book at some point in the future and AI advancements are moving quickly, I'm hesitant to offer any specific AI tools that you should use. Because many AI platforms represent startup businesses, I recognize that their efforts might fail as quickly as they began.

» I feel on slightly safer grounds offering some organizations that have arisen and are explicitly dedicated to promoting AI literacy among educators.

- AI for Education (www.aiforeducation.io)

- Teach AI (www.teachai.org)

IN THIS CHAPTER

» Focusing on key engineering ideas for STEM

» Taking a big-picture look at engineering design and activities

» Breaking down the engineering design process

» Exploring other approaches to design

» Advancing coding with robotics and physical computing

Chapter **6**

Encompassing Engineering Solutions

E ngineering design principles are a key element of a modern approach to scientific education. This new focus represents one of the most substantial changes in recent years and is central to the transition from talking about science as a standalone discipline to focusing on STEM as an integrated way of solving problems in the real world.

This approach manifests in the NGSS by elevating the disciplinary core idea (DCI) of engineering design to a status equal to the other DCIs including physical sciences, life sciences, and Earth and space science — the more traditional academic areas of science.

In this chapter, I discuss how to center innovation, design, and invention as key engineering elements of the STEM classroom. I discuss the NGSS for the engineering design DCI across the grade levels, and also present fabrication tools that you can incorporate as part of STEM lessons. And I dive into the concept of the *engineering design cycle* —the key thinking process to follow when looking to engineer a solution to a problem — as well as how to apply other engineering design elements.

To end the chapter, I focus on robotics and related engineering tasks that often show up in the classroom as a way to teach and reinforce students' computer coding skills.

Centering Innovation and Invention

The NGSS prioritizes engineering alongside traditional science concepts. The inclusion of engineering design at a status equal to the other more traditional science DCIs is a hallmark of the new prominence of engineering. In addition to the engineering design DCI, several of the practices and crosscutting concepts that I discuss in Chapter 3 are also tied into engineering.

Embracing design principles

The problem-solving methods that educators think of for science are at the heart of the engineering design DCI. Like it is with the other DCIs in the NGSS, (as I note in Chapter 4), engineering design is also broken out into standards. But unlike those other standards, you don't find discrete performance expectations that students can accomplish within a single year. Instead, the standards are *grade banded* (which means one set of standards intended to be covered over multiple years), similar to the computer science standards that I discuss in Chapter 5.

As in the standards I discuss in previous chapters, this vertical articulation of skills across the grades is intended to help reinforce the importance of making sure that students are engaging in it from an early age. The difference through the vertical progression of these standards is more about the depth of understanding how the engineering design process works, as opposed to fixating on the teaching of entirely new skills.

Early elementary (kindergarten through second grade) engineering:

>> **Ask and explore:** Identify problems through questions and observations.

>> **Draw it out:** Create and use simple sketches and models of object shapes and how they can help solve problems.

>> **Compare results:** Look at data from tests of a possible solution to determine which one is working better or worse.

Upper elementary (third through fifth grade) engineering:

>> **Describe problems:** Use given needs or wants and resource criteria and constraints to define a simple design problem.

>> **Create solutions:** Brainstorm possible solutions for a problem that fit given criteria and constraints.

>> **Improve based on tests:** Test design solutions and use results to identify and implement improvements to the original design.

Middle school engineering:

>> **Clearly define design problems:** Set clear-cut design goals and limits based on resource constraints and other limitations.

>> **Compare and refine solutions:** Evaluate the effectiveness of different designs using a well-defined process, including testing methods and results, and then use those results to combine, refine, and iterate new and improved solution designs.

High school engineering:

>> **Break down problems:** Divide complex real-world problems into smaller components that provide more manageable engineering goals.

>> **Explore global challenges:** Identify large-scale problems and set clear goals that take into account various concerns and constraints associated with the problem, including environmental, economic, scientific, and social concerns.

>> **Weigh trade-offs:** Use evidence, testing, and reason to evaluate constraints, concerns, and possible side effects related to proposed design solutions to large-scale, complex problems.

>> **Test with simulations:** Use models and computer simulations, including reasonable assumptions, to test the impacts of proposed solutions to large-scale, complex problems.

Students are not expected to gain full proficiency in these engineering design skills within a single school year. These engineering skills, more than the other science skills, are truly more of a marathon than a sprint. A physical science concept may be fully covered (and hopefully learned) in a single unit, but that's not so with these standards. Students engage with these engineering design skills in a variety of real-world scientific contexts over multiple years.

The fact that engineering design standards span multiple years demands that educators introduce these concepts to students at an early age. Teachers are extremely busy and — particularly in the earliest grades — a teacher may understandably believe that students aren't ready to engage in engineering sorts of tasks. However, if young students do not engage with them early-on, the prophecy becomes self-fulfilling and these students will not be prepared to engage with engineering tasks later on.

Adopting the tools of building and fabrication

While the DCI is called *engineering design*, the standards don't just stay in the conceptual realm. As early as the K–2 grade band, students are expected to create physical models of their designs and test multiple designs to judge strengths and weaknesses based on the data.

When standards for third through fifth grades say that students should generate and compare possible solutions, you can interpret the possible solution as the design itself — but where is the fun in that? The intention is that students will often actually generate — that is to say, build — a prototype of their designed solution.

But you do find a hierarchy in design tools and skills through the standards:

>> **From very early in their engineering education,** students should be building objects that have the goal of performing functions that are solutions to specific problems. This means that, starting at an early age, students will need to become familiar with tools used to construct things.

Certainly, young students may be able to construct things without any complicated tools at all. If constructing with cardboard and masking tape, the only tool a student really needs is a decent pair of scissors.

>> **As the engineering students get older,** the tools that they access and become familiar with will increase in significance and complexity.

Tools they may engage with range from standard construction and carpentry tools (hammers, screwdrivers, saws, and so on) to more sophisticated and tricky equipment (hot glue guns, soldering irons, drills, for example) to modern high-tech fabrication equipment (3D printers and laser cutters). (See the nearby sidebar "Safety First.")

Broadly speaking, the fabrication of a product takes place in two ways:

>> **Additive fabrication:** Adding materials together.

Examples include combining materials (for example, with nails, screws, or glue), pouring cement/plaster into molds, and 3D printing.

>> **Subtractive fabrication:** Removing material from an initial material.

Examples include cutting, etching, drilling holes, and sculpting from stone.

Though these are clearly two distinct types of fabrication, real-world fabrication results in much overlap. If you create something with modeling clay, for example, you likely alternate in real time between additive and subtractive techniques. You add modeling clay to the work, sculpt the clay, and remove pieces; you repeat these steps as needed until you achieve the desired result.

WARNING

SAFETY FIRST

When working with tools and equipment, follow safe practices. Consult with your school's safety officer about any requirements, including the presence of appropriate fire prevention equipment and first aid supplies in the work area. Students should wear appropriate protective gear, such as safety goggles, based on the needs of the project.

Schools must store dangerous equipment in locked areas and the maintain the security of those areas.

While some items — flammable chemicals and circular saws, for example — are inherently dangerous, some others create more borderline cases in which educators must exercise their judgment. A person can hurt themselves or another person with a hammer or a power drill, for example, but it may not present the same risk as a circular saw.

Access to these tools is a privilege, not a right, and irresponsible use of them should result in having that privilege revoked. Have a clear policy on what it takes to get permission to use any regulated tools, and what sorts of actions will result in them being taken away.

When in doubt, err on the side of student safety.

Recognizing the main divisions: Mechanical and electrical engineering

When covering concepts in engineering, you have two large umbrellas of content, based on the type of system you are designing and analyzing. When you focus on a mechanical system (machines involving force and movement), you are exploring *mechanical engineering*. But when you focus on an electrical system (components that manage or use electrical power), you're in the realm of *electrical engineering*.

Work in the STEM classroom should touch on the basic principles of both types of engineering by having students construct both mechanical and electrical devices throughout their education. Students who are to become proficient in engineering will need to understand principles of both types of systems and be able to switch between them as needed. And although mechanical and electrical engineering are separate disciplines that have some distinct principles, you also find a huge amount of overlap between them.

A single device may well require some elements of both types of engineering because mechanical and electrical components work together in many modern devices. For example, much of the design of a robot centers around mechanical principles of moving wheels and arms, but the motors that move those robotic wheels and arms are connected to an electrical power source and get inputs from various electrical sensors. And electrical engineering is a key part of the section "Physical Programming: Coding Meets Engineering" about physical computing later in this chapter.

REMEMBER

Conceptually, the mental process of designing devices under either (or both) types of engineering is largely the same. The engineering design cycle that I discuss in the section "Engaging the Engineering Design Process" later in the chapter applies to designs in both types of engineering.

Engineering and physical science

Because engineering is fundamentally a study of how to exploit physics for human advantage, you find a perfect opportunity (when teaching the engineering part of STEM) to reinforce many basic physical science principles that appear in the science standards (see Chapter 4). These include

> **Force:** An action that changes or maintains the motion of an object. Force equals mass times acceleration.

> **Energy:** The capacity for doing work, consisting of both *kinetic energy* (energy of motion) and various types of *potential energy* (stored energy).

Work: Work is the energy transferred to or from an object that occurs when a force acts on and displaces the object. It equals the exerted force multiplied by the distance the object moves.

TIP

When you teach the E in STEM, you must make sure that students recognize a key principle at the center of engineering: the idea of *conservation of energy*. Energy is never created nor destroyed during any physical process, but it just changes form. Students need to understand that they can't actually build a mechanical device that generates more energy than what is put into it, even though the usefulness of the device may give that impression. For example, a pulley and lever system may allow you to lift a particularly heavy object by turning a crank to distribute the weight across multiple ropes, but that's an efficient use of energy, not a creation of new energy.

In a mechanical device, a useful concept to determine is the *mechanical advantage* it produces, which is the ratio of the *output force* to the *input force*. You find three possible outcomes for this mechanical advantage ratio:

>> **Greater than 1:** The device produces an *amplification* of force.

>> **Equal to 1:** The input and output forces are identical, so the device has no mechanical advantage.

>> **Less than 1:** The device produces a *reduction* of force.

REMEMBER

Again, you'll want to keep in mind (and remind your students) that you don't actually get more energy out of the mechanical device than was put into it. You may amplify the force (on the output side), but the overall energy will never be greater than the energy that goes into a device, due to the law of conservation of energy.

Why you want to produce a mechanical device that amplifies force is (hopefully) obvious, but why would someone want to produce a device that reduces the input force? The reduction of force in a mechanical devices comes about because, when operating the device, you actually produce more movement with less force. You can see an example of this outcome when you ride a multi-speed bicycle. You shift the gears so that you can spin the pedals — and ultimately the wheels — more times to cover more distance without putting any extra force into it.

Exploring simple machines

A basic concept in engineering is the idea of *simple machines*, which are machines that have few moving parts (or none at all) and change the direction or magnitude of a force. Simple machines are the foundation for much of what you do in mechanical engineering.

Most commonly, educators talk about six types of simple machines, as covered in Table 6-1. I say "most commonly" here because, technically, you can view the pulley, screw, and wedge entries in the table as extensions and combinations of the wheel and axle, lever, and inclined plane entries.

TABLE 6-1   **Six Simple Machines in Mechanical Systems**

The Machine	Its Description	Examples
Wheel and axle	A round object (often disk-shaped) that is able to rotate around a rod.	*Tires on vehicles, doorknobs*
Lever	A rigid body (such as a bar or board) that rotates around a pivot point, or *fulcrum*. A lever system consists of an applied force and a load force. The geometry of the situation changes the direction and magnitude of the applied force relative to the load force.	*Playground see-saw, wrench, hammer*
Inclined plane	A rigid surface oriented at an angle with one side higher than the other, which reduces the amount of force required to move a load a given vertical distance.	*Ramp, playground slide*
Pulley	A wheel and axle system designed so that a belt, chain, rope, or cable can move along with the wheel. This arrangement changes the direction of the applied force. Multiple pulleys can combine together to significantly change the magnitude of the output force.	*Bicycle chain system, window blinds, elevator cable system*
Wedge	A moving inclined plane that exerts a force between two objects to either force them apart or secure them together.	*Door stopper, nail, axe head*
Screw	A wedge that is twisted around a cylinder in a helix shape. Rotating the screw with a minimal force can generate a large force in the direction of the turning screw.	*Screw, bolt, drill bit, bottle cap*

You create *complex machines* when you combine two or more simple machines. A bicycle is a complex machine consisting of two wheels and axles, levers for pedals, and a pulley system of chains between the pedals and the rear axle. (Hopefully, your bicycle also has brakes, which consist of more simple machines working together.)

Engaging the Engineering Design Process

At the core of any engineering or design task is the *engineering design process*. This is a fairly well-defined process in engineering, but it's also one of those sets of activities (like the scientific method I discuss in Chapter 4) that can vary in different contexts. But in general, any creative design process to engineer a device ultimately passes through these stages of development in one form or another.

Outlining design process steps

In its simplest form, the engineering design process followed in STEM projects breaks down into these six steps:

1. **Ask**

   Clarify the goal of the design. Ask questions about

   - The problem or the need being addressed

   - The resources available

   - Any necessary constraints

   And conduct any initial required research.

2. **Imagine**

   Brainstorm as a student group to identify the most appropriate solutions to the problem. Discuss the benefits and drawbacks of the different solutions.

3. **Plan**

   Having identified a general solution, solidify the details of how you plan to implement it. Develop a list of steps needed to solve the problem. Steps may include creating initial designs or models of a prototype solution.

4. **Create**

   Build a prototype or other initial attempt at the solution, for testing purposes.

5. **Test**

   Conduct testing of the prototype solution.

6. **Improve and repeat**

   Analyze test results as the basis to identify areas of the solution prototype that need improvement. Cycle back to repeat Step 6 as needed until the solution is satisfactory.

You can get more details on each of these steps in the section "Focusing on Engineering Design Process Steps" later in this chapter.

These steps are generally done in order, as shown in Figure 6-1, although some backtracking can occur. For example, in the middle of planning your design, you may realize that you have fundamental questions (which you didn't ask initially) or that some element of your imagined design won't work the way you intended. These non-sequential "back to the drawing board" moments are just part of the process when designing an unknown solution.

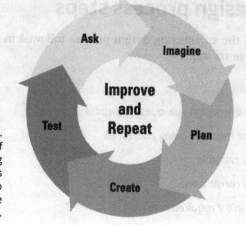

FIGURE 6-1.
This example of the engineering design process shows how to move through the six phases.

Examining design process activities

In Chapter 4 I describe the scientific process as a complex and non-linear set of activities that fall into three broad categories. And the engineering design process is also complex, and its inherent activities also fall into those same three broad categories:

>> **Investigating** means not only getting the information you need to initially define the problem, but also performing tests of a design to get information to inform the analysis part of the process. This activity overlaps most strongly with the Ask (Step 1) and Test (Step 5) parts of the engineering design process.

>> **Evaluating** involves not only running tests of your idea, but also having discussions with others about the merits of relative designs. This part of the process can have a strong emphasis on communication, both presenting your ideas as well as listening to and evaluating the ideas of others. This activity overlaps most strongly with the Imagine (Step 2), Plan (Step 3), and Improve (Step 6) parts of the engineering design process.

>> **Developing explanations and solutions** is the creative aspect of the project, in which the designer brainstorms new ideas or actively creates their solution. This activity would overlap most strongly with the Imagine (Step 2), Plan (Step 3), Create (Step 4), and Improve (Step 6) parts of the engineering design process.

WARNING

These ideas are important for the teacher to have in the back of their minds, but be cautious in putting too much emphasis on students memorizing them. Just because teachers have a nice list of six steps that are useful to follow, the real creative process of designing solutions isn't required to follow those steps.

Teachers usually need that reminder more than the kids do. (This runs the risk of the same over-emphasis that I discuss in Chapter 4 related to memorizing the scientific method.)

In Chapter 9, I introduce the 5E instructional model that includes five distinct phases of instruction, and you might be tempted to connect those phases directly to the stages of the engineering design process. The 5E model represents a way to teach a new concept, based on neuroscience and the psychology of learning, whereas the engineering design process demonstrates a process that anyone would go through when creating a new design.

Focusing on Engineering Design Process Steps

In the section "Engaging the Engineering Design Process" earlier in the chapter, I briefly introduce the process steps and activities involved in designing for STEM engineering projects. In this section, I break down those steps and explain them further.

Ask: What are we doing?

The first step in any engineering task is to have a clear idea of what your project goal entails. In the Ask step of the engineering design process, the student gets the information that helps define that goal, including any design constraints they're working under.

Asking the "What are we doing?" often leads the students to other questions. They may run into content and terminology related to the task that they need to learn before they can really proceed too far into addressing the task itself. In this important phase of the engineering design process, you can incorporate a lot of the initial content learning related to the STEM project. (I cover more about this part of lesson development in Chapter 9.)

As opposed to the initial investigation step in a scientific task, an engineering task is often centered around a practical problem that usually requires a physical solution of some kind. *Note:* You can apply this process to a digital project that results in no physical construction, like designing a computer simulation.

TIP

Some presentations of the engineering design process include a separate Define step before you go into the Ask step. You may want to break out this step separately, but the parameters and constraints of the problem should be included among the things that the student is asking about in the Ask step of the process presented in this chapter.

Asking specific questions

The following questions are ones about the specific problem or need that students should ask and have answered during this process step:

>> What is the particular problem?

>> Can the problem be specified more precisely?

>> What are the key elements of the problem that should be focused on?

>> Who does the problem affect the most?

>> What is currently being done to address this problem?

>> Who has the power to affect the situation?

>> What available tools or technologies address (or could address) this problem?

>> Is there a way to test solutions on a smaller scale?

>> How can the problem best be articulated and communicated?

>> What is the final test of this design?

The questions in this list are similar to those laid out in *A Framework for K-12 Science Education* (National Academies Press 2012), when they give a detailed description of what students should do in relation to the science and engineering practice of asking questions and defining problems.

Balancing student and teacher involvement

REMEMBER

The standards tell us that part of the engineering skills that students need to learn include knowing how to ask these questions and find answers to them. An engineering task in which a teacher tells the students the solution they have to design and hands them the answers to all of the questions in the Ask step, is not aligned to the engineering design standards for modern STEM education. Teachers may have their greatest involvement during this part of the process, but even this step should be largely student-centered.

The balancing act for questioning in this step can be challenging, especially at first. You want to come away with a clear definition of a problem or goal, but you also don't want to define things so precisely that only one single engineering solution exists.

For example, some STEM kits designed for assembling a project can really only be functionally assembled in one way, and — you deviate from the intended design — then you are unlikely to end up with a working prototype. These kits may be worthwhile to work with as a way of learning new concrete skills, but they aren't particularly useful as a way of working on the engineering design process. The student isn't designing anything if the only question they're asking is "Can you pass me the instructions?"

Imagine: What could we do?

After students identify and define the problem that they're working on, they should proceed to trying to imagine as many possible solutions as they can.

Students can take the Imagine step phase individually, in groups, or both. Having students perform an initial brainstorm individually to come up with ideas often makes sense; then they can get together in small groups or as a class to discuss the ideas they had.

You should highlight two points that are somewhat in contention during the imagining step of the process:

1. Every student's idea is valuable and needs to be heard.
2. Not every idea will be used on the project.

Cultivating soft skills

Before getting too deep into the project, this imagining part gives you an opportunity to really cultivate students' soft skills, such as collaboration and patience. You should encourage students to support each other and listen carefully to all of their classmates' ideas.

In particular, you need to teach the kids to hold onto their initial ideas lightly. They should be willing to let them go if they hear another idea that they think will work better, and that isn't a practice that comes natural to many kids. It is part of building a learning environment where students view their learning process as continually fluid and ongoing. Encourage the students to also keep a record in their journal or engineering notes about any ideas that come up during the process, even if they aren't used in the project.

Emphasizing creative thinking

Part of the reason that you don't want to over-define the problem and the constraints is that you want the students to feel free to think creatively during the imagine portion of the project. They may come up with ideas that are not feasible with the resources that you have, but they may think outside the box and come up with real innovations that approach the project's core challenge from a new angle.

Consider this example from an internet video of a company promoting their innovation for cities that don't have much space to plant trees. The company developed a form of microalgae that metabolizes carbon dioxide into oxygen. They propose replacing park benches with new benches that contain a large tank filled with microalgae, so that each bench could convert as much carbon dioxide into oxygen as a 20-year-old tree does. The benches are also (in my opinion, at least) more aesthetically pleasing than many traditional benches. (Probably more expensive, too, but that is a separate challenge.)

While most people working on this issue may have imagined solutions to the problem "How do we get more trees in cities?" The innovator who came up with this bench solution was working on the issue "How do we get something into cities to convert carbon dioxide into oxygen?"

The bench solution doesn't replace the need for more trees, or even the need for more trees within cities. But it's a great example of how the defining of the problem (the Ask step) matters for the Imagine step in the process. A definition of the problem that's too narrow will close off possible options that may mitigate, if not solve, the problem.

Plan: Okay, let's do this!

After your students have a set of ideas in place, it's time to move forward with deciding on which of the ideas you're going to use. Sometimes the Plan step will be pretty superficial, and sometimes it'll be lengthy and detailed — depending not only on what you're requiring from the students but also on their own natural inclinations.

Evolving a plan

The plan that the students develop should naturally evolve out of the discussion that began during the Imagine step of the process. They're selecting from among the various ideas presented, modifying them as necessary, and then getting ready to actually build or implement the solution.

Depending on the context of the problem, you may be able to combine different ideas for a solution. Maybe one student had a good idea for how to design a machine to pick up an object, but that machine isn't as practical as someone else's design for moving the object across the room. You could either build two different devices to handle this (if that works in your situation), or if the students need a single device to handle both, they could combine elements from both designs.

Asking for resources

For part of the planning stage, students should develop a good idea of what materials or tools they need to complete the project goal. They should make a clear list of what they need, including quantities, before they move on to actually building their project.

TIP

Students will almost certainly be off the mark in the materials and tools they're asking for. Knowing that you have limits on the resources available in the classroom, you should expect that you'll get students who decide (halfway through the project) that they need more material. Suppose that students initially request 10 craft sticks and then decide that they need 20; that's fine, and you should provide the extra craft sticks. But suppose that students decide they need 1,000 craft sticks (when they initially requested 10); that's a good time to make them revisit the material constraints they're working under.

REMEMBER

This chapter focuses on engineering and relates to building physical objects and devices, but this engineering design process applies to a variety of other design-related tasks. You may find that the materials and tools needed for a project are digital instead of physical, such as access to public domain graphics and graphic editing software.

Create: Actually do this!

This next step involves having the students actually create their engineering solution, or a prototype of it. Although some modeling and building work in preparation may take place during the planning stage, this Create stage gives students the opportunity for the hands-on work. This hands-on piece of the project is one of the hallmarks that people think about when they think of STEM education.

Controlling the chaos

This step also brings the controlled-chaos aspect of STEM education to the forefront. Teachers can find that dealing with this chaotic environment can be a challenge, both emotionally and logistically. For example, when you begin the creating step with students who haven't been exposed to STEM projects before, fights over materials can break out.

In one of the first projects I ran as a STEM coordinator, I brought several third-grade groups together to do an engineering project. In addition to me, four third grade teachers were also in the room, so I felt like we'd really be able to keep things under control. I set up a hot glue station, so that each group of students could send a single person over to use the hot glue gun to attach projects parts together.

That plan was an utter disaster. Everyone wanted to use the hot glue gun. Rather than sending single people, whole groups would swarm the hot glue gun station.

Being ready to adapt

The following day, I eliminated the hot glue gun as a means of attaching parts from the project. Instead, each group received a roll of masking tape. But third graders seem to have trouble with rationing masking tape. On day three of the project, I peeled off arm-long strips of masking tape, four per table, and stuck the ends onto the table. This worked generally fine (although a handful of particularly tape-happy groups did end up asking for some more).

Be ready to modify the project plan as needed if you're finding a problem with the use or quantity of resources. Just like teachers expect the students to find solutions to problems, they should model this behavior by acknowledging to themselves and the students that something didn't work. Then they can change their strategy accordingly.

Test: Did it work?

After the students create their initial build, they can proceed to test it to find out whether their creation can actually accomplish the task or solve the problem that the students designed it for. Very rarely will a first prototype do exactly what the students hope that it will.

As part of the initial framing of the task at hand and the solution being developed, students should know what their test will ultimately look like. This should come out during the Ask stage of this process (if not before students even move into the engineering design phase). They cannot design a solution to meet the goal of the test, after all, if they are not aware of the goals of the test.

In the case where a group does a great job and accomplishes the task with their first prototype, it may be useful to have ideas on hand about how to modify the challenge to keep those students engaged.

Identifying tests that match the project

Project testing can take a variety of forms, and one thing to consider is what are the relative expectations for project success. For example, can all of the students succeed at the tests? Can they all fail to provide a workable solution? Is the project competitive so that someone is guaranteed to come in first?

If the project is to build a robot that can pick up an object, carry it 50 feet, and then drop it into a basket, in principle, every single group in the class could achieve the goal (pass the test). Or, in this situation, having none of the groups succeed is also possible.

But other tasks are designed to have a clear winner, because they are set up as a competition. If you're building towers and the tallest tower wins, you could have these outcomes (though the first is most likely):

>> Some group will eventually build the tallest tower and win the competition.

>> Multiple groups build towers that reach the ceiling. In that case multiple groups create such a good design that they don't lose within the confines of a classroom test.

But the expectation in these situations is that a single winner will usually emerge.

Figure out if you want to have a set success criteria that multiple student groups can meet, or if you want a competition that would have a specific victor. Plan for tie breaker criteria if a competition test ends up too close to call, such as the winner being the tower with the narrowest base.

Testing results as a STEM learning tool

TIP

This testing phase offers another point (like debugging programs, which I discuss in Chapter 5) where you can emphasize that making mistakes — and even failing — is still progress in the students' STEM learning journey. You can pull out the Thomas Edison quote here.

I have gotten a lot of results! I know several thousand things that won't work. You'll want to establish this tolerance of mistakes and failure as a cultural expectation in the classroom well before the student's prototype falls apart, of course. I cover the idea of how to destigmatize failure in Chapter 9, but the testing phase of a STEM engineering project is a prime place where teachers and students will need to embrace that mindset.

After you have the results of the initial test in hand, of course, you aren't done with the STEM project. No! One of the most important elements is still to come: using the results to iterate your solution.

Improve and repeat: Keep doing it

The creative process is iterative. I learned this in my early days as a writer, through the phrase *all writing is rewriting*. The phrase is certainly true in writing, but it's also true in every creative endeavor. If you are creating something new, then you've got to get started on an initial step and then figure out how to improve it, until you reach a point where you find that your creation is good enough to accomplish your goal.

At the opposite end of this concept, though, is another hard lesson: No project will ever be perfect. I know award-winning authors who look back at their most popular novels and just think about the parts that they wish they could re-write because they have a better idea of how to handle some aspects of the story.

Fighting the pace of education

Threading this improve-and-repeat needle into a STEM engineering project means that teachers want to give the students at least one opportunity to learn from their test and modify their design. Achieving this last step can be a real challenge, particularly since teachers are always starving for time. One of the most natural responses in the world is for a teacher to express that they've covered the material in the lesson, the kids did the project, and it's time to move on.

But part of the problem with modern education is that kids are always moving on to the next thing. They do not get appropriate time to reflect on what they have done and internalize the lessons that they could learn from their experience. They are exposed to the material, taught the lesson, and then moved along to the next lesson. In Chapter 9, I lay out the neuroscience research about learning. The importance of taking time to mindfully reflect on a new concept (for an extended period of time) is shown by the research to be a crucial component of acquiring new knowledge and skills.

Allowing for iteration in a STEM project

The iterative step in STEM is crucial for students to really come to terms with any mistakes they made in that first round of testing. They should reflect not only on what they did, but how they did it.

Did they rush some element of the design process?

Did their project fail because, early on, they made a design choice that didn't make sense?

Did someone in the group try to tell them that a different design was better?

As the group reflects on their design — and the results they got from the test — they need to consider the degree to which they want to modify the prototype for the next test. No one wants to go back to the drawing board at that point, but maybe doing so is warranted.

REMEMBER

Even if you don't have time for the students to fully re-do their design from the beginning, at the very least they should have time to meet as a group and discuss their first design. Maybe instead of a making time for a complete rebuild, you let the group explain to you what they would do differently if they were given the opportunity. If you're seeing enthusiasm at this prospect, then you can decide how much time you want to commit to the Improve and Repeat step of the engineering design process.

Other Approaches to Engineering and Design Cycles

The engineering design process I describe in the preceding sections has two main benefits: It works and it's short. But it's not the only way to lay out the steps of this process. You may be using resources or a curriculum that describes the steps of the engineering design cycle in different terms. What you call the parts of this process isn't particularly important, as long as you're getting the students engaged in critical design thinking.

Like with many processes and tasks, you'll find no single correct way to break out the steps. I've seen some versions of the engineering design process that have as many as 12 steps — although that level of division frankly seems a bit over-designed for my tastes. And some processes use flowcharts to emphasize repeating steps as needed.

Listing out too many of these design approaches would be overwhelming, especially since they largely mirror each other in most respects. But I go over a couple of examples so that you can see how the basic engineering design cycle that I outline in the previous sections relates to these other structures.

PLTW design process

One example of an alternate design process is provided by Project Lead the Way (PLTW), one of the leading STEM curriculum and professional development companies in the United States. The six-phase design process often associated with their curriculum was developed based on work at the University of Maryland. I list the phases (or, steps) here, along with parentheticals mapping them back to the phases (or, steps) of the earlier engineering design cycle.

1. **Define the Problem** (Ask)

2. **Generate Concepts** (Imagine)

3. **Develop a Solution** (Create)

4. **Construct and Test a Prototype** (Create and Test)

5. **Evaluate the Solution** (Test and Improve and Repeat)

6. **Present the Solution**

This breakdown of project phases has a benefit of being not only a design process, but one that is easy to break out into the flow of a lesson plan for students to follow. In that sense, the PLTW process is both an engineering design process and an instructional model.

Justin Gary's Core Design Loop

One intriguing approach to design from outside of the K–12 education space comes from game designer Justin Gary in his book *Think Like a Game Designer* (Aviva Pub 2018). This approach gives a practical glimpse into a successful design process for a commercial industry. Over the course of designing dozens of successful games, Gary has developed a process that he calls the Core Design Loop (depicted in Figure 6-2), which he applies not only to game design but also to any creative endeavor (including his own book).

Here are six steps in the Core Design Loop, with extremely brief descriptions:

1. **Inspiring.**

   Coming up with initial ideas through exploration and study.

2. **Framing.**

   Determining constraints on what you are designing.

3. **Brainstorming.**

   Refining initial concepts and constraints with others.

4. **Prototyping.**

   Creating an initial rough draft of your product.

5. **Testing.**

   Putting your prototype through as much testing as you can.

6. **Iterating.**

   Implementing feedback from the testing as quickly as possible to start the cycle again.

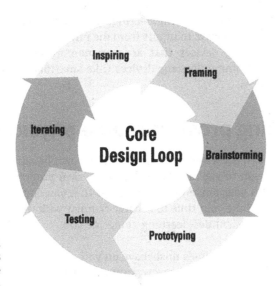

Source: Justin Gary, 2018/with permission of AVIVA Publishing

FIGURE 6-2.
The steps
of the Core
Design Loop.

Gary's method of running a successful game design and publishing company highlights the iterative nature of any design activity. Designing and producing a game requires going through this loop multiple times, for each stage of the game, including (but not limited to)

> **Creating the basic rules,** and then refining the full set of rules

> **Drafting the initial design of the components** (the board, the pieces, and so on) to make sure that your components clearly fulfill everything you need them to

> **Applying final polish** to be sure the product looks like something people want to purchase

Backtracking to earlier design loop stages happens anytime you realize something isn't working.

Physical Programming: Coding Meets Engineering

Over recent years, a range of physical objects have emerged that allow students to take their knowledge of coding outside of the purely digital realm and use it to interact in amazing ways with the physical world. This design space for programming objects that sense and interact with the physical world is known as *physical programming*, or sometimes *physical computing*.

This physical aspect takes the coding knowledge (emphasized throughout Chapter 5) and combines it with engineering, to create complex systems that can respond in programmed ways to inputs from the physical environment. Examples of physical computing devices that are common include cars, smart home appliances, mobile communications devices (like smartphones and tablets), and keyless entry devices.

Introducing programmable physical objects

Each of these new objects and systems have their own benefits, drawbacks, and quirks. As you begin to explore the realm of physical programming — both on your own and with your students — remember that you don't need to introduce all of the systems. Take your time to become familiar with them, and let the students explore the possibilities, learning alongside you.

TIP

New technology can sometimes misbehave on you, so always have a backup plan in place for the STEM lesson if the programmable technology doesn't work out as expected. If you run into technical problems, you can

>> **Have the students write out the steps of their plan for the system they're programming.** They can always describe their plan in writing to think through their process.

>> **Troubleshoot the technical problem.** The issue may be as simple as needing to replace batteries, for example. Fixing a simple problem can give you the time to resolve the situation to proceed with your lesson.

>> **Focus on the thinking part of the lesson.** A substantial issue that you can't easily fix allows you to continue teaching the thinking skills that are central to the lesson, even though the equipment isn't working properly at the moment. You can troubleshoot the equipment later when the students aren't around.

I touch on some general categories of physical computing products in the next sections, but I don't dive deeply into specific products. New products are continually under development. You can find lists of specific products that you might want to have available in Chapter 18. For guidance on which products work better for different ages and grades, check out Chapter 13.

Robots and drones

Probably the most obvious physical computing system that students engage with is physical robots, and in recent years, you have no shortage of options. Robotics options have been around long enough that several of them have established curricula that come along with the physical robot, and the curricula is often offered for free online. In addition to what we think of as typical robots, the increased prevalence of remote drones with programming options gives another way for students to work on their programming skills.

Here are some aspects to consider when introducing students to robotics, drones, and remote-control vehicles.

>> **Determine up front whether you want the students to design and build their own devices, or work with something that is pre-built.** Obviously, if you're working with an entirely preconstructed robot, then you're able to dig into the coding end of things, but students won't necessarily get much engagement with engineering principles.

Prebuilt robots include brands such as Dash, Sphero, and Ozobot. When introducing these robots, in particular, I have seen some teachers introduce them through remote control applications. A benefit to this approach is that students can learn about the robot's functions before digging into the coding.

>> **Take a coding-centered approach to working with robots.** When introducing robots, you can present the robots alongside the code so that, in order to initially engage with the robots, the students *have* to learn the basics of how to code them.

You can then later introduce them to the remote-control options. The students will internally think of these objects as something that you code, but which you can also control remotely. This is the result you want. If you introduce students initially through the remote-control features, the students may think of them as remote-control toys that they can also control with code.

If you're looking for discussions of specific robotics systems appropriate for different grade levels, you can jump to Chapter 13.

Microcontrollers and microcomputers

A variety of new affordable small-scale computing devices (about the size of a credit card) may revolutionize what you can do in the classroom. The first of these devices are microcontrollers, which are essentially small computers consisting of a single integrated circuit. You can attach them to devices to perform a specific function. The second device is a microcomputer, which is similarly compact but can perform multiple functions.

Microcontroller products (see examples in Figure 6-3) have come out to popular acclaim over the last couple of decades, and they continue to be refined so that they're even more user friendly and appropriate for educational use. These include

>> Makey Makey (https://makeymakey.com/)

>> micro:bit (https://microbit.org/)

>> Arduino (https://www.arduino.cc/)

FIGURE 6-3.
The micro:bit version 2.0 microcontroller (left) and the Arduino Uno R3 microcontroller (right).

Photos courtesy of Andrew Zimmerman Jones

Microcontrollers are great if you need a single function for your STEM project. Makey Makey became famous for being able to turn almost anything into a musical instrument, with a classic viral project of creating a functioning piano keyboard out of bananas. If you need a sensor that detects moisture and sounds an alarm, then a microcontroller can easily do the job for you. You would just need to have a moisture sensor and an alarm to hook into it (although a recent version of the micro:bit comes with a speaker built into the integrated circuit).

REMEMBER

But microcontrollers are not a full computer and cannot run complete programs the way a computer does. For that, you'd need a microcomputer, like the Raspberry Pi (https://www.raspberrypi.com/). You can hook this little device into other components and create a small, but powerful, versatile computer that can run a variety of programs.

Many of these small computing products weren't originally designed for education, but a number of entrepreneurial approaches can result in creative (and potentially educational) uses for them. I discuss some specific kits associated with these products in Chapter 13.

Chapter **7**

Crunching the Numbers with Mathematics

deally, within the greater context of STEM, mathematics isn't just about basic rules of arithmetic, but instead, it's a way of thinking about getting a deeper understanding of quantitative structures and relationships.

In this chapter, I work hard to lay out a foundation for the reader who may not have a strong mathematics background but must teach it anyway. I discuss the reason that math is important, both on its own and as a fundamental aspect of STEM instruction. I go deeper with some tips on how to think mathematically about the subjects you're teaching, including how to approach STEM subjects with an emphasis on mathematics.

Thinking About Why We Learn Math

You can generally classify a new math concept in one of three categories:

» **Directly useful:** Practical mathematics, such as what you'd need to calculate your taxes or measure a room for construction.

>> **Potentially useful:** A crucial concept that isn't useful now but might at some point be useful if you study a specific subject. For example, suppose that you learn about the concepts of vectors and matrices, and then later find those concepts essential (and therefore useful) in higher level physics, mathematics, and linear programming.

>> **Indirectly useful:** A way of thinking and reasoning that is transferable to other contexts, perhaps as the basis of problem-solving, computational thinking, and logic.

Mathematicians and other people who love math tend to love it because of the things that fall into the third category (indirectly useful). I've never met a single person in my life who said, "My love of math started with my 7 times tables!" That's the first category, by the way.

The danger when presenting mathematics in STEM education is that it can easily be overwhelmed by the first category (directly useful). If that happens, you take the most abstract and universal of the four STEM areas and turn it into the most concrete, practical, and lifeless of the areas.

Knowing that Kids Will Use Math in the Future

Throughout my life, I've occasionally heard people express the view that kids don't really need to learn math anymore, because they have calculators. What is the point of making kids learn their times tables and memorize addition quantities when they'll always be able to find those solutions with a device that is close at hand? And, yes, this viewpoint often comes from kids, but it's a surprisingly common refrain from adults, too!

And, in a sense, people who hold this viewpoint are right. Most of the math that previous generations learned during the majority of their class time in elementary schools is no longer essential. Technological advances make simple calculations trivially easy, except on those rare occasions where your cell phone battery dies. It makes little sense for students to spend a massive amount of time on the basic skills of arithmetic *if* the point of those lessons were those standalone skills.

The Common Core State Standards (CCSS) don't focus on teaching students these rote skills, and instead, they center on overall fluency and proficiency in thinking mathematically. (See the nearby sidebar "Where are the Math Standards?") You might expect that mathematics standards would require this proficiency (thinking mathematically), but other standards also emphasize this thinking.

WHERE ARE THE MATH STANDARDS?

Unlike the preceding chapters in this part of the book, this chapter doesn't describe the math standards by individual grades or even domains. I have reasons for this different approach. First, math is a more high-stakes subject than science (because of the related evaluation and testing), and so, I have little doubt that most teachers have already been exposed to the math standards. Second, listing out the science, engineering, and computer science standards takes up way more space than I like, and the math standards would just eat up book pages without providing much benefit.

I do recommend becoming familiar with the CCSS math domains, which I list in Chapter 3. You can view the individual grade level standards at the Common Core mathematics website (www.thecorestandards.org/Math). If you want to become more familiar with your local mathematics standards for individual grades, you should be able to access them through your state government's education website.

REMEMBER

Mathematics concepts don't just appear in the CCSS for math, but they're woven throughout the NGSS and the CSTA computer science standards. Future careers in many fields will require a high degree of quantitative literacy, computational thinking, problem-solving, and data analysis — which are all central aspects of mathematics.

Math in science and computer science

Saying that mathematics is the language of science is a cliché, but it has become a cliché because of how much truth the statement contains. The gold standard of many science investigations involves writing out a clear definition of a concept — in a mathematical form — that makes a clear, quantitative prediction that can then be tested in some form.

This connection between mathematics and science shows up throughout the science standards. Several of the practices for the K-12 science education framework (see Chapters 3 and 4) are explicitly mathematical in nature:

Developing and using models

Analyzing and interpreting data

Using mathematics and computational thinking

Obtaining, evaluating, and communicating information

The math-science connection is also true for several of the NGSS crosscutting concepts:

Patterns

Scale, proportion, and quantity

Systems and system models

Stability and change

Some connections may seem obvious, but others require a bit more thought on how math and science relate for

>> **Models:** As one of the mathematical practices in the CCSS, modeling is an aspect of mathematics that teachers have become much more familiar with over recent years. The term *model* can be incredibly broad, meaning anything from a physical scale model to a mathematical equation to a computer simulation. All modeling of physical systems or problems require mathematical skill, although the skill level required varies depending on the type and complexity of the model.

>> **Ratio, proportion, and scale:** Ratio and proportion make up a central theme of the mathematics CCSS, particularly across the middle school grades. This shift represents a transition from the arithmetic thinking in the lower grades (particularly division and multiplication) into thinking about relationships between quantities in upper grades. This concept ties into modeling, since you often choose to create a model that is proportional to the real-world situation you're modeling.

>> **Stability and change:** Mathematics provides a way to identify which elements of a system remain the same and which change, and to clearly quantify the amount of change taking place. This measurement of change is the whole basis of calculus, which came about in part because Sir Isaac Newton needed a mathematical tool to discover elements of classical physics, including his laws of motion and universal gravitation. (How's that as a science connection for you!)

Similarly, computer science skills are well connected with mathematics and computational thinking throughout all grades. Fundamentally, computers and computer programs work through performing operations on numerical entities. The manipulation of bits in the computer is ultimately a mathematical activity. Computer Science Practices from the CSTA computer science standards also resonate with mathematics:

Recognizing and defining computational problems

Creating computational artifacts

Testing and refining computational artifacts

REMEMBER

Both the science and computer science standards — which reflect the goal of preparing students for careers in the future — include a central role for mathematics and mathematical thinking.

Psst, they know if you hate math

Some fantastic teachers out there love mathematics and engage in math concepts in extremely thoughtful ways. I don't want to diminish that observation at all when I say that the opposite is also true: many teachers outright loathe mathematics.

This situation makes sense. A person whose passion is helping kids grow and learn (like a teacher) is not necessarily a person who is inclined to be passionate about working with numbers. And someone whose passion leans toward numbers is often drawn to a field other than teaching (particularly teaching in earlier grades). Teaching, as a profession, hasn't done a great job of drawing math-passionate people into it.

WARNING

But the lack of passion for (or outright dislike of) mathematics does carry over to the students. Particularly in early grades, students think that their teachers are right about pretty much everything.

The dislike of math is closely tied to another trait of many elementary teachers: math anxiety. For years, while working in mathematics assessment, I ran committees of teachers who reviewed mathematics test questions in middle school. Invariably, a committee member would frantically come up to me, explaining that they were a third-grade teacher and weren't qualified to review sixth-grade math items. These frantic committee members were elementary teachers who were terrified that they wouldn't be able to keep up with sixth grade mathematics.

TIP

Whether your internal belief is that math is boring, scary, or hard, the fact is that your beliefs can carry over to the students — but so will your enthusiasm (genuine or not) for the subject. If needed, fake it till you make it.

The hard truths about the hard stuff

Traditionally, the goal of mathematics education aspired to get the students through the Algebra, Geometry, and Algebra 2 sequence of courses in high school. The CCSS defines high school standards for mathematics, including a recommended distribution of standards across these three traditional courses.

The reason to target that classic sequence of mathematics is to prepare the student for calculus in college. Over the last few decades, a more common approach is for college-bound STEM students to take calculus in high school, often earning college credit along the way.

Noting the layered nature of math education goals

The underlying goal of traditional high school mathematics education has been to prepare students for calculus. This goal is odd, because calculus isn't always a required course in education programs, even in some mathematics education programs. (I have more on this point in the section "Matching standards and goals with STEM" later in the chapter.)

I remember interviewing college graduates from a mathematics program at a prominent university who had never taken a calculus class. The university said that the graduates were qualified to teach high school mathematics, but they'd never even taken the course that showed them the ultimate point of traditional high school mathematics courses! And as a result, the graduates don't understand why the things they are teaching in Algebra 2 matter.

The frantic third-grade teacher I discuss in the section "Psst, they know if you hate math" earlier in the chapter, who was unfamiliar with grade six mathematics, may run into similar problems of not understanding why they teach specific math concepts. That is, they might not realize that the fraction concepts they introduce in third grade lay the groundwork for the more significant proportional reasoning that the sixth graders face.

The misunderstanding about how foundational mathematical concepts are needed to support later skills became explicitly clear to me when I was working with the Indiana Department of Education (IDOE) on streamlining the state's content standards. The state legislature had mandated reducing the number of standards by 25 percent, but then left it to IDOE to determine which standards to eliminate. The department made recommendations and had a public comment period. Among the commenters was a teacher suggesting the elimination of standards about partitioning shapes into equal pieces. The teacher considered it a useless, time-consuming activity that students weren't very good at.

What the teacher didn't seem to realize was that partitioning of shapes lays the foundation for the introduction of fractions. Rather than being a useless, time-consuming activity, partitioning shapes is an important activity in that grade to prepare students for future work. And if students were bad at it, that was an even more significant reason why the standard needed to be retained.

Seeing where the math standards lead

This layered nature of math goals is part of the reason I think that looking ahead to where a content area leads is important. I have mapped out the vertical articulations of the standards across grades for science (see Chapter 4) and computer science (see Chapter 5). In those cases, the goal of the standards was to define what a student needed to know by the time they graduate high school and provide standards leading up to that level so that students are prepared when they graduate. The mathematics standards in the CCSS are no different

The goal of mathematics education under the CCSS (or the state standards that often closely mirror the CCSS) is to get students prepared for the standard algebra and geometry sequence in high school. In other words, to be college and career ready in high school mathematics.

Think for a moment about what this means. The underlying assumptions of the CCSS is that if a student is not proficient in their grade level of mathematics standards, then they are not at that moment on track to become college and career ready in high school.

Matching standards and goals with STEM

One challenge in defining appropriate math education standards involves the meaning of the phrase *college and career ready*. This phrase can mean something different to different students. The high school mathematics standards are anchored around the algebra and geometry sequence because that's tradition, but that sequence of math concepts isn't essential for every student to become ready for their own college or career path.

Consider four different groups of students who have post-graduation plans and the mathematics that they would need to thrive in their chosen path.

Post-Graduation Plans	Math Proficiency Required
College for STEM careers	Education beyond Algebra 2 in high school to prepare for the calculus probably needed in college
College for a non-STEM careers	Completion of Algebra 2 in high school
Non-college for a STEM career	High-level math proficiency; subjects vary because of the wide variety of math skills required by various STEM fields
Non-college for a non-STEM career	Proficiency in basic mathematics (true proficiency through eight-grade math); not necessarily a deep understanding of higher-order functions

When looking at these general needs to make these students college and career ready, I'd say that being on-track with the CCSS puts a graduating student in a good position for the second and third groups in the table. The students in the first group should actually exceed the CCSS a bit (perhaps even taking calculus in high school), and students in the fourth group can likely thrive without gaining full proficiency under the high school standards.

REMEMBER

The problem with defining standards in earlier grades is that you don't have any idea which students will fall into any of these four college and career groups. As a teacher, you may have a sense of where a student might fit, but they have a lot of runway to cover between the mathematics proficiency acquired in grade 3 and the mathematics proficiency that they'll have by the time they hit high school.

The STEM approach promotes embedding as many of the mathematics concepts as you can within authentic, real-world projects that are relevant to the students. You still have to cover all of the math standards, but STEM makes mathematics into a tool to solve problems. Mathematics is a means, rather than an end in itself.

Illuminating What We Talk About When We Talk About Math

In contrast to people who say that students don't need to learn math (see that viewpoint in the section "Knowing that Kids Will Use Math in the Future" earlier in the chapter), I sometimes hear from the other end of the spectrum — the people who complain that kids need to spend more time memorizing their times tables. (These same people, one of whom gave birth to me, are also often obsessed with cursive writing. Hi Mom!)

But this other-end-of-the-spectrum group seems to have the same basic conception of mathematics as the people who don't understand why math is important. Both groups view the core of mathematics to be computation and memorization.

For mathematicians, mathematics isn't primarily about computation and memorization. It's about understanding relationships between quantities. It's about problem-solving and being able to break reasoning into discrete steps. Teachers who have a deep understanding and background in mathematics can map the contours of mathematics, seeing where the concepts are heading and how they fit together.

Beyond computation and memorization

The reason that so many people dislike mathematics is that, honestly, for decades education focused more on arithmetic and memorization of rote facts or shortcuts than on a comprehensive approach to mathematics.

REMEMBER

In a STEM class, the emphasis cannot be on computation and memorization. Don't get me wrong. A lot of computation *will* take place in a STEM classroom, but that won't be the emphasis. Students should generally have access to calculators (to help with the computation part), but lessons should be built around using mathematics in a specific task or project.

I'm also not saying that there's absolutely nothing that a student should memorize. Measurements, in particular, come to mind here because making and working with measurements is a regular part of the planning stage of many STEM projects. So for the memorization piece, you probably want to at least try to get students to remember that 12 inches equals 1 foot, and that 1 yard equals 3 feet. And you definitely want them to have a sense of how the metric system works.

However, if students go through their whole lives having to look up those relationships (inches to feet and yards, for example), that is hardly the worst hardship they'll have to endure. The important thing is that they are comfortable working with those sorts of quantities and can fluently move between various units, even if it includes taking the time to look them up. (I keep an Amazon Echo device in my kitchen, used primarily to convert between teaspoons, tablespoons, ounces, cups, pints, and quarts.)

Related to that topic, different sets of standards set different requirements for what students need to know about measurement conversion:

>> **The CCSS has a fifth grade standard about converting within a given measurement system,** but nothing about converting between systems. So the CCSS indicates that a fifth-grade student should be able to convert centimeters to meters, but not necessarily convert centimeters to inches. They have no standard that explicitly indicates conversion between systems, although middle school standards related to applying ratios could use conversions between standard and metric units as a problem-solving context.

>> **Indiana also has explicit standards in fifth grade for in-system conversions (matching the CCSS),** but they also have a written a sixth-grade standard about conversion between systems. If that sort of item were on the state test, however, the test specifications indicate that the cross-system conversion would be provided.

TIP

Because of potential differences in the material you need to present, you should look up particular skills and standards in your state's mathematics frameworks, as well as how those skills are assessed on your state's test specifications.

Organizing and representing data

To implement mathematics in integrated STEM, you may often have students working with data and, can you focus on mathematics as a tool for how to organize and represent that data. I'm a huge fan of data analysis as a cornerstone of mathematics, and certainly throughout STEM, one of the recurring themes should be integrating data literacy at all grades.

As discuss in the section "Matching standards and goals with STEM" earlier in the chapter, the definition of being *college and career ready* is built around the idea that high school students need to be ready to complete the classic Algebra, Geometry, and Algebra 2 sequence of math courses in high school, which prepares them for calculus. Calculus remains important. The director of a college engineering department told me that they were pleased with the practical skills that come out of many STEM programs, but find that many of those students are often still behind on what they need to know mathematically for a college engineering program.

Making way for data analysis

In recent years, a growing movement among mathematicians and education reformers aims to shift that high school emphasis (for the non-STEM track students, in particular) from a calculus-based model of mathematics to a greater focus on data analysis and interpretation.

While some Algebra 1 curricula are good about incorporating data analysis throughout their lessons, the fact is that, in a course called Algebra 1, the data analysis is almost always going to take a back seat to the emphasis on understanding linear functions. But you really could teach many of the same skills with the emphasis on the data. Consider these approaches:

>> In Algebra 1, students traditionally learn about functions, and then about how to apply those functions to data as a linear model.

>> Alternatively, the linear equations could be used as a tool in the service of modeling linear data relationships. You still cover all the same math concepts about the linear (and eventually non-linear) functions, except now you're giving a student reasons why they have to do this.

This approach is consistent with the STEM-based approach in other sorts of projects where you focus on an authentic task and then bring in the study of the knowledge and skills needed within the context of that task. If you do that, then students are significantly less likely to ask, "When am I ever going to need this?" because they need the tool right now to complete the task they're doing. (They might still ask "Why do we have to do this?" if the task isn't relevant to them, but I offer more about that question in Chapter 9.)

Displaying data in association with math skills

Seeing the progression of math skills through data is, I think, particularly useful — because of how the relationship can so closely tie into integrated STEM lessons. In this section, I list some of the key skills related to creating and interpreting data displays, across the grade levels.

Early elementary data display skills:

>> Count and group objects (kindergarten)

>> Organize counts by groups (first grade)

>> Answer simple "how many" questions about group data (first grade)

>> Create simple line plots, bar graphs, and picture graphs (second grade)

>> Solve simple addition, subtraction, and comparison problems using data given in a bar graph (second grade)

Upper elementary data display skills:

>> Solve one- and two-step ("how many more" and "how many less") questions using bar graphs (third grade)

>> Create scaled line plots, bar graphs, and picture graphs including fractional values (third grade)

>> Solve fraction problems using data given in line plots (fourth grade and fifth grade)

Middle school data display skills:

>> Create data displays on number lines, including box plots, histograms, and dot plots (sixth grade)

>> Looking at two visual displays of different sets of data, informally describe visual similarities and differences (seventh grade)

» Generate scatter plots of data (eighth grade)

» Identify and describe patterns of data presented in scatter plots (eighth grade)

» Relate linear trends in scatter plots to a straight line that could reasonably fit the data (eighth grade)

» Present and interpret information about frequency and relative frequency within two-way tables (eighth grade)

TIP

You can have data several times during a STEM project, particularly at the start of the project when you're gathering information about the project constraints and then also at the end when you've completed testing. These opportunities are excellent times to focus on the data and discuss the most appropriate way to represent it for comparison, to reinforce these data literacy skills.

Displaying data is hardly the most important thing about the data, and the mathematics domain of statistics and probability has several standards (starting in sixth grade) that focus on the types of questions you ask to get statistical data, how to gather statistical data, and what sort of actions you can take to summarize the data. Teachers can weave these crucial skills throughout many STEM projects.

Critical thinking, reasoning, and logic

I want to close out the chapter with that third category of math concepts that I mention in the section "Thinking About Why We Learn Math" earlier in the chapter — concepts that are indirectly useful. This category is the fertile compost of mathematics, the problem-solving, logical reasoning, and computational thinking that undergirds everything else. And it also has a role throughout STEM, to the point of being explicitly called out as fundamental in the math, science, and computer science standards.

The indirectly useful category of math concepts is also the hardest to quantify and the hardest to teach. For example, teaching students how to tell when combining fractions together makes a problem easier is much more difficult than simply telling them how to add two fractions together. And if you're like that teacher who said to me, "I love STEM, but I hate mathematics," it's a gut punch.

Hopefully, I have somehow conveyed in this chapter that mathematics deserves a little more love than it's getting. But, even if I've won you over to the cause, what I've certainly not done within this single chapter is give you the information and tools you need to really understand the depths of mathematics.

Fundamentally, the problems with math education can only be fixed by having teachers of math who love and appreciate math. One way to do that would be to increase the wages of math teachers significantly, so that brilliant mathematicians are more inclined to head in the direction of education, instead of going into finance, computer science, or economics. I don't believe that the pay raise to entice brilliant mathematicians to become teachers is likely to happen, but the next best thing is transforming hesitant math teachers into full-blown lovers of mathematics.

Toward that end, as a reward for having made it all the way through a chapter that you may have dreaded, I offer recommendations of four fantastic books that are guaranteed (okay, not *really* guaranteed) to enhance your appreciation for the richness of mathematics:

>> *Is Math Real?: How Simple Questions Lead Us to Mathematics' Deepest* Truths by Eugenia Cheng (Basic Books 2025)

>> *The Joy of X: A Guided Tour of Math, from One to Infinity* by Steven Strogatz (2013)

>> *The Calculus Diaries: How Math Can Help You Lose Weight, Win in Vegas, and Survive a Zombie Apocalypse* by Jennifer Ouellette (2010)

>> *Zero: The Biography of a Dangerous Idea* by Charles Seife (Penguin Books 2000)

And if these books don't win you over, I take another stab in the next chapter when I talk about how to integrate math together with other content areas.

IN THIS CHAPTER

» Digging into integrated STEM

» Using technology to aid in reading and writing

» Discovering the past through STEM

» Looking at societal issues with STEM

» Exploring the arts with STEAM

Chapter **8**

Mixing It Up: Integrating STEM Components

While STEM is described in terms of four subjects that are linked together, the point of combining them into a single term is to erase the dividing lines between the subjects. In the previous four chapters, I (mostly) cover the specific subject areas and lay out what students need to learn in each of them. My goal now is to convince you to pay as little attention as possible to the dividing lines between those content areas. That is, I encourage you to approach STEM as a holistic approach to knowledge and understanding.

STEM isn't a curriculum, and it isn't just another element that you tack on to existing lessons. STEM is a way of structuring and delivering instruction that centers on the student's ability to apply their knowledge, skills, and creativity with the goal of seeing the relevance and relationship of the many core ideas that they're learning. I cover aspects of designing lessons in more detail in Chapter 9, but in this chapter, I discuss some general themes that come up when integrating content from different subject areas in STEM lessons.

In this chapter, I explore concrete ways in which the different areas of STEM overlap with each other, and I explain how to incorporate those overlaps into any classroom. I describe several ways that teachers should explicitly incorporate technology literacy as part of reading and writing instruction. I also present a project-based way of approaching modern civics instruction and historical under-standing that focuses on solving problems with STEM. And I dig into STEAM, which incorporates the arts into STEM to enrich both the arts and the STEM educational experience.

Combining STEM Areas

The fact that the four subject areas (science, technology, engineering, and math) combine into a single term, *STEM*, depicts how much overlap exists between them. In the classroom, though, they are commonly taught as completely separate areas (if they are even taught at all). That teaching approach does a disservice to both the subjects and the students because it really isn't the way that these subject areas operate in the real world.

If you look at these four areas historically, their progress is closely tied together. Ancient civilizations learned how to advance beyond simple machines into complex ones by growing their understanding of mathematics and the natural world. As their understanding grew, civilizations built not only new devices, but also larger cities and more complex societies. And they developed scientific and technological advances in agriculture to feed the people in those cities.

TIP

During the Scientific Revolution — followed by the Industrial Revolution and then the Information Revolution — you can see advances in all four STEM areas moving along with each other. (This tidbit also becomes useful when you think about how to approach history and social studies, but that's later in the chapter.)

REMEMBER

Trying to break the STEM subject areas apart into distinct and easy categories might make teaching individual concepts easier, but doing so steals away a lot of the context that gives meaning to the knowledge itself.

When using models and simulations

One of the most powerful ways in which STEM areas overlap involves the use of models and simulations. As I discuss in Chapter 7, the idea of modeling is central to how teachers present mathematics throughout all grades in the Common Core State Standards (CCSS) for mathematics (which provide the basis for most states mathematics standards these days). Using models and simulations to explore a concept, phenomenon, or task is central to all four of the STEM areas — and one of the best ways to incorporate them together.

A gold standard for approaching a modeling or simulation project is for the students to study a phenomenon, develop a model of their own design, and then use that model to further advance their understanding of the phenomenon. That process is, understandably, quite a heavy lift, and may not be something that's a realistic expectation of many students in most classes (particularly depending on the grade level of the students).

REMEMBER

But the point of identifying a gold standard isn't to always reach it. The gold standard is often used as a reference point for more modest efforts that fall short of that ambitious high mark. A ton of modeling and simulation tasks can take place in any classroom with resources teachers have at hand. And these tasks can help expand the student understanding of the phenomenon.

Asking and answering key questions

When using a model or a simulation in a STEM lesson, you can explore the following key questions:

>> In what ways does this model/simulation match the phenomenon well?

>> In what ways does this model/simulation match the phenomenon poorly?

>> What differences would I expect between this model/simulation and the actual phenomenon?

>> Are there constraints I could put in place that would mean the model/simulation and the actual phenomenon match up better?

Considering a specific example is often useful. Suppose that students are designing a paper airplane with the goal of understanding the basic principles of aeronautics. Questions they should ask would include the following (along with some possible answers students might come up with):

>> **What parts of the paper airplane matches an airplane well?** They have similar wing structures and overall shape.

>> **What parts of the paper airplane matches an airplane poorly?** Paper airplanes are made of (duh) paper instead of metal, so they are much lighter. Paper airplanes are also much smaller, and they don't have engines, or in fact, any moving parts.

>> **What differences would you expect between the flight of a paper airplane and an actual airplane?** The paper airplane is going to glide a short way and then fall to the ground, but a regular airplane can keep moving as long as it has fuel.

>> **Are there constraints you could put in place that would mean the paper airplane and the actual airplane match up better?** If you were just gliding in an airplane without an engine, it would probably match up better with the paper model.

You can find a lot of different types of questions to ask about your model and simulation, and students will come up with many answers to those questions that are different from what I propose in the list.

REMEMBER

The point of asking (and answering) questions involves getting students to think about the connection between the model, the simulation, and the actual phenomenon itself. This useful critical thinking about the limits of the model helps develop student's critical thinking muscle regarding other areas, not just in STEM but also in analogies that come up in reading and the social realm.

Simulating phenomena with coding

You could consider other ways to model airplane flight. Students who are familiar with coding — even in a basic programming language like Scratch — might want to do a computer simulation of a gliding airplane. This approach wouldn't be directly relevant to the physics of gliding an airplane, but it would allow you to test out the ways in which different magnitudes of downward motion (how fast the airplane falls) appear relative to the horizontal motion (how far it goes). You could then have students compare the simulated glides to the observed glides that they see in their paper model tests.

TECHNICAL STUFF

The coded computer simulation for a gliding airplane could potentially offer a hint about the relative magnitude of the gravitational acceleration on the paper airplane, if you wanted to go deeply into the analysis.

When testing hypotheses and solutions

A model and a simulation may give you a trial run for fine-tuning your hypothesis and solutions into measurable activities, but the next step up is implementing them by testing. This testing phase is another case in which you find a major opportunity for interaction among the four STEM disciplines.

Science — The aspects of the natural, physical world that must be understood and manipulated as part of the solution, including the scientific theoretical framework that supports the solution.

Technology — Tools involved in the solution.

Engineering — Building of any devices needed for testing of the hypothesis that are not already available.

Mathematics — Precise measurements and calculations required as part of formulating and testing the hypothesis. Numerical or geometric models may be generated as part of this process. Mathematics will also be needed for the analysis of the results to determine if the solution is effective.

The previous modeling phase may have been more abstract, but the testing phase has more real-world considerations, which may make teaching it easier in some ways and more difficult in others. Planning for this is part of a STEM project is what I focus on in Chapter 9.

Of course, as I discuss in Chapters 2, 4, and 9, one of the real benefits of a STEM project comes from incorporating not only a testing phase, but also an improvement and iteration phase. In this last phase, students take their test results and figure out how to act on them to refine (and hopefully improve) their project elements and results. Ideally, students have enough time allotted to do the refinement and then do another test, to confirm whether their changes have improved the project in the ways that they had intended.

Reading, Writing, and STEM

One concern often expressed about an emphasis on STEM is that it marginalizes the importance of the *softer skills*, including those related to communication. The truth is that communication should be an integral part of every STEM lesson. The science, mathematics, and computer science standards all include practices (see Chapter 3) that emphasize the importance of being able to communicate the thinking related to these subjects.

REMEMBER

If a student has a solution, even a working solution, but cannot explain the solution, then they aren't yet demonstrating full proficiency with the skills in question.

Many STEM projects incorporate communication in the form of public speaking because the students must explain or present their results to the group. A class may also require a written report, which would touch on writing skills.

The importance of STEM background knowledge

While the STEM classroom has ample room for promoting reading and writing skills, it's important to recognize that those communication-oriented classes also have room to incorporate the STEM subjects. Evidence suggests that stronger STEM skills provide a basis for stronger reading skills.

Reading and writing standards are split into two areas: literature (or fiction) and informational text (or non-fiction). For the moment, I want to focus on the non-fiction part of things (although, because I'm a science fiction fan, rest assured that I get back to the role of STEM in literature).

Considering the standards

The CCSS has a general "Reading: Informational Text" domain that is vertically articulated all the way from kindergarten through twelfth grade, but in the sixth through twelfth grades, those standards are explicitly articulated as literacy standards in "History/Social Studies" and "Science and Technical Subjects." And many of the state English language arts standards follow this format, just as they follow the CCSS format for mathematics.

In general, you can think of informative writing as tending to fall in these categories (which break out history from social studies a bit):

Modern Culture/Events: Something people are doing in the world today

History: Something people did in the past

Science: Something going on in the natural world, which may or may not directly impact or involve people

And, of course, a piece of informative writing can combine these categories. (My anti-knowledge-silo campaign is also cross-disciplinary!) You could assign an essay that connects something happening today to a historical event or societal context, for example. Or you could hit all three categories with an article about how something going on in the natural world affects people, how they respond to what's going on, and how they responded to similar situations in the past.

TIP

In all these situations, educators must prioritize giving their students a broad context of underlying knowledge if they expect the students to correctly read and interpret informative passages or to complete meaningful, relevant written assignments.

Looking at related research

The definitive research on the relationship between comprehension and a broad context of knowledge goes back to the 1987 "Baseball Study" conducted by education researchers Donna Recht and Lauren Leslie. In this study, the researchers wanted to understand how dependent reading comprehension was on the topic covered in the reading material.

Gathering groups of junior-high and middle-school students, they separated them into four groups with these characteristics:

>> High general reading ability with high baseball knowledge

>> High general reading ability with low baseball knowledge

>> Low general reading ability with high baseball knowledge

>> Low general reading ability with low baseball knowledge

The students read a half-page passage describing an inning of baseball and then demonstrated their comprehension of it by recreating the inning on a model base-ball field.

Here are the results of the groups' efforts:

>> **The first group in the list** (who had a high level of reading ability and baseball knowledge) performed the best at the task. The fact that great readers who knew baseball had no problem recreating a model of what they'd just read is not surprising.

>> **Students in the last group in the list** (who weren't good at reading and didn't know about baseball) were largely unable to recreate the inning on a model baseball field. This result is also not surprising.

>> **Students in the second group** (who had an overall high general reading ability but low baseball knowledge) performed no better at recalling facts about the passage or summarizing what had happened on the model baseball field than the students who had low reading ability and low baseball knowledge (the last group). In other words, the fact that these students didn't have background knowledge about baseball completely overrode any benefit they had from being good readers. This result is surprising!

Prior to this 1987 study, literacy educators held a pretty strong belief that reading ability was context independent. If a student knew how to read, they'd be able to sort out the important details of the topic even with no prior knowledge of it. In this instance, they might not know the definition of a short stop, but they'd be able to describe what that person did after they read the passage. But the study results showed that wasn't the case.

>> **Students in the third group** (who were poor readers but knew baseball well) showed a stronger ability to summarize what had happened in the passage than did students in the second group. Knowledge about baseball fundamen-tally drove the understanding more than raw reading ability. This result may not be really surprising.

REMEMBER

This recognition that content knowledge is essential to reading has become one of the cornerstones of the modern understanding of the science of reading and of a movement to inform literacy education with what research shows about how students acquire linguistic and written knowledge. If educators want students to be able to read and interpret writing about STEM areas, then the students must have a foundation that allows them to understand the context and supporting details.

TIP

Take the results of this research about comprehension and knowledge base as an important reminder that you must take care to be sure that you're assessing the skills that you intend to be assessing. I cover more on this topic in Chapter 11.

Researching and writing with technology tools

One other way that teachers can more effectively incorporate STEM concepts into language arts education is through an emphasis on STEM tools to assist in research and writing of essays. This approach doesn't automatically turn the essay into a STEM project, but it helps promote the idea of a holistic, unified understanding of knowledge and skills.

The most significant technological research tool used today is, of course, the internet, and whether you want them to or not, most students are using it. Anytime I do research, I still run to the library and end up with a bag (or two) full of books that I flip through, but — even alongside my old school approach — I definitely do a ton of research online (including identifying which books I want to find before I ever go to the library and, often, requesting them in advance so they'll be waiting for me when I arrive).

Despite my best efforts, I have never convinced either of my sons to use physical books as sources for research papers. I'd go with them to the library to find sources, and even check out some books with them, but they had no interest in using them to do research that they could otherwise do on the internet.

Developing online research skills

REMEMBER

Using this amazing Internet research resource effectively and ethically is a component of both digital literacy and media literacy, and growing proficiency in those areas should certainly be considered alongside STEM. Many standards, including the CCSS for English language arts (ELA), emphasize reading, listening, and media literacy skills that are useful when conducting research online.

Here are just a handful of the skills that the CCSS ELA standards require of students:

Locate information relevant to a given subject

Distinguish valid and invalid information

Cite specific textual evidence for claims

Break down components of an argument

Compare and contrast different sources

These research skills — to engage with deep texts and gain knowledge from them, and to break apart arguments into their component parts — are key skills that students also develop in STEM courses. The skills are not separate and distinct, but instead, they complement each other well. Both applications of these research skills motivate students to think critically about subjects, whether they're dealing with a physical object, a scientific theory, a math equation, a video, or a written essay.

Writing about what you find out from research

The writing part of dealing with technology tools (as distinct from the "research" part) involves synthesizing the gleaned and validated information together into a meaningful output. And, even in this part of the process, a number of technological tools are helpful.

First and foremost, teachers must encourage students to use the editing functionality of their word processing program. That is, have students actually generate a first draft of the written work — with the understanding that it will not be perfect — and then take another pass to edit the work. Again, this use of technology resonates perfectly with the overall goals of STEM education, because in STEM, you never assume that the initial prototype or design is going to be the same as the final one. That iterative step, with the goal of finding and correcting errors, is just as important in writing as in STEM!

Fine-tuning what you write with technology tools

Teachers should also explain other technology tools — such as spellcheck and grammar check in a word processing program or apps such as Grammarly — that students can use to help fine-tune their writing efforts. And the explanations can't happen just once. Students need to see the editing tools in operation multiple times to pick up how best to use them. While just explaining to students that the tools exist seems simple, maybe you've noticed that these tools have become immensely complicated in recent years and can require some work to use with proficiency.

Before I submit chapters in this book to my editor, I run them through not only a spell check and grammar check, but also a check for options such as Clarity and Conciseness. I'm able to do this by using settings such as Formal Writing, as well as Professional and Casual. Because this book sort of qualifies in all three categories, I check all three settings to determine if I want to change anything before sending off the chapter. (To my chagrin, I *always* find something.)

Of course, most students will not make full use of these technology editing tools, but they absolutely need to know the range of tools that are available. That way, they're prepared to write (and refine) something when it actually matters to them. The goal of developing skill with using technology communication tools in school isn't that they write a great essay in class: The goal is that they have the tools to write something competently (or better) when they need to outside of class.

Including communication technology literacy as an element of instruction in school for all students is also an equity concern, because more affluent students will be more likely to have access to these paid resources at home. This situation is another example of how less affluent students can easily fall behind when they don't get the same level of instruction and access to tools that affluent children use regularly. See Chapter 15 for more about this and other equity issues.

The giant elephant in the room on any discussion of technology in writing is artificial intelligence, or AI. The big fear is that students will just use AI to generate their essays and be done with it, and sadly, teachers can't do much about students who are inclined to cheat in that way. See the end of Chapter 5 for more discussion of AI and how it can be used in the classroom. The goal of teaching students to use a range of technology tools (including AI) effectively and ethically in their writing is to make sure that they know when it's appropriate and when it isn't.

Reading as the basis of STEM

In addition to using STEM education as background content for understanding reading passages, you also find influence going in the opposite direction. Students working on a STEM project need to gain information, and they can find much of that information in written resources. The students must be able to read and interpret those resources to grow in STEM.

The prevalence of explanatory videos can make this point something of a challenge to get across to students today. As a gamer hobbyist and amateur game designer, I've discovered that learning a new board game by watching a video of someone playing it is easier than actually reading the rulebook. This fact is true for a ton of things, from plumbing projects to cooking recipes.

REMEMBER

When you're delving deeply into a project, you can still find real benefits to having a written reference source. For one thing, unless you've memorized the video timestamp of a specific piece of information, skimming a written resource to review that information is much easier than finding it in a video. And so, having students write down the timestamp on the video — along with a quick comment about what happened there — is a good and efficient way to make notes about a video for reference later. (I cover more about this point in the next section on media literacy.)

Obviously, reading informative written sources that cover science and technical subjects is one way to use reading in STEM, but you should also be on the lookout for ways that you can connect literature with STEM. For example, you can

>> **Explore the technology mentioned in the fictional reading.** If it's a technology that people don't commonly use (such as the spinning wheel and spindle in both the original fairy tale and Disney versions of *Sleeping Beauty*), have your students consider modern equivalents.

>> **Recreate a scene from the reading.** You have many ways to approach this recreation, for example, by building puppets or a miniature diorama, creating a digital graphic, writing a computer program, programming robots, or using other available technology.

>> **Create a video, PowerPoint slide deck, or infographic explaining key themes of the reading.** Include a data display to really bring it home!

You can base these types of STEM projects on fairy tales in lower grades and progress to more sophisticated literature as students' grade levels increase. Many of these ideas, though, integrate STEM not only with literature, but also with various forms of the arts, as I covered in the section "STEAMing up the Arts with STEM" later in this chapter.

Media Literacy as STEM

Today's language arts standards often include media literacy standards, and this is another place where you find a huge potential overlap with STEM — particularly with the "T" part.

As I mention in the previous section, society is at a stage in which people may interact with digital media and video a lot more than with written media. Videos that demonstrate and explain how to do things are incredibly useful, and you need to teach your students how to use them as effective resources as — part of their growing media literacy.

TIP

Plan to work on the practical skill of taking notes while watching a video early in students' education, that is, as soon as they are able to write. One important thing for students to realize is that simply watching a video won't ensure that they understand everything in the video. And the hands-on aspect of STEM really can be useful because — when they try to replicate a project described in a video — they quickly and clearly discover how little of the necessary information they absorbed.

In addition to being able to retain information from videos and making notes for later reference, students need to know other media literacy skills, like how to assess the reliability of a given source of information. Teaching these methods gives you an excellent opportunity to reinforce the ways in which computer technologies can impact society (and also apply the computer science standards I discuss in Chapter 5).

Promoting Justice for All: STEM and Society

The ultimate goal of a STEM classroom is to have students engage in authentic projects to solve problems in a real-world context. These problems are often scientific- or engineering-related, but teachers know that society has other types of problems in the world — including social problems. STEM education can be a means for exploring, defining, and solving those problems, as well.

The exploration of history and modern civics provides an opportunity for students to identify problems that need to be understood and solved. Ideally, students will use their own interests as motivation to identify these questions and problems. That way, they will (by definition) meet the benchmarks of authenticity and relevance that make for a great STEM project!

If you take the route of having students identify and define a problem and then offer a solution, be aware that the solutions the students land on might not be the ones that you expect. You should encourage students to find and explore their own approaches to understanding the problems, as well as finding their own solutions.

Suppose that students decide they want to investigate nuclear power as a safe and clean form of energy production. And if you don't personally support this view of nuclear power, you can legitimately offer students evidence that might challenge their perspective. But it's the students' project. If they find arguments in favor of nuclear power to be more persuasive, then they should be allowed to make that case. (Presumably, this would be a project where they are not, in fact, building their own nuclear reactor. Regardless of which side of the debate you come down on, that would be a step too far.)

TIP

Civics projects that overlap with STEM don't necessarily need to go all the way through the process to design a solution to the problem (although that would be great!) but can emphasize the define-the-problem portion of the science and engineering practices.

STEAMing Up the Arts with STEM

A big reason to incorporate the STEM approach to education into the classroom involves the aspect of play. Specifically, engaging in play is one of the most effective ways to connect someone (particularly young people) with the learning experience. Another aspect of education that benefits from the play aspect is the arts. As such, combining the arts and STEM provides benefits to both areas.

Some people prefer the acronym STEAM in place of STEM, to explicitly emphasize the connection to the arts. As I mention in Chapter 2, I personally am not a fan of this, mostly because I feel that the play and creativity inherent in the arts automatically comes along for the ride in a good STEM lesson. Also, I believe too much explicit emphasis on the "arts" part of the project can lead away from building an educationally rigorous STEM lesson. I've seen far too many cases in which a STEAM project results in little more than an arts and crafts project that has a slim and tenuous connection to a science context — but doesn't actually teach STEM principles.

Whether or not you embrace the STEAM acronym, both teachers and students will benefit from experiencing a rich integration of STEM with the arts. (For the remainder of this chapter — because I am talking about the arts — I switch to using the STEAM acronym. But don't be confused!)

One thing to keep in mind when approaching the integration of arts and STEM (to make STEAM) is the necessity of including all teachers who are involved. The visual arts, music, or other arts teachers in your school may already be working on a project that can be a natural fit for STEAM integration. They may have insights from their expertise and background that will make the process simpler and the resulting lesson better.

Visual arts

Visual arts have a sizable capacity to bring in other STEAM principles. Art teachers with an interest in STEAM make for some truly impressive STEAM teachers. This observation is, in part, because art teachers are able to fully embrace the controlled chaos of a STEAM classroom in a way that more traditional teachers find challenging.

An art teacher is used to the basic structure and progress of a STEAM project:

1. Give a basic introduction and instructions about the tools to use and the task at hand.

2. Let the students do their best to complete the task with the tools you provide.

3. Circle around the classroom, offering help and consultation where needed.

4. Collect tools, clean up, get students organized and ready to move on.

I'm sure that art classes exist in which teachers spend most of their time lecturing, but I've never witnessed one. (Nor would I want to.)

Many of the design principles that are important to creating an effective engineering project also resonate with artistic principles. The field of architecture is a particularly good example of where artistry and function merge together (hopefully) seamlessly and create a robust area for exploring various features that highlight the structure-and-function crosscutting concept from the NGSS.

In Chapter 12, I cover the idea of creating a true *makerspace* (a creative place in your school where students can make things) in more depth, and this is another example of how visual arts education really has a place alongside other work in STEAM. Using a laser cutter to etch a three-dimensional design on a metal water bottle is a feat of creative artistry as much as it demonstrates technical proficiency with the necessary equipment and software.

REMEMBER

One element that is crucial to a STEM project is the idea that the project is iterative. If you're doing a STEAM project in the arts, be sure to incorporate an opportunity for the student to review their project design and modify it. The test in that case may be a peer review process to get feedback from other students in the class.

Music, theater, and musical theater

Outside of a handful of elementary school plays, my first introduction to theater was through a technology angle rather than through the arts. While I was in high school, a local community theater was short on people to run the sound and light boards. A friend of mine performing in their upcoming play thought I'd be pretty good at it, and that's how I first got recruited as a theater tech.

If you've ever been involved in any sort of live performance, you probably realize just how much technology and engineering goes into the whole process. Building the sets is an engineering challenge. Getting the lighting and sound set up right are major technological hurdles, with constant modifications (iterations) going on until the day the performances begin (and sometimes beyond). Once, I participated as a tech in a show where the crew had to rebuild a broken chair leg during the intermission.

TIP

Live performance teaches the soft skills of perseverance and grit that are needed in STEM education. Each performance is really an iterative experiment, with the performer adapting based on the results from the previous attempts.

One other possibility for STEAM integration is to flip the connection and use music as a springboard to learn about science. The creation of music itself provides a basis for understanding the physics of sound waves and harmonics. Students can learn these principles, and then design and build their own instruments, with various features — perhaps even using technology to analyze them. So that provides yet another opportunity for creativity and exploration!

3

Employing Approaches to STEM Education

Dive into creating a STEM lesson or project and use authentic, hands-on activities to engage students in a holistic approach to learning.

Zoom out from an individual lesson to look at creating a full STEM curriculum that involves aspects of pacing, scope, sequence, and reinforcement of learning goals throughout the school year.

Consider the ways that you can assess student performance within STEM lessons and curriculum, as well as how to assess the STEM program itself.

Look into ways that you can expand a typical STEM lesson to really engage students deeply with STEM principles both inside and outside the classroom.

IN THIS CHAPTER

» **Exploring the basis of learning**

» **Starting a new lesson**

» **Structuring STEM lessons**

» **Building an inquiry-based culture**

» **Prioritizing collaboration**

Chapter **9**

Engaging Student Minds in a STEM Lesson

After you have a firm handle on what you need to teach, you have to figure out *how* to actually teach it. One big benefit of STEM education comes from its emphasis on student-centered learning. More traditional approaches to education are teacher-centered, with the teacher actively delivering the learning and the students taking the role of passively absorbing information. The teacher certainly has an important role in a student-centered classroom, but that role is to structure the STEM lesson that creates teachable moments and facilitates the students' exploration — not to hand out information to the students.

To steal a phrase dating back to at least 1993 (when it appeared as the title of an article in the journal *College Teaching*), teachers go from *sage-on-the-stage* to *guide-on-the-side*. In a student-centered classroom, the student becomes the active agent of the learning process.

Throughout this chapter, I refer to a lesson, but don't think that you must complete an entire STEM lesson in one class session. In fact, the research on the neuroscience of learning suggests that doing so isn't particularly effective. By lesson, I mean a sequence of class sections, connected together by a single project or unified set of STEM topics. You can use this same process to create an entire unit of connected lessons, as well. Expanding beyond a single set of connected lessons into a full curriculum is a more central focus of Chapter 10.

In this chapter, I explore how to create a STEM lesson. I cover recent findings about how the human brain learns new information, discuss how to find starting points for creating a STEM lesson, and show how to build a lesson from those kernels of ideas. I also explore some specific instructional models that help you structure a lesson flow and walk you through some key student behaviors that you want to your lesson structure to encourage. Along with lesson structure, I discuss the importance of aiming to support student collaboration and development of key employability skills as part of the STEM lesson.

Unpacking the Learning Brain

The goal of this chapter is to design lessons specifically in the realm of STEM; these lessons attempt to leverage the current research-based understanding of how the human brain learns new things. In short, the process of *learning* involves getting information that a person doesn't possess in their long-term memory to record itself reliably into their long-term memory. If this happens, the person has learned the information.

Transitioning input into long-term memory

So, what does neuroscience tell us about how learning happens? You find five steps to this process.

1. **Sensory input:** Sense something, and electrical impulses of that experience make it to the brain.

2. **Sensory register:** The brain evaluates whether the sensory input is worth devoting mental energy toward. If not, the person doesn't even pay attention to the sensory input.

3. **Immediate memory:** For a brief period of time (about 30 seconds), the brain begins passing the information biochemically to recreate the experience for later consideration.

4. **Short-term working memory:** By consciously focusing on experiences, for a period that typically ranges from 5 to 20 minutes, people draw stronger connections related to the experiences, which creates pathways with other memories and knowledge that make retaining the new knowledge more likely.

5. **Long-term memory:** After a memory (or piece of information) has been retained sufficiently, it passes into long-term memory. The knowledge bits in long-term memory can still deteriorate over time, but now, when people reflect on the knowledge, they solidify an established connection, as opposed to building a new one.

As you read over these steps in the process of converting input to memory, you can probably think of a time when a mental path experience went awry. How many times has a student (a child, a spouse, or a parent) been so focused elsewhere that they don't even receive the sensory input from a person talking to them? Or if the sound does enter their brain, they're so focused on other things that they just mumble a thoughtless *yeah* in response, while the brain doesn't engage with the experience at any conscious level.

REMEMBER

The core takeaway from the sequence of gaining knowledge is that getting an idea into the brain always requires a time in which the learner is actively reflecting on the knowledge. Listening to someone lecture for 20 minutes while thinking about afterschool plans doesn't get the information into the listener's long-term memory.

Following through with repeated exposure

Getting the knowledge and experience into long-term memory is a heavy lift, but it certainly isn't the end of the story. After knowledge resides in long-term memory, you have to repeat exposure to that knowledge to strengthen the connections that the remembered information has to the rest of the learner's mental model of the world.

REMEMBER

Following through with repeated exposure is why having teachers who know the flow of content across grades — as described for science throughout Chapter 4 — is so critical. A well-structured STEM lesson connects any new information to the existing knowledge that students have about a specific concept, so that their mental connections can grow stronger. To accomplish these connections, the teacher constructing the STEM lesson needs to have a clear sense of what the students do and do not know.

Here's an example of the flow of physical science concepts in the NGSS. The concept of *force* gets introduced

>> **Early on (kindergarten, in fact)** as an understanding of push and pull

>> **As a return concept later on (third grade),** where the force is being exerted by magnets

>> **Even later in (fifth grade),** with that force being exerted by gravity

All of these repeated approaches to aspects of force reinforce the foundational idea that pushes and pulls are the things that change the speed and direction of an object's motion.

By middle school, students should be able to build a mental model of the world that understands the important ways that all forces on an object work together to move it, even if the student never studies physics in high school to formalize this knowledge into mathematical laws.

Ensuring the connection of concepts

Treating the standards of each grade as a standalone set of ideas means that you may teach about magnets in third grade without ever explicitly connecting the idea back to physical pushes and pulls that the student already knows about. Some students, of course, may make this conceptual connection on their own, but some will not. Teachers must structure the STEM lessons so that the students recognize these connections and highlight that discovery when that happens.

Though my background is in physics and mathematics, I've often thought that if I had it to do over again, I might well choose to focus on psychology rather than the hard sciences. But, in this version of reality, I'm neither a psychologist nor a neuroscientist. If you want to dig more deeply into the underlying psychology and relevant research, consider reading books such as *Child Psychology & Development for Dummies* (Wiley 2011). For research-based approaches to general lesson planning and instructional techniques, you should consider *Instructional Design For Dummies* (Wiley 2024) and similar books. (See the sidebar, "A Six-Phase Learning Model.") You can also find a lot of great research about learning through play, but I get to that in Chapter 12.

A SIX-PHASE LEARNING MODEL

Researchers at the educational nonprofit McREL International have translated the science of learning into a six-phase learning model. This model applies to a wide variety of learning situations, and following it clears the way to get new memories all the way into long-term memory.

1. **Become interested:** Students need to feel comfortable in the learning environment and then connect either emotionally or intellectually (or both) with the subject of the lesson.

2. **Commit to learning:** Students need to recognize that they gain something by learning the new material, even if that something is just satisfying curiosity.

3. **Focus on new learning:** Students need to be given time to actively engage with the new material.

4. **Make sense of learning:** Students need to be able to take the new information in chunks and connect it to existing mental models they have of previous information.

5. **Practice new learning:** Students need to work with the new information repeatedly, over a period of time, in a variety of forms and contexts.

6. **Extend, apply, and find meaning:** Students need to apply the new knowledge, exploring the boundaries of their mental models that incorporate the new information. This exploration can prompt new questions, which can draw students back into phase 1 for new information (while still extending the previous information).

The STEM lesson models throughout this chapter represent different ways of walking students through the same mental learning steps. Terminology for the steps isn't always the same, but the psychological steps are similar. Those who want to explore this learning model in greater depth can find it described in the book *Learning That Sticks: A Brain-Based Model for K–12 Instructional Design and Delivery* by Bryan Goodwin (ASCD 2020).

Inspiring a STEM Lesson

The hardest part of creating a STEM lesson is figuring out what to do. The possibilities are literally endless. And like you do with the student projects, using constraints to limit your choices is helpful. You know the concepts that you need to teach, and that knowledge will give you a lot of guidance about the sorts of STEM projects you'll be looking to do.

Starting points for STEM lessons

When trying to create a STEM lesson from scratch, your initial inspiration can come from three basic directions, as outlined in Table 9-1.

TABLE 9-1   Inspiration for STEM Lessons

Source	Description	Examples
Content	Content standards specifically define the learning objectives, and so, are a great place to start in forming a lesson.	Energy and motion, natural selection
Problem	You identify a problem or need within the classroom, school, or community, and build the lesson around that.	Reducing food waste, designing a more efficient parent drop-off flow through the parking lot
Task	You want students to learn a specific task or skill that is likely to be used as a foundation for later projects. Then you build a lesson around developing that task or skill.	Measuring angles, using a 3D printer, coding robots

MODIFYING PUBLISHED LESSONS

This chapter covers how to create a lesson from scratch, but you will often find initial inspiration through a pre-existing lesson. You can find tons of great STEM lessons and resources (see Part 5) that you can draw from to get started, especially until you feel more comfortable building a lesson from the ground up.

Avoid cookie-cutter lessons. You don't want to just walk all students through a step-by-step process, with the goal of every student having exactly the same final product. Also, analyze the eight elements in the section, "Refining STEM project ideas," to see if any changes are needed to improve the lesson.

Identify the learning objectives and the crucial components of the lesson. Are there any learning objectives that you want to add or modify? Can you change some elements of the lesson to provide the students with greater flexibility? Can you adapt the lesson to use a wider choice of supplies?

For example, rather than having every student build a structure with just craft sticks, you could offer students different materials — including some craft sticks (but not enough to build the whole thing) along with straws, pipe cleaners, cardboard, and other materials — so that each student's design can be different.

TIP

Keeping a science journal for yourself as a way of tracking lesson ideas is a great way to develop the habit of looking for inspiration while you go about your day. I regularly hear a news report on the radio that seems like a great hook for a lesson and make note of it in my journal. You can also do this digitally on social media by creating a page or other platform (like a Pinterest board) specifically to follow and share useful science reports and sites, so that all of these resources and ideas are easy to track down in a single location.

Of course, you can always start a STEM lesson by taking an existing lesson and modifying it. You still have to choose the content and format of the lesson, and you can look at the sources in Table 9-1 for inspiration. You can find out more about modifying STEM lessons in the sidebar, "Modifying published lessons."

Refining STEM project ideas

After you have an initial idea around which to build a project or lesson, ask yourself some key questions about what elements you need to instill in the lesson to make it into a good STEM project. In the manifesto in favor of a maker-based education, *Invent to Learn: Making, Tinkering, and Engineering in the Classroom* (2019), the authors (Sylvia Libow Martinez and Gary S. Stager) highlight eight elements of a good project.

>> **Purpose and relevance:** The prompt to engage with the lesson should have some level of personal meaning to the student.

>> **Time:** You must allow enough time to complete the full project, including not only the planning step, but also all of the execution, testing, debugging, iterating, and other steps required. Some steps may take place outside of class time, but circumstances vary as to whether that is an option.

>> **Complexity:** Ideally, a project pulls together different knowledge and skills, driving students to synthesize their understanding from previously unconnected areas.

>> **Intensity:** All kids have a capacity for intense focus when properly motivated, and a good project is one that draws students' focus for an extended period of time.

>> **Connection:** Working together on the project should help draw the students together through teamwork. Even when a student is completing an individual portion of the project, they can confer with and learn from others in the class.

>> **Access:** Students need access to the materials or tools required to complete the project. If you have a fully stocked STEM lab or makerspace, this access may be easy, but if you're working with fewer resources, then you need to plan ahead so that you have sufficient options for the students.

>> **Shareability:** The final product of the lesson should be something that the students share with the class and, indeed, something that they *want* to share.

>> **Novelty:** Projects should not just rehash what students have done in previous years. As younger students begin engaging more in STEM, this puts greater responsibility on teachers in upper grades to come up with more sophisticated projects.

Obviously, you will have some lessons and projects that don't rank high on each of the elements listed, but you can look at each one and try to identify where you can strengthen lesson elements.

Consider a task-based inspiration that a teacher may have for a classroom. Suppose that a teacher wants to introduce the students to a 3D printer for the first time early in the year; in this case, students need a lesson that includes some sort of project to walk them through the particulars of how the printer works. Students may initially do simple printing (such as a keychain or nametag), but the teacher will want to include some design requirements in the lesson to encourage real student involvement.

Although 3D printing a nametag or keychain is a fairly well-defined project based around learning a clear skill, students still have ample room for flexibility and creative expression. Students should have input regarding the size and shape of their project, for example, and the font and text that appears on the nametag. Also, they can decide whether to print their full name or a nickname. And students may not have flexibility to select any color under the sun, hopefully they have some color options to choose from. For this sort of project, the inconsistencies between the outcomes will give the class opportunities to see a variety of design and fabrication styles.

Surface, deep, and transfer learning

Throughout construction of the STEM lesson, you want to think about the level of learning that the students engage in during the lesson. The level of learning comes in explicitly when you consider the types of evidence and questions that you plan to use to assess student performance and involves the Depth of Knowledge (DOK) of the evidence. The point of addressing the DOK is to ask questions and elicit evidence to determine various levels of understanding. I talk more about DOK in Chapter 11, when I discuss assessment.

But because you'll want to elicit evidence of different levels of understanding from the student, you need to incorporate those different levels into your instruction. In Chapter 2, I mention Dr. John Hattie's Visible Learning research, and it provides a good model for thinking about different levels of learning. Hattie identifies these three levels of learning.

Surface learning: Initial conceptual understanding of a concept, including related process skills and vocabulary.

Deep learning: Conceptual understanding that involves making connections between different, but closely related, practices and ideas, including planning and implementing investigations that lead to elaboration, revision, and generalization of understanding.

Transfer learning: Sophisticated conceptual understanding that allows transfer of thinking in one area into another area, by recognizing the connections between them.

One thing to keep in mind about all learning models is that they're constantly being refined. For example, in Hattie's 2014 book *Visible Learning*, he discusses "surface, deep, and constructed understanding." You find no mention of "transfer learning" or "transfer understanding" in the index. By 2018, in *Visible Learning for Science, Grades K–12*, Hattie and his collaborators had transitioned to this new terminology.

TIP

Like with the Depth of Knowledge, the key point here isn't to say that one type of learning is significantly more important or better than another. You cannot have transfer learning about a subject until you have done the surface learning and deep learning, after all. What a model like this makes explicit is that if you spend all your time on surface learning, then you aren't actually reaching your true objectives in educating young people.

You want to do everything you can to move between these levels of learning within a lesson, but you also won't necessarily reach transfer learning levels with students in a single lesson. In my example from the last section (designing and 3D printing a nametag), you wouldn't expect that introductory lesson to provide much transfer learning. But out of that lesson, students now know how to print text on an object, which may be a skill that students leverage in a future lesson to expand it into another area. Sometimes you plant knowledge in the fertile soil of one lesson to promote the transfer of knowledge that you cultivate in a later lesson.

Studying Up on STEM Teaching

After you identify the starting point of the STEM lesson (see the section "Starting points for STEM lessons" earlier in the chapter), the next job is to structure the full lesson. The goal of a STEM lesson is to facilitate the students' movement through the steps of the learning process and get the necessary information into long-term memory.

REMEMBER

In a STEM lesson, you should structure a lesson to be student-centered, rather than teacher-centered. The teacher's role is to facilitate learning, not hand out information to the students. The teacher creates learning opportunities for the students to discover the knowledge and skills that achieve lesson objectives. The students should be defining the questions and the paths toward finding answers to those questions.

Educators have developed a variety of approaches (or instructional models) to creating STEM lessons over the years. Using a series of steps outlined in a model approach can really help with lesson development. But keep these points in mind as you do:

>> **If you modify the approach, do so carefully.** The danger with following a series of steps is that they give the illusion that you must follow them precisely every time you build a lesson. You can make changes to the models, but do so thoughtfully.

The phases of the instructional models are there to make sure you're walking the student's mind through the learning process, so if you make a change, be sure to have a solid reason for it, like providing information at a crucial point for the student to introduce it into their project.

TIP

>> **Use the model design to emphasize key learning objectives.** Educators often create these instructional models by using the method of *backward design*, in which you begin by identifying the learning objectives, then the evidence, and then the lesson and activity itself. I review the process of backward design in greater detail in Chapter 10, but for now, the critical first step is to identify the key learning objectives for the lesson.

POE model

If you are looking at a quick one- or two-day lesson, a solid approach that you can use to structure the lesson is the *Predict-Observe-Explain (POE)* model.

Here are the three stages of a STEM lesson that uses the POE model.

Predict: Students have an initial introduction to the topic and provide their initial thinking on what may happen in relation to the topic. This stage is intended to stimulate thinking about the topic and make students alert for what to focus on as they proceed through the lessons. In this stage, you can give students an opportunity to discover any misconceptions about the topic that they may have when entering the lesson.

Observe: Students have firsthand experience with evidence, often through direct activities and observations, or possibly through data provided. Ideally, students perform the activities and gather the data, although in some cases, the data may come from external sources or a classroom demonstration.

Explain: Students generate scientific ideas based on the data from the Observe stage. Claims that students make during the Explain stage should be evidence-based, though they may not yet know the proper terminology for the concepts. But at this point, students should identify and correct misconceptions that came up in the Predict stage.

The teacher's role in the POE model is to facilitate discussion. Teachers would not lecture on the topic but might write down students' initial thinking on the board during the Predict stage. And teachers can make sure to retain the initial thinking somewhere so that they can return to review it during the Explain stage. In this way, the students can evaluate their own thinking. Table 9-2 spells out the student and teacher roles more explicitly.

TABLE 9-2

Student and Teacher Roles during Different Stages of the POE Model

Stage	Student	Teacher
Predict	Provide initial thinking on topic.	Facilitate discussion.
	Predict what will happen in relation to the topic.	Provide group and individual means of recording student thinking.
	Identify elements of interest related to the topic, such as what sort of data to look for.	Prompt students with questions to engage and elicit their thinking, including anticipated misconceptions.
	Participate in discussion, recording predictions and notes as needed.	
Observe	Conduct experiments, tests, observations, or other activities.	Provide experiments, tests, observations, or other activities for students.
	Gather and represent relevant data.	Give guidance on gathering data and related expectations.
Explain	Generate ideas and conclusions supported by evidence.	Facilitate discussion.
	Identify supported and non-supported claims from the earlier Predict stage.	Review back to notes to check earlier predictions against evidence.
	Discuss and review ideas with other students.	Prompt with questions to engage student thinking.

The POE model guides students to directly confront their initial thinking and adapt that thinking (including any misconceptions) in response to evidence from the observations. This STEM-like approach is more hands-on and iterative than a traditional teacher-centered lecture approach, or even a more straightforward classroom demonstration.

REMEMBER

Specifically, the main benefit of this approach (and the 5E approach that follows) is that you help the students recognize that they are coming into the activity with some preconceptions about it. Their role is to test those preconceptions, and either confirm or modify them accordingly.

5E model

Another common STEM instructional model is called the *5E* model, which is so named because the five stages (or phases) of this instructional model all begin with the letter E.

> **Engage:** Students first encounter and engage with the instructional task. The goal at this stage is to ignite student interest in the activity, possibly connecting with past learning experiences.

Explore: Students directly engage with the phenomena and materials, building their own understanding of the central concepts. This stage usually happens in teams, so that the students are communicating and learning from each other.

Explain: Students communicate their growing understanding to the wider group, giving them a chance to both reflect on their own learning and also draw understanding from what other groups have discovered.

Elaborate: Students apply the new knowledge and understanding gained in new ways, trying to make connections to other related concepts and applying the understanding in innovative ways.

Evaluate: Students and teachers use various diagnostic tools to determine the amount and depth of learning that has taken place.

The 5E model was originally developed by the Biological Sciences Curriculum Study (BSCS). The research of Rodger W. Bybee, PhD, is often cited as most central to the 5E model from his years spent as the executive director of BSCS.

You may notice that the 5E model, like the POE model, doesn't prioritize the role of the teacher in the learning process. No explicit portion of the instructional model involves having the teacher tell students the information they're supposed to learn in the lesson. The process is designed so that the students will extract understanding and knowledge through the course of the lesson. The teacher is present to facilitate that process, not to dominate it.

Engage

The Engage portion of a STEM lesson focuses on getting the student interested in the task at hand. Some students have the mental fortitude to focus on something that is boring — just because a teacher tells them they have to — but a look around any typical classroom will show that this isn't the dominant situation. Unless the students see a reason to care and pay attention, they will likely tune out. This stage gives teachers the opportunity to capture students' interest.

This task of engagement succeeds best when it's tied to an *intrinsic motivation*, like curiosity, rather than an *extrinsic motivation*, like grades or other rewards. And so, establishing a culture of curiosity in the classroom is key. If your class, school, or district can create this culture, then you have an established pool of social credit that you can draw on. Through this culture of curiosity, students become used to finding that projects are interesting, so they give you the benefit of the doubt. Until that culture is well established, though, this introductory part of the lesson is your shot to generate that interest. Don't throw it away.

One way to think about the Engage stage involves the student, the environment, and your (the teacher's) leadership. In this stage, you're trying to disrupt the students' understanding of the world — within an intellectually and emotionally safe environment — in a way that will motivate them to want to learn more to restore a sense of understanding the world. Ideally, you create a mystery that draws the student into a teachable moment. If a student thinks that they understood something, and you show them that they actually don't understand it as well as they think, then you provide them with intrinsic motivation to follow along in the lesson. People are inclined to want to solve a mystery.

If you've studied psychology, you might recognize the intrinsic motivation described here similar to principles described by Jean Piaget. Piaget claimed that a central part of learning was trying to develop cognitive structures in response to this mysterious disruption between what you feel you should know but don't actually know (yet). Though this concept doesn't precisely match with the rigorous neuroscience evidence of learning discussed in the section "Transitioning input into long-term memory" earlier in the chapter, it is still somewhat useful as a mental model. Like it is with many things, Piaget's model was a good attempt at an initial explanation of learning using the limited evidence that Piaget had at the time. It isn't a wrong model, so much as an incomplete one.

In project-based learning, the unknown mystery is often centered around the project's goal. "How do you keep a bridge from collapsing?" or "How can you germinate seeds in cold weather?" or "How can I build a light circuit that turns on when it gets dark?" all provide mysteries for the kids to investigate, with generally limited amounts of intellectual unrest. On the other hand, making an object hover off the ground with magnets can seem like sorcery to a first-grader.

Be careful about just assuming that everyone will be interested in the subject of the STEM lesson. Suppose that your Engage stage is very quick. If you're doing a lesson on rocketry, for example, you might start with a video of a rocket going off, and then expect that you have everyone in the group immediately interested in how to build their own rocket. Having a more thorough plan to engage the students is better — in case the class response to the rocketry video is apathy. If they're all on board, though, you can decide in the moment to jump straight into the Explore stage.

Explore

In this phase of the 5E model, students get the chance to try to resolve some element of the mystery on their own by taking the time to explore their understanding of the core mystery revealed in the Engage stage.

REMEMBER

The teacher's role in this phase is to initiate the exploration and also provide necessary background information. A student might need to either review existing knowledge, like what they've previously learned about plants, or gain entirely new information, like how to use a new piece of equipment.

Students typically work in groups during this phase, in part to give them the opportunity to begin initial discussions of what they're observing. Ideally, students take this exploration time to identify things that they know and don't know related to the mystery they're investigating. They will hopefully have a list of questions that come out of this stage.

Explain

The Explain phase involves the students pulling together their explorations into the first initial stage of understanding.

REMEMBER

An embedded culture of curiosity should again guide you through this stage. You are almost certainly limited on time to complete the lesson, but that doesn't mean you can just pick out the groups with the most correct initial research to give their explanations. For the students who do not yet have correct explanations (the ones who most need help here), the crucial element of this stage is hearing the reasoning about the other (correct and incorrect) explanations.

TIP

As students give their explanations, they will identify correct (and incorrect) concepts that they don't yet have (or don't remember) the vocabulary for. Make notes of the groups that use these concepts and refer back to these concept with the correct vocabulary during a direct instruction part of the lesson. You can help the student by naming the concept that they came up with, which also gives them a sense of ownership.

Remember when Samantha described how the current changed when the magnet moved near the wires? A man named Michael Faraday noticed that in 1831, too, and he called it electromagnetic induction.

Not only will Samantha be much more inclined to remember who Michael Faraday is, but you now have a springboard for an entire unit on how power plants work. Congratulations!

Elaborate

In the Elaborate phase, students move beyond the initial context of their exploration to figure out how the idea applies in different areas. And teachers should continue to make related lesson activities achievable — but also challenging — for the students.

During this phase, the teacher continues facilitating, and what that looks like can vary widely. Students are likely still working in groups, although now, they may be alternating between simulations, written material, internet searches, and other forms of study and investigation to find out more about the subject.

TIP

Not every single STEM lesson you create has to go to the full depth of the 5E model. In some cases, you might just want to do a fun activity, rather than engaging with all phases of the full 5E model. That's perfectly fine, as long as you at least balance the more limited fun activity with full 5E lessons in which students reach all levels of complexity, which is really what differentiates 5E from other models (including the earlier POE model). I cover more about balancing lessons when I discuss how to develop a full curriculum in Chapter 10.

Evaluate

Various types of formal and informal evaluations — from observations to scored exit tickets — may exist throughout the entirety of the lesson, but in the Evaluate phase, the student performs a final set of activities that informs the teacher about whether they have sufficiently grasped the concepts being taught.

A deeper exploration of STEM assessment is the focus of Chapter 11. One key element of evaluating, though, is that you should consider this Evaluate stage during all phases of planning the lesson. You want to build the lesson largely around the evidence you're going to expect to see in the final Evaluate phase, so that you are setting the students up to successfully generate that evidence of their knowledge.

OpenSciEd instructional model

I cover the general POE and 5E models in the previous sections, but a wide variety of STEM instructional models are available. Pretty much every single developed STEM curriculum has its own spin on how to structure the lessons, and the educators who developed the curriculum usually have research to back up their structure. In this section, I dig into an example of a structure used by a specific curriculum, OpenSciEd (`https://openscied.org/`), so you can compare it to the more general models.

OpenSciEd uses a *storyline* approach to their instructional model. It is an inquiry-based approach, with instructional units available for free download and also packaged through certified distributors. Similarly, you can gather your own supplies or purchase them as classroom kits.

Instead of talking about stages or phases, OpenSciEd breaks their flow of lessons down into *routines*, which they describe as activities that play specific roles in advancing the storyline with structures to help students achieve the objectives of those activities. The lesson structure focuses on five routines outlined in this list, and I include parentheticals with the 5E model phases they most closely connect to.

Anchoring Phenomenon routine: This initial routine establishes the core phenomenon that the student will investigate throughout the unit. (Engage)

Navigation routine: Students make connections to their initial questions about the phenomenon. (Explore and Explain)

Investigation routine: Students develop plans to gather additional information needed to answer questions about the phenomenon. (Explore and Explain)

Problematizing routine: Students engage with the topic to extend or revise their thinking, identifying areas that need to be rethought or explored further. (Explain and Expand)

Putting the Pieces Together routine: Students connect the learning from a variety of their lessons and routines and determine whether they yet have a solution or need to repeat routines. (Explain and Evaluate)

THE FLIPPED CLASSROOM

Another popular educational model in recent years is "the flipped classroom," where students are provided with pre-recorded lectures or online resources to view outside of class. This reserves the class time for more engaging work, like group discussions, hands-on activities, and classroom projects.

In a way, the flipped classroom is a very traditional learning experience, where the student's job is to gain the information outside of class. I had many classes where I was assigned reading, and the entirety of the classroom time was devoted to discussing the reading as a group.

The issue now, as in those earlier classes, is that students may not engage with the material, either because they just don't want to or because of access issues outside of school (thus creating an equity concern). You'll almost certainly have some students coming to class prepared and some not. Your school may also have policies about homework, particularly in younger grades, which make this approach difficult.

As you can probably tell, this OpenSciEd flow involves repeating several of the steps throughout the process, guided largely by the students' ownership of the process. But lessons structured this way are also lengthy units that dig very deeply into a subject, spanning weeks of class time. OpenSciEd curriculum has great options for STEM teachers (particularly since you can use units at no cost), but their depth may not be suitable for every teacher, particularly if you're just starting out with STEM projects.

Getting Students to Ask Questions

From their earliest ages, children are question-asking machines. That is true until they learn that asking questions frustrates people (particularly grown-ups) and they stop asking them. But intellectual curiosity is the cornerstone of learning, so one of the goals of STEM education is to keep students asking the questions, and give them a framework to look for the answers.

One benefit of this method is that the students are constantly asking themselves questions, but they are also identifying themselves as the agent who is in charge of answering them. They may ask you (the teacher) some questions, to be sure, but you aren't setting up a situation in which you're the person who provides all the answers.

REMEMBER

And not having the teacher as the sole information source is good, of course, because even the wisest teacher doesn't have all the answers to all the questions that students ask.

Guiding question boards

In the interest of creating a curiosity-driven culture in the classroom, I recommend creating a place of prominence for asking questions. Of course, an individual lesson, unit, or project will no doubt have a set of related questions, so having a question board specific to a project makes sense. But I like to go further than that and have a standing question board.

Practically speaking, having a board for questions gives you the ability to control a discussion, particularly if a completely unrelated question comes up. You can acknowledge the question, write it on the question board, and then return to the topic at hand. The student feels validated but hasn't completely derailed the discussion with an irrelevant side question.

WARNING

The students feel validated only if they have a reason to think that the questions on the question board will, in fact, be addressed. Students will quickly notice if questions go on the board only to be ignored, and that situation is basically equivalent to ignoring the question. If the question board becomes a wasteland for topics you (the teacher) don't want to deal with in class, it will do no good for you or the students.

You don't necessarily need to answer all of the question-board questions in class, but you want to take some time to get back to them. You also don't need to address the questions at great length in class. As you go through the questions on the board, you can ask if any students would like to investigate them, either by looking up information online or by asking someone else at home to help them.

Soliciting group feedback

When I began teaching in the nonprofit Project SEED, the most notable thing that an observer would see in a Project SEED classroom was the students actively engaged nearly continuously throughout the entire class session. If I could pass along a single skill to every teacher in the world, it would be that methodology of engagement. I can't pass it along to everyone, but I can offer it to you.

Eliciting visible active participation

The continuous, active engagement in a Project SEED classroom involved communications controlled by the use of student hand signals and direct instruction (from the teacher) for student responses.

>> **To "agree" or say "yes" to something,** students would raise both arms straight up in the air and wiggle them around, which looked sort of like a third-grader as a football referee indicating a field goal.

>> **To disagree,** students would place their hands one over the other in front of their chest and move them back and forth. The first thing teachers did on the first day of class was to teach these hand signals.

>> **Virtually every time that a Project SEED teacher spoke,** they would (unless they forgot) include a clear direction about how the students should respond:

- "Julia, before you give me your answer, I'm going to be watching to see if the class agrees or disagrees."

- "Hands up nice and tall if you think you know how to solve this problem."

- "When I point at the equation, show me with your signals if you agree or disagree with the answer written on the board."

In short order, students began to use their hand signals without prompting. At that point, the teacher's job was to acknowledge and praise it, reinforcing the desired behavior. "I didn't even ask, and I can tell what Juan is thinking about that." Suddenly, other kids remember the signals and begin responding as well.

Asking the right kind of questions

In classrooms, you commonly hear a question like, "Who knows what types of rocks they were talking about in that video?" The teacher is trying to get great information, but the question is an utter waste of time. Even if every single student was paying attention to the video and knew the information, they have no idea how they're supposed to respond. Is the teacher wanting them to raise their hand? Are they supposed to call out "Me!" or are they supposed to say the name of the rock?

REMEMBER

The lack of hands waving in response to the "rock" question could result because students don't know how they're supposed to respond or because they weren't paying attention to the video. If you instead said, "Raise your hand if you heard the type of rocks they were talking about in that video," then you'd instantly see at least how many kids are paying attention to you and think they know the answer. A complete lack of hands raised means they don't have the information. (Maybe it never made it into their sensory register.)

The Socratic elements of the Project SEED lessons were entirely built around the group feedback of being able to gauge agreement and disagreement (from the position of hands and arms). Though Project Seed teachers rarely taught this explicitly, in almost every class, students would develop a signal method in which they held one arm horizontal and another vertical, forming a right angle, to indicate "I partially agree and partially disagree."

REMEMBER

In any classroom, this partial agreement is intellectual gold because it shows that a student is thinking in a nuanced way about someone else's thinking. They recognize that they agree with part of the explanation but disagree with other parts of it. When kids do that, you must acknowledge their partial agreement and praise it. Then get them (or someone else) to explain the part they agree with and the part they disagree with.

For hands-on STEM lessons, using this approach is a bit more of a challenge since these question-based responses don't easily translate into individual or group hands-on work. But even within a STEM lesson, you have points where you ask students questions. And establishing immediate response as part of the classroom culture is a great way to make sure that you always take the temperature of the class on the lesson ideas under discussion.

Including direct instruction

Even without a central role for the teacher (giving a lecture and providing all the information the students need), STEM lessons still contain elements of the structure that require passing along information to the students (probably information that they don't already have). You can easily view a student-centered class as one in which the teacher never provides any direct instruction — and some models (such as Socratic teaching) can, in the extreme, fall into that domain.

But the research suggests that having the teacher provide direct instruction to the students is always a significant role. Balancing that with question-asking, student-centeredness, inquiry-based education, and discovery learning is a challenge. In the 5E model, for example, direct instruction about the core concept typically comes during the Explain portion of the lesson.

REMEMBER

Be sure to plan to get the student explanations *before* you tip your hand regarding the correct explanation. This sequence is probably one of the hardest conceptual changes to make, because teachers naturally feel that the point of the lesson is to get the correct information into the students' brains. But the learning science outlined in section "Unpacking the Learning Brain" earlier in this chapter clarifies that rushing to the correct-information step doesn't actually help get that information into the brain. If the teacher just plans to give them the explanation anyway, the whole lesson exploration is kind of pointless from the students' point of view.

TIP

You can work-in direct instruction after the students have the opportunity to explore the lesson topic themselves. They have hopefully developed questions around the phenomenon they're exploring, as well. You can then tie the direct instruction into answering the students' questions.

Probing background knowledge

When introduced to a new concept, the students don't have the foundational ideas (let alone the vocabulary) to formulate questions. Part of the early stages of a STEM lesson should be structured to get preliminary explanations from the students, which establishes their baseline understanding.

Consider this (extreme) analogy: You time travel to the streets of New York in 1900, hold up a modern smartphone, and say, "Does anyone have any questions about how to use this?" The people who hear you will be perplexed because they lack absolutely any context to ask informed questions about the smartphone you're showing them. They know about telephones, of course, but the telephones that they interact with involve wires and bulky structures. And frankly, many functions of a modern smartphone that a person might ask about have nothing to do with its function as a telephone.

REMEMBER In almost every situation, students will have more relevant background knowledge about the topic you're addressing than my hypothetical New Yorkers. As part of the introduction to the lesson or unit, establish the habit of explicitly drawing out students' current understanding. But know that their current understanding is almost certainly incomplete.

Sometimes when you probe the students' background knowledge, you realize that you're dealing with students who actually do understand the concept incredibly well. Maybe their previous class or school covered the concept in such depth that they already grasp the key learning objectives. At this point, getting their questions about the concept becomes key, because they can identify gaps in their understanding — and inform the direction you can go with the lesson to fill in those gaps.

Here are some steps to keep in mind for outlining lesson progress:

1. **Confirm that the understanding you see spans the entire class.**

   What is more likely is that you have a handful of students who have advanced familiarity with the subject matter. I once introduced a robotics lesson in third grade only to discover that two or three of the students in the class had attended an afterschool robotics club, and so, they had an immense amount of experience coding robots. I had to establish a balancing act between allowing these students to thrive as the experts, but also covering the lesson material for all the other students.

2. **Determine the engagement of the students.**

   If students already know the concepts, then you may need to modify and expand the lesson. For example, if you are planning a lesson to introduce 3D printers to the class by making nametags — and you learn that the class already did that in their art class last year — then students may have no interest in (once again) making name tags. You may be able to engage the students with a slight change (say, creating little 3D printed signs with a short, inspirational quote instead of their names) or modify the lesson more significantly.

3. **Consider the best way to leverage the lesson to reinforce the students' knowledge.**

   You have two main options here: Treat the lesson as a short example of something they already know (in which case you'll probably get through the lesson quicker than expected) or use it as an opportunity to dig much deeper into their understanding and mastery of the related concepts and skills. Understanding the gaps in students' understanding is crucial to making this decision.

Finding out that students have too much background knowledge can be a challenge to the STEM project. But probing the background knowledge and finding out that students aren't actually as proficient in the background concepts as you were hoping is also a challenge. Again, you want to explore this lack of background to make sure whether it's a real deficiency, or the students just need some motivation to remember the things they know.

In a knowledge-deficit situation, you may need to modify the lesson to spend more time on the core foundational concepts, essentially re-teaching concepts that you'd been hoping they would already have established. Although it's easier said than done, try not to get frustrated about this. It's not your fault that the students have these gaps, but you have to deal with it if you're going to teach the kids what they need to know.

REMEMBER

Identify points of the STEM lesson you planned that connect with the discovered gaps in student knowledge. You may also need to identify new learning objectives for the lesson.

Ensuring time for student feedback, iterations, and reflection

Teachers are always short on time. The final stages of a STEM lesson, in which students reflect back on what they've done and what they've learned, are one of the easiest portions to speed through or skip over entirely. The students did the thing, after all, so can't you all get on with your day?

If you check out the learning science part of this chapter (in the section "Unpacking the Learning Brain" earlier in the chapter), you see that this part of the lesson design is crucial for strengthening the connections around those new concepts. Students have to reflect on the new knowledge, what they discovered about it, and how it fits into the rest of their mental model of the world.

Until you study this idea in depth, you may not see its importance. For years, teachers didn't explicitly allow for this segment of learning, and some students were still able to achieve high performance in classes.

But if you think about it, the highest-performing students are high performing precisely because they do this connection and reflection of knowledge as a matter of course. They have a running narrative in their minds that asks questions, analyzes, and reflects on the things they're doing and learning. Their minds have always been alerted to connections with ideas they've already learned about.

Some of the high-achievers have been taught this, of course, but rarely is it something they were taught explicitly within the confines of a classroom — or else the whole class would be doing it. Some mix of nature and nurture is responsible for the students who do this reflection naturally.

REMEMBER

Now teachers recognize that their jobs include training students to question, analyze, connect, and reflect on learned knowledge. Explicitly. From the earliest ages.

Embracing Collaboration and Student Roles

One final element to consider in the stew of creating STEM lessons is making sure that the lesson comes across as a team exercise among the students.

One of my jobs as district STEM coordinator is to help make sure that the schools have sufficient supplies for their STEM activities. One day, a few months into the job, I got a materials request that seemed unusually large. I looked over the lesson, finding that each student group needed about three small mirrors for the project. (The lesson involved reflecting a laser beam.) A quick estimate of how many student groups I'd expect in a room and how many classes were doing the project made me realize that this request was for about four times as many mirrors as I would have expected.

I followed up with the teacher and discovered that she was having each student complete the project individually instead of in groups. She explained that, in the wake of COVID in particular, the sixth-graders doing the project just couldn't get along with each other. It was easier to just have them do the project individually than work in groups.

And she was absolutely right. Sixth-graders (particularly after COVID) are not well socialized to work together in groups. It is definitely easier to do projects individually, as there will be fewer disagreements and fights.

But some of the learning objectives in that lesson related explicitly to working in groups, providing feedback to collaborators, and demonstrating the ability to take on different roles. By having students complete the task individually, the lesson became easier for the teacher at the expense of some of the most important learning objectives.

TIP

Do not let students pick their own groups and, at the same time, don't think you can outthink the group dynamics. If you assign the smartest kids to be in groups with the struggling kids, they'll both recognize what you're doing. Randomly assign the students into groups and be sure that they know you're randomly assigning them. Playing cards make a great way to do this, although you can find online randomization tools (see https://wheelofnames.com) to use.

PLANNING FOR MISTAKES, MISCONCEPTIONS, AND FAILURE

Part of the goal of an inquiry-oriented learning environment is that the classroom culture is very accepting of mistakes, misconceptions, and even failures.

One major purpose of education is to establish a safe place to explore new ideas and make mistakes. If I'm undergoing surgery, I definitely want to have a surgeon who made the worst professional mistakes of their life *while they were in medical school*. I do not want a surgeon who never made mistakes in medical school, because if something goes wrong on the operating table, they're less likely to know how to react to it.

In any lesson, you know that certain misconceptions will come up. Think through the lesson about what the most likely misconceptions are for students to bring up. And after they come up, do not immediately knock them down, but take the temperature of the class to identify how many other students believe the same thing. Get various students to explain their reasoning.

Many brilliant humans, including Aristotle, believed that heavier objects fell faster than lighter objects, until Galileo disproved it. Your students will almost certainly have the same sort of misconceptions, until disproven to their satisfaction.

Chapter **10**

Designing a STEM Curriculum

While many teachers drop STEM into their class as standalone lessons or projects to supplement the teaching of their core curriculum objectives, the growing importance of STEM has led some districts, schools, and teachers to plan out a more comprehensive STEM curriculum. In this case, the hands-on learning of STEM really takes center stage throughout the year. (See the sidebar, "High-quality STEM units" later in the chapter.)

In this chapter, I use the term *curriculum* to apply to any extended series of teaching that covers a scope and sequence spanning multiple STEM concepts. The STEM lessons I discuss in Chapter 9 should cover multiple class sessions and days, but a STEM curriculum is measured in the span of weeks and months. You may also find that tackling a STEM curriculum in smaller chunks, such as chapters or units, is useful. And you can then combine the chunks to map out the curriculum over the course of a full school year.

In this chapter, I walk through many elements of creating a full STEM curriculum. First, I talk about looking back at the content standards outlined in Part 2 of this book, to establish the basis for a curriculum to serve as an anchor. I then explore ways that you build out the rest of the curriculum around those core anchors. Finally, I help you to plan out a cycle of revision and iteration of the curriculum for the future.

Focusing on the Standards Through a New Lens

In modern education, the foundations of instruction are academic standards. These are the high-level academic goals established as the basis for education, and a curriculum should be built with the intention of effectively meeting these standards.

A curriculum is aligned to the academic standards if, over the course of receiving the implemented curriculum, the students will learn the full depth and breadth of the academic standards.

Identifying key academic goals

For a STEM curriculum, making sure that everyone involved is on the same page is crucially important because (as I discussed at length in Chapter 2) STEM means different things to different people. Some people think that STEM includes math class, while other people think that you aren't actually *doing STEM* unless you're building something.

Asking questions to determine expectations for STEM

Here are some questions to ask yourself (and your team) about what should be included in the STEM curriculum:

» Are students receiving a separate curriculum intended to cover science, mathematics, or other core content, with the STEM curriculum as a supplement?

» Is the goal of the curriculum to teach the STEM content or to use STEM to teach 21st-century skills, group collaboration skills, career competencies, or other necessary non-academic skills?

» Which sets of standards should the STEM curriculum be aligned with?

» Are all STEM disciplines to be integrated?

» How will teachers incorporate the STEM lessons alongside any other responsibilities?

» Will teachers be expected (and have time) to collaborate on the planning and implementation of these projects?

>> How will supplies be provided for STEM projects, including technology and digital supplies?

>> What sorts of grades will be provided out of the STEM lessons?

>> What steps can be taken to make the STEM lessons inclusive for all students?

Exactly right answers to many of these questions don't exist. You can build great STEM programs around a wide range of implementation strategies. At the outset of your investigation for creating a STEM curriculum, you may not be able to answer all of the questions in the preceding list, but they're good starting points for the discussion.

You want to be sure that the key stakeholders are on the same page about the goals and strategy. If the principal and district officials think that STEM is replacing the science curriculum, but the teachers think of STEM as a supplement to the science curriculum, then you want this to be discussed at the planning stage rather than down the road.

Discerning core learning objectives

After you talked through the questions in the preceding section as a group — and you're sure that team members are (mostly) on the same page about STEM — you can move on to identify your core learning objectives. These objectives will almost certainly come from the set of standards that you identify through the questioning. A learning objective doesn't have to be a direct quote of a standard, although it certainly may be. The performance expectations of the NGSS, in particular, make great foundations for learning objectives.

Learning objectives should include everything that you're identifying as essential from the STEM curriculum and can include a mixture of the following:

>> Academic standards (including process standards, practices, and crosscutting concepts)

>> Social and Emotional Learning (SEL) objectives

>> Employability and 21st-century skills

>> Practical skills

REMEMBER

At this initial stage, you should home in on the essential elements (such as foundational knowledge and skills) that you want to achieve through STEM. Those elements are what you'll be building the curriculum around. You can take time later on to fill in non-essential elements (such as peripheral information), in an effort to get full coverage of the skills. But as long as you're prioritizing the most essential elements, you've got a great starting point.

Designing with the end in mind

When you use this end-in-mind approach, you start with the learning objectives as part of a design process called *backward design*. In this process, you create the curriculum with the goal in mind and then construct a series of educational experiences that move toward that goal.

Backward design moves through three stages.

>Stage 1: Determine Learning Outcomes
>
>Stage 2: Identify Students' Learning Evidence
>
>Stage 3: Develop STEM Lessons and Activities

This design method is largely based on the book *Understanding by Design, Expanded Second Edition* (Pearson 2005) by Grant Wiggins and Jay McTighe, although it has also influenced Rodger Bybee and other researchers over the years. As I mention in Chapter 9, you can use this backward design at a smaller scale to design individual lessons, as well as the full curriculum.

Stage 1: Determine Learning Outcomes

A major benefit of this approach occurs because, when you begin with learning objectives, you make sure that the core learning is central to the design process. If you begin with individual STEM activities or lessons, then you may completely miss satisfying the core learning objectives. Many of those STEM activities or lessons that you find in old resource binders or for free online are years old and may have been designed around different learning objectives and standards.

REMEMBER

Having a unified STEM vision is helpful at this point because you must begin to prioritize a specific learning path toward your objectives. If, at this stage, you indicate that your core learning objectives for the STEM curriculum are to cover all of the science standards, the Common Core State Standards (CCSS) for mathematics, and the Computer Science Teachers Association (CSTA) computer science standards, you just won't achieve that goal.

More significantly, the standards are not written so that they are all equally central to student education. Some standards exist specifically because they support other standards. Yes, you want to cover them (I get to that in the next section), but they aren't core learning objectives.

Chunking out the curriculum into different units or chapters may be useful at this point as you identify core learning outcomes that naturally combine well together. A unit's unifying ideas may naturally present themselves — such as physical science versus life science — but it isn't always spelled out so cleanly. Here are a couple of examples:

>> **Decide that you want to build a unit around the crosscutting theme of structure and function,** for example. That unit will include both physical science and life science activities, as well as various engineering and mathematics activities related to it.

>> **Focus your unit on solar energy,** which allows you to combine physical science together with Earth and space science as well as engineering and technology, and maybe even some investigation of how plants use solar energy.

Stage 2: Identify Students' Learning Evidence

After you determine the learning outcomes at the center of your curriculum (or units or chapters), you move on to determining the evidence of student performance that you'll want to generate.

This evidence falls into two components:

1. Identifying what evidence would support a conclusion that the students have attained the learning outcomes.

2. Identifying how you intend to get that evidence.

You can support some learning outcomes by having the students answering questions on a quiz or test, but other outcomes may need a physical product as evidence.

At this stage, you don't have to identify every single exit ticket, project, or question that you're going to use to evaluate the students throughout the STEM curriculum. Instead, you identify the key elements you will need as output from the students, and these will provide the basis for the formal assessments you do within the individual lessons.

In short, during this second stage of the design process, you begin to develop the Evaluate activities for the 5E model (which I present in Chapter 9), before moving on to develop the rest of the lessons in Stage 3. You can find more information about establishing this evidence-centered approach to assessment in Chapter 11.

Stage 3: Develop STEM Lessons and Activities

With the goal of the learning unit in place and the evidence that you want to see from the students in mind, you can now construct the individual lessons.

Chapter 9 focuses on building individual lessons, and those principles apply here, too. But when you simultaneously create multiple lessons within an overall curriculum, you get the benefit of planning out effective curriculum coherence. Trying to achieve this coherence when you focus on standalone STEM lessons and activities is more difficult.

If you are using the 5E model from Chapter 9, you will have already planned out how to gather evidence for the lessons (the Evaluate step) in Stage 2, so now you're moving on to the Engage, Explore, Explain, and Elaborate phases during Stage 3 of the design process.

REMEMBER

The goal of these 5E learning stages is to set the learning objectives into the student's long-term memory and solidify those connections sufficiently so that they stick around and emerge when you check for them. You must plan for any evidence of learning that you expect to get from the students later.

Anticipating contingency plans

Things will go wrong with your lessons during implementation, and planning for how to address the problems that you can anticipate is ideal for the curriculum. Here are a handful of problems that can happen regularly and that you should plan ahead for:

>> Equipment failures

>> Videos and other online resources becoming unavailable

>> Running short on key supplies

Ideally, when planning lessons, you're able to think ahead about these issues. For consumable supplies, you can frequently swap out materials for others, particularly those that serve cosmetic purposes. With some attention to detail, a teacher can look through a lesson and realize that the missing glitter from the material list won't actually hinder the students with their project. (In fact, my estimate is that many elementary teachers are happier with a little less glitter in their lives.)

Here's an example of the sort of problem that can crop up unexpectedly. I had an elementary school lesson in which students used the free Microsoft Flip (formerly FlipGrid) online tool to create videos. But over the summer of 2024, Microsoft announced that they were retiring Flip. As I went into the fall semester of 2024, I found that students could still largely accomplish the actual lesson goal. Because all of the instructional materials indicated that students would use Flip, I had to communicate with teachers across the district and offer a list of possible alternatives, including the option of using Google Slides to create a flipbook animation that you clicked through.

Setting the Scope, Sequence, and Pacing

During the design process I describe in the previous sections, you will inherently discuss the scope of coverage and the specific order, or sequence, of the material that you want to teach. Some concepts are naturally covered in a certain order — because they build on each other — but you generally have some flexibility with the approach you take.

As you develop the scope and sequence of what you cover and identify individual lessons, instructional materials, and projects to reach your learning objectives, you can also identify the pacing of how to move between the concepts.

When you map out the central learning goals that you expect the STEM curriculum to cover, you most likely still haven't identified every concept or topic that you need to teach. And ideally, you want to find ways to connect the non-STEM-specific standards and learning goals to the STEM lessons that you already have planned. Alternatively, you can use these other concepts or topics as bridges between STEM lessons.

You have a number of factors to take into account while planning out your non-STEM curriculum. And as always, you may realize in the middle of implementing your lesson plans that you could have connected your lessons with STEM differently, and possibly better. That's something you can fix in future implementations, but you should adapt as best you can to the circumstances you're in during implementation.

Considering formal and informal requirements

One thing that you must consider while planning out your curriculum across the year is whether any formal requirements determine when you must cover certain topics. The most obvious formal requirement throughout the year is the timing of different types of testing. And obviously, you want to cover related material *before* a student is held accountable for knowing that material on a high-stakes test.

If you have formative or interim assessments, planning for scope and sequence of coverage can become a little more complex. You can use a formative assessment to identify gaps in student knowledge. And getting that data earlier in the process — before you're too far into the STEM curriculum — can be useful. For example, you might identify areas where students are struggling in math and then find ways to incorporate more math into your STEM projects to help with those struggles.

REMEMBER

Informal requirements may have more to do with the timing of your STEM lessons because of the themes you plan to work into the lessons.

>> Is one of your lessons a study of the human body that involves skeletons? In that case, you might consider it an informal requirement that this lesson falls around Halloween.

>> Maybe you want to study circuits and LED lights around Christmas time, to use the prevalence of lighted holiday decorations as a way to help engage the students in the concept.

>> You can also look for other calendar events that may connect with STEM activities, for example, by planning a circle-themed lesson that coincides with National Pi Day (March 14).

Other calendar-related guidance might impact your choice for sequencing or pacing. This influence can depend on the weather in your area, which may dictate when certain objectives are easier to achieve outdoors and when you want to focus on indoor activities.

You should also look for ways to incorporate the STEM lessons with your other curriculum goals. For example, I went through the flow of each grade's reading curriculum and identified places where connections could be made. During a reading unit about farm animals, I incorporated a STEM lesson about birds. Rather than keeping the toucan used as the basis of the original lesson, I introduced the concept by discussing chickens (a barnyard animal), and then transition to talking about toucans. In another lesson, a reading unit about the major rivers of China provided context for a STEM unit about building a boat that won't sink.

TIP

Tying your STEM curriculum into learning in other content areas in the way I describe in this section helps support conceptual connections that the students' brains are making. But you can also use these ties to help solidify buy-in from other school staff and departments that may not be quite as onboard with the amount of time taken up by STEM projects.

Using gaps to your advantage

As you identify the core learning objectives, you see a variety of other standards and learning objectives that you could have used but decided not to make central. Incorporating these non-central standards and objectives is a good way to look for supporting lessons that reinforce the core concepts while still maintaining strong alignment to the academic standards.

Involving previously introduced concepts

Looking backward and forward in the vertical articulation of standards across grades can enable you to identify other gaps that may prove helpful for filling out your curriculum. When you find a gap, you can introduce a concept that appeared in a previous grade and will appear again in a future grade. But for this in-between grade, you can tackle that concept from an entirely different angle that is relevant to the grade's standards and learning objectives.

Regarding the cognitive research covered in Chapter 9, an approach like bringing in previous (and future) concepts will provide the major benefit of reinforcing students' mental connections, and preventing the brain from pruning them out. Students can also connect the new learning objectives with the existing mental models that they have from that previous knowledge.

When the previous concepts didn't stick

The danger of reintroducing previous concepts, of course, is that the students may never have actually learned the concepts all that well previously. In that case, you may have to do some extra work to help establish that knowledge foundation. But because the concept isn't central to your core learning objectives, the lack of knowledge isn't a crucial problem (in the current lesson) if the students are a little shaky on a concept from the previous year.

TIP

If you find that many students don't show the base knowledge of a previous concept, you're also likely to find some students understand it well. These students can provide some explanation about the concept for the other students. And because this knowledge isn't the core of the lesson, you can just reinforce the correct explanation of the previous material and move on with the new material.

WARNING

If the previous learning is so far off the rails that none of the students have any knowledge about the reintroduced concept, you may want to consult with some other teachers about how best to proceed, though not necessarily the teachers who were responsible for teaching the concepts in the previous year. (Those teachers may be sensitive at the suggestion that the students didn't learn what they taught at that time.) If you're able, ask colleagues and mentors whether they feel that taking time out of the grade-level work to fix misconceptions is worthwhile. It may well be, depending on where that concept leads in the vertical articulation of learning standards.

One other thing to keep in mind when planning out the scope and sequence of your curriculum is the relationship between surface, deep, and transfer learning, which I discuss in Chapter 9. You probably want to sequence your lessons so that more surface-oriented lessons tend to happen earlier in the year, laying the foundation for students to draw connections between the deeper layers of understanding later in the year.

Revising and Iterating Your Curriculum

As you find with most endeavors in the world, your first attempt will probably not be the best attempt. That applies not only to the work the students are doing, but also to the lessons and curriculum that the teachers are providing. Whether you're implementing a pre-developed STEM curriculum or one that you've created yourself, you'll want to find ways to evaluate whether it's doing what you'd like it to do.

Therefore, just like you consider evidence for the students' understanding of the learning objectives, you need to consider evidence that you will use to evaluate your curriculum. Schedule time into your implementation, preferably with any other educators who are also working with this curriculum, to get feedback on what is working right and what could be improved in the future.

Our schools send out two teacher surveys per year asking for feedback on the STEM curriculum. These surveys include not only questions about their feelings regarding the implementation, but also questions in which they give an assessment of the students' feelings and reactions.

REMEMBER

HIGH-QUALITY STEM UNITS

A common phrase in educational design is "high-quality instructional materials." Developers, researchers, and others use the term *high-quality* to distinguish between instructional materials that don't have a solid research basis and those that have been refined and tested through research. Often, instructional materials, including many of those made by teachers, are not actually (by this definition) high-quality.

I'm not inclined to use this buzzword throughout the book, for one simple reason: I assume that anyone reading this wants to produce high-quality lessons, units, and curricula. Any guidance I give takes the high-quality goal for granted.

No instructional materials that you create will start off as high-quality instructional materials straight out of the gate. Just like the engineering design process and the 5E instructional model (see Chapter 9) incorporate the idea of imperfect initial drafts that are refined through iterative trials, this method is exactly how you arrive at high-quality instructional materials.

Responses to the surveys can reveal room for improvement, such as

» **Additional teacher training:** Some teachers have significant complaints about the curriculum or implementation but also relate stories of great student success and engagement. The teacher successfully implemented the lessons, but did not feel comfortable doing so. These responses indicate a solid curriculum with room for additional professional development opportunities.

» **Appropriate material support:** The survey also provided useful information to revise implementation. One frequent complaint was that sufficient supplies were not provided. In the following year, I printed out supply lists for each project, with space where the teachers could note if any supplies had been insufficient. When I collect the STEM kits together, these supply lists will provide yet another means of feedback, letting teachers tell me exactly how much of each individual supply they will need for those project in future implementations. If your school implements STEM projects at scale, centralizing material gathering and distribution might be more productive than having each teacher gather their own supplies (even if they can hopefully be reimbursed for them).

TIP

You have alternatives for getting feedback on STEM curriculum. Depending on your teaching situation, a formal survey might not make the most sense. Perhaps you could take some time at a department meeting to discuss how the STEM curriculum is going and get some feedback from other department members. If someone expresses concerns or criticisms about STEM, though, you should ask for specifics and take notes on what the school can do to address them.

Ultimately, you want to continually refine and develop the STEM curriculum as new resources become available or as resources you previously relied on become unavailable. You should view the curriculum as a living document that is constantly evolving, not something that stays set after its initial creation.

IN THIS CHAPTER

» **Identifying goals of assessment**

» **Using assessment to guide learning**

» **Assessing academic skills and knowledge**

» **Measuring life and career skills**

» **Considering peer review and evaluation**

Chapter **11**

Measuring and Assessing STEM

I n order to teach any subject effectively, participating in an ongoing system of measuring the student's current understanding of the material is crucial. This ongoing process of gathering evidence about what a student knows, understands, and can do is what we mean by *educational assessment.*

Unfortunately, the same flexibility and student-centered approach that makes STEM education so beneficial to student learning also creates a challenge for the teacher trying to figure out how to assess that student's understanding. A student may well be able to complete a complex engineering task, but may not have access to the language to explain their method during a formal assessment when the project is over. This situation makes traditional forms of assessment difficult and, more importantly, inaccurate.

Because of the flexibility in designing a STEM lesson (see Chapter 9), no single cut-and-dried *rubric* (a set of criteria used for evaluating student work) is appropriate in every situation. Writing this chapter would have been a lot easier if I could have given a clear sample rubric that you could just change for your specific assessment situation, but that isn't the case. Instead, this chapter I focus on describing factors that must go into designing a rubric, but you must complete the actual designing of the rubric individually, based upon the lesson(s) that you design.

In this chapter, I provide guidance about assessing and evaluating student success within a STEM curriculum. I discuss the importance of clearly defined learning goals that also represent the targets for assessment. I also discuss how to use ongoing assessments during the learning process to provide feedback to students and guide their learning. I explore the difference between assessing academic skills and knowledge versus evaluating social skills, including both collaboration and employability skills. And I take a brief look at how you can have students provide self-assessments and team evaluations as part of the assessment process.

Knowing (and Assessing) What You're Trying to Teach

The primary consideration when looking at what you are assessing in a STEM lesson is to have a clear idea of the learning objectives. If you used the backward design process outlined in Chapter 10 to build your STEM curriculum, you began by clearly laying out those learning objectives in Stage 1. In Stage 2 of that process, you determined the evidence you will use to evaluate performance toward those learning objectives.

If the goals for your STEM curriculum include preparing students for any assessments, you will want to review assessments to be sure that you are targeting the goals. For example, you should incorporate the terminology and concepts that will be in the assessment, both as part of your instruction and as part of the evidence you expect from the students.

Indiana's Department of Education recently began incorporating computer science questions into the state's Learning Evaluation and Assessment Readiness Network (ILEARN) Science assessment, which is administered to students in fourth and sixth grades. Some teachers were shocked to discover that sixth-grade students were asked about binary numbers, but the item specification documents for the ILEARN Science test clearly indicate that this is a valid way to assess one of the Indiana computer science standards. Checking the expectations of any testing (assessment) in advance is a way to avoid running into this problem.

TIP

In assessing the NGSS (found at www.nextgenscience.org), keep in mind that you'll want to assess along all three dimensions of the standards: the Disciplinary Core Ideas, the Crosscutting Concepts, and the Science and Engineering Practices. The NGSS performance expectations list out the related concepts that are also part of the learning objectives associated with the concepts.

Assessing types of evidence and types of students

Educational assessment should be based clearly on gathering evidence about the student's knowledge, understanding, and ability related to the learning objective. As you plan the lesson, identify the evidence that you expect the student to provide. Evidence can include the following:

>> **Student creations**

Constructions, prototypes, models, diagrams, designs, journals, and final work product

>> **Student behaviors**

Level of focus, active participation in discussions, effective teamwork, and clear effort at self-improvement

>> **Student responses**

Exit tickets, worksheets, quizzes, tests, including defining key vocabulary terms, explaining key concepts, or describing a complex process

As you can see, it's appropriate to incorporate more traditional assessments like worksheets, quizzes, and tests as part of a STEM unit, particularly to check understanding of key concepts. But because the learning objectives should cover more than the facts of the lesson content, the evidence materials should include opportunities for the students to reflect on their experience and expand their thinking.

Ideally, assessments for STEM lessons expand beyond the traditional form into more performance-based approaches, perhaps by having student groups participate in a conference with the teacher to discuss their process, almost like a performance review with a supportive supervisor. (Those who have experienced poor supervisor interactions might find that a triggering analogy.)

For the evidence that you're seeking, you'll want to lay out a clear rubric. When you consider all the possible options that I introduce earlier in the section — across the course of the lesson — the idea of bringing it all together into a single rubric may seem overwhelming. But you have a lot of flexibility in how you want to weigh the different evidence elements.

One benefit of the breath of skills and abilities that students demonstrate during a STEM project is that your scoring rubric can take into account different types of student achievement. Consider these three students, all of whom were engaged with the project and understood it well:

>> **A quiet student** who doesn't describe the project well verbally and isn't speaking up much in the group but has a particularly well-written description of their process.

>> **A student with poor language skills** who provided little written or verbal descriptions, but whose journal has diagrams that depict all the different steps of the process, and accurately match the final design built.

>> **A student who internalizes the learning experience** and so provides little written or verbal descriptions during the project because they were focusing intently on the building process. This student can describe each step of the process in great detail, including justifying design decisions.

These three students depicted here are providing evidence of their understanding in very different ways, and it's likely that no single approach to assessment is going to capture and reward their individual learning processes. If you give only multiple-choice exit tickets, or look only at the written project reflection, you will be missing part of the whole picture of understanding.

Considering levels of knowledge, learning, and understanding

When translating the learning objectives into the sort of evidence that demonstrates student understanding of the material, the teacher needs to consider the different depths at which students will learn the material. Some elements of STEM education involve teaching vocabulary and basic definitions, and others involve students unlocking deeper connections between wildly divergent concepts.

One big danger in teaching STEM is to think that all knowledge is created equal. It most certainly isn't. This condition manifests sometimes as assessing only at the most superficial level of understanding — such as key vocabulary terms or facts — without exploring deeper and more profound levels of understanding. Toward this end, I talk about the *cognitive rigor* of an assessment, or of an individual question or task.

TIP

The goal of talking about cognitive rigor is to make sure that teachers include both straightforward and complex questions, not only in the classroom but also in formal assessments. A mix of cognitive tasks allows for a fairer and more well-rounded assessment of the students.

> » If every single question requires the recitation of memorized facts, then students aren't getting a deep understanding of the lesson content, and the resulting shallow understanding will become evident when looking at questions against the cognitive rigor categories.

> » If every single lesson task requires a full research paper, on the other hand, then it may be challenging to identify students who actually know some of the basic facts but don't do well on written assignments.

Approaching cognitive rigor in STEM lessons

Throughout the assessment world, one of the most common approaches to cognitive complexity is known as Depth of Knowledge (or DOK), a cognitive rigor model developed by Dr. Norman Webb in 1997. The DOK model focuses on four levels of tasks.

> **DOK Level 1: Knowledge Acquisition (Recall and Reproduction)** — Provide a well-established bit of information, either from memory or by implementing a simple and memorized procedure.

> **DOK Level 2: Knowledge Application (Skill and Concept)** — Implement a known skill or concept in a relatively straightforward way to arrive at the answer.

> **DOK Level 3: Knowledge Analysis (Strategic Thinking)** — Apply reasoning strategies to develop a method to complete the task or come to a conclusion, usually with some large degree of flexibility or ambiguity in the methodology to be used.

> **DOK Level 4: Knowledge Augmentation (Extended Thinking)** — Think extensively about how knowledge can be used and applied in different academic and real-world contexts.

The focus here isn't knowledge, but the complexity of the behavior being asked of the student. How is the student engaging with the skill or knowledge? What sort of question do they face, and what sort of output will satisfy the question? A standardized test, for example, will almost never have the time and complexity for a question that elicits DOK 4 thinking; that is more for a science project, research paper, or book report.

Identifying cognitive rigor in STEM lessons

WARNING

These different levels in the DOK may seem, at first glance, pretty well-defined and static, but they absolutely aren't; they are highly context-dependent. I once had a boss who told me of a conference where the DOK creator Norm Webb presented on the subject, with a slide that had an example of an item for a given DOK level (1 through 4). In the middle of talking about the slide, Webb paused and looked at the slide, then told the audience that he'd changed his mind. This example was actually a different DOK than he'd thought.

Teachers in workshops can have protracted debates about the DOK alignment for any assessment question. The best practice method of determining the DOK is to ask a group of teachers what level they think the DOK is and then to take the rounded average. Rarely is the vote unanimous, even after training intended to calibrate the teachers' ratings.

Even something as simple as the solution to a basic multiplication problem can shatter the illusion of DOK simplicity.

>> A third-grade student may have to think hard about how to multiply two one-digit integers by working through the process of multiplication as repeated addition.

>> A sixth-grader, hopefully, can just answer the question from memory of times tables. What would probably be a DOK 2 question for the third-grader becomes DOK 1 question as soon as the student memorized the multiplication fact.

REMEMBER

The goal of the DOK framework isn't to nit-pick the exact DOK level of each and every question and task. You want to look at the tasks and use the DOK (or other cognitive rigor approach) to be sure that you've got a mix of complexities in your tasks and assessments. If your lesson includes nothing but things on the borderland between DOK 1 and DOK 2, then you need to consider if you're really pushing for enough strategic thinking among your students.

Focusing on grade level skills

The focus of the assessment should be on the grade level skills that you are trying to teach to the students, so it's important to keep those grade level standards in mind when considering the scoring of the evidence.

Consider this example: In Chapter 5, I mention that teachers could use flowcharts to organize and compare algorithmic thinking for students before grade 6, which is the point where flowcharts show up explicitly in the computer science standards. I completely stand by this, but here's an important thing that you then have to consider: How should the use of flowcharts figure into assessment prior to grade 6?

Introducing concepts before they appear in standards

A middle school computer science standard exists that explicitly includes using flowcharts to describe algorithmic processes. In grade 6, it would therefore seem perfectly appropriate to assess a student on whether they understand the various components of a flowchart and are using the notation correctly. But prior to grade 6, the standards indicate no expectation of proficiency with the concept of flowcharts. It would be inappropriate to penalize a student's grade for not being proficient in a concept that the standards don't indicate they should be proficient with yet.

WARNING

For this reason, a lot of teachers (often guided by well-intentioned state and local policies) will only teach concepts that are specifically aligned to the standards in their grades. But this sort of zero-tolerance policy short-changes the students by limiting the ways in which they can gain exposure to topics that may help their understanding of the concepts they're working with.

Matching evidence to learning objectives

In the flowchart example from the preceding section, suppose that you're working on step-by-step instructions for something with a third-grade class. You reach a step in the process where some sort of loop occurs, so you decide instead on a series of steps. It now makes sense to introduce the concept of a flowchart to represent the instruction. If the student uses a rectangle instead of a diamond to represent a decision point, but you can understand what the student is trying to represent, then the student shouldn't be penalized.

You can absolutely explain to the third-graders that a different sort of shape represents a decision point in a flowchart. You may well have several students in the class who make this same mistake, in which case it's useful to bring up figure use as a topic for discussion with the class as a whole. When you do

>> Be clear that the use of figures can be confusing.

>> Ask students whether they have a way to remember which type of figures to use.

>> Take advantage of the great learning opportunities here for a good teacher to exploit.

But because proficiency in the exact way to build a flowchart isn't expected of grade 3 students, students who fall short of that goal aren't showing a lack of grade 3 proficiency. They're actually showing a lack of middle school proficiency, which is perfectly fine and expected in third grade!

The important distinction here is between the learning objective and the *evidence* of the learning objective. The standard (and thus the valid learning objective) in grade 6 is explicitly that students "use flowcharts . . . to address complex problems as algorithms." A flowchart with correct elements is evidence of that learning objective.

In grades 3 through 5, however, the standard is "1B-AP-08. Compare and refine multiple algorithms for the same task and determine which is the most appropriate." Students can use a flowchart to organize their thinking as part of the evidence they provide, but an accurate flowchart isn't the objective. An accurate comparison is. If students in grades 3 through 5 use flawed flowcharts to provide accurate comparisons — and you can tell what they're intending to communicate — they're giving you evidence that they've met the learning objective. A flawed flowchart in grade 6 doesn't provide the evidence of meeting the learning objective.

Offering Formative Assessment as Feedback

Though the 5E model (described in Chapter 9) contains a final Evaluate step, effective instruction embeds various formative assessments throughout the entire instructional cycle. This trail of assessments offers a means of gaining knowledge about the student's understanding and progression. You must know where the students are in their understanding so that you know whether they're absorbing the lessons that you are providing.

You can accumulate this knowledge through continual classroom assessment, both formally and informally. The goal here is to establish communication and feedback for the student, not to achieve a given letter grade at each point along the way.

If you're doing STEM right, students will be pushing their limits, and this means you will occasionally have students who fail drastically. The way that you provide feedback on this evidence of failure is crucial in determining whether this students viewed the feedback as humiliating proof of their inadequacy or as an amazing, teachable moment that they can take away from the experience. Throughout this book, I write about the importance of establishing an inquiry-based culture that values making mistakes, and central to that culture is how you handle those mistakes when they come up in the course of the lesson.

Some mistakes are expected and are almost required as part of the lesson. For example, in an early robotics session, students were trying to get a robot to approach a wall and then turn right and continue in that direction. They quickly realized, though, that the turn-right code block caused their robot to turn right indefinitely, so it never began moving forward. This failure is one that isn't at all unexpected, and instead, it serves the purpose of teaching the need to choose a code block that directs the robot to "turn right 90 degrees." This mistake provides the basis for talking about looking at all of the code block options.

But some mistakes are more magnificent than this because they result — not from something inherent in the lesson — but from the student taking a big swing at the goal of the project. These ambitious failures could completely derail from the sorts of solutions that you were expecting the students to offer, and if you aren't careful when you provide feedback, you could discourage this out-of-the-box thinking.

When these magnificent-failure situations happen, you want to be sure to praise the ambition, rather than focusing exclusively on the fact that the project failed at the goal. You don't ignore the failure, though, because you want this to be a learning experience. Ask the student what they could have done differently, centering on what they learned from the project, rather than what you think they should have learned.

The Hard Skills: Assessing Content Knowledge

Some of the more straightforward concepts to assess are academic content skills, which are usually outlined fairly explicitly in the academic standards (as I discuss throughout Part 2). These skills and the associated knowledge are the cornerstone of what teachers are taught to assess throughout their own education and training. STEM makes the process a little more complicated because it involves not only traditional question-based assessments, but also evaluation of projects and student work in group situations.

Keeping science notebooks

You can reap several benefits from keeping a scientific notebook, either one notebook for the entirety of the STEM curriculum across the year or shorter project-based notebooks. Notebooks enable the student to record their own journey through the learning process, documenting ideas and understanding as it develops. It also motivates a reflective process that is at the heart of learning.

Like many other aspects of a STEM curriculum, having students take clear and accurate notes is a cultural step that needs to be established early in the class. It is both a habit that students must develop and a skill that you must explicitly teach.

Prioritizing notetaking

Because notetaking is a skill, if you intend for your students to maintain a science notebook as part of your STEM curriculum, you will want to identify this as one of your learning objectives for the early units in the curriculum, as described in Chapter 10. A goal of early units will be to teach the students that recording their thinking clearly in the journal is an expectation in the class.

Though a variety of digital and online tools allow for taking and managing notes, the research suggests that students should take notes within a physical notebook. And because this notebook will include designs that they may need to edit, students should use a pencil.

Physically writing notes helps solidify the information within the student's mind (see Chapter 9). The inherent slowness of writing down notes helps with this process because most people don't write fast enough to record all the information verbatim as it is delivered. Instead, the notetaker must listen to the information, mentally process and analyze it, and then proceed to summarize it in a form that will be useful to them later on. For some writing-related accessibility purposes, though, some individual students may need to record their notes digitally.

Defining a notetaking structure

The degree to which you want to establish a formal structure for the science notebook can vary greatly. Here are a handful of types of science notebooks that can be the basis for your class's notebooks.

>> **Lab notebook:** Keeps careful records of science experiments, often across multiple trials and variations. The book may have a high degree of structure, which can provide a benefit because kids will know what they're supposed to put in it.

>> **Engineering notebook:** Emphasizes engineering over science. This type of book includes design notes and sketches, as well as details about tests of different prototype designs. It may also have a high degree of structure.

>> **Field journal:** Focuses on documenting natural experiences. The content in this type of book is not intended to be particularly replicable, so there is less structure. It is often smaller so that students can easily carry it with them on outdoor expeditions.

>> **Interactive notebooks:** Designed specifically for school, where students receive input from the teacher and are responding. This type of book is for highly structured content, usually around individual lessons.

Whatever you call your notebooks (or journals), you can mix up these types of notebooks to the degree that you're comfortable with. The teacher is the only person, after all, who might judge the student if a lab entry follows a sketch of a natural observation.

The structure you provide can range from formal layouts to asking the student to provide "I notice/I think/I wonder" statements on the page. In this case, you can try out some different formats to see what works best for you and your students.

If you really want a deep dive into science notebooks, I recommend *Science Notebooks in Student-Centered Classrooms* (NSTA 2022) by Jessica Fries-Gaither. In addition to a lot of guidance on how to handle classroom science notebooks, the Appendix contains some great printable resources specifically to help structure and maintain school notebooks.

Reviewing students' journals or notebooks

At some point in the process, of course, you'll need to collect the journals and review them. This review gives you two important opportunities:

>> You, as the teacher, gain a sense of how well individual students and the class as a whole are following along with the material. Teachers can then adjust the structure of the later STEM lessons (or tasks in the current lesson) in response to any widespread misconceptions.

>> The students can receive specific feedback from you, possibly with advice or guidance on how to proceed in their thinking and notetaking format.

You'll want to review journals relatively early in the 5E instructional model — likely during either the Explore or Explain phase. You can give whatever sort of feedback is appropriate at this point in relation to structure and neatness, but formal grading of content can be trickier. The goal of the journal is for the student to make sense of their own thinking, and if you see that they're doing so, then the notebook is doing its job. Depending on the grade level you're dealing with, expecting students to maintain a well-written journal may be more or less realistic.

Focusing on the necessary academic goals

In the process of developing lessons and curricula (described in Chapters 9 and 10), you will have identified core learning objectives for the academic goals you're trying to teach. These should obviously be the focus of the assessment that you're conducting, and you will have identified necessary evidence in Stage 2 of the backward design process.

Your evidence and the rubrics that you develop should provide students with a variety of ways to demonstrate that they've met the learning objectives. Some students will have made it clear in the classroom discussion that they understand the core concepts — even if the formal exit tickets, quizzes, and maybe even their final project doesn't work as well as expected. Others may have said very little, but their project shows a clear understanding of the principles at work.

REMEMBER

The goal of the project in the lesson should be to give the students every opportunity to demonstrate that they've achieved the learning objectives. The goal of the rubric is to evaluate student work in such a way that only a student who fails to provide any evidence in support of the learning objectives would do poorly on it.

Allowing practical knowledge and skills to count for something

A major benefits of STEM education is that it can engage students who do not normally thrive in a traditional academic environment. This may happen because the students can leverage more practical knowledge and skills toward a productive goal in the classroom. Students who zone out during a lecture and may not have the foundation needed to grasp the full depth of the academic concepts, may still do extremely well within a STEM lesson because they are approaching the concepts from a non-academic angle that works for them.

Teachers need to be sure that their methods of scoring take these non-traditional approaches to the lesson into account and give credit for the level of engagement that the student is bringing to the exercise.

I don't mean to belittle academic conceptual knowledge. College engineering professors have told me that one concern with the emphasis on hands-on STEM courses is that they don't also emphasize the foundational mathematics, So you have students coming into college engineering courses who are great at assembling things or using 3D printers but without the solid mathematics grounding to actually support the needed work. When you're designing an electrical system, being able to calculate the effective resistance of a series of resistors in parallel is crucially important, after all.

PRACTICAL VERSUS ACADEMIC SKILLS

In my undergraduate college career, I had only one class I had to drop out of because I was doing poorly. It was Introduction to Electronics. I'd done great in the conceptual courses, where I had to write out and solve the equations for electrical systems, electrodynamics, and electromagnetism, but I was never able to successfully make the jump to using that conceptual knowledge to build a circuit. My father-in-law, who worked in construction his whole life, can do all sorts of rewiring work around the house, but he couldn't tell you the difference between how you add resistances together if they're in a parallel or a series configuration.

On some level, this practical ability to work with electronics is more immediately helpful than the more conceptual understanding of how electronics works.

Letting students show their thinking

One of the most important things in assessing within any area is to give the students motivation to do deep thinking. If you don't ever give them the opportunity to demonstrate that deep level of thinking to you, though, the student will not realize that it is valued. As I discuss in relation to the depth of knowledge (see the section "Approaching cognitive rigor in STEM lessons" earlier in the chapter), if the only thing you ask about is surface recall or basic skill proficiency, then the students will think that's all they're supposed to be getting out of the lessons.

You should treat input from the students about why they thought or decided something with just as much importance as what they thought or decided. This point ties into the idea from Chapter 9 about how learning works. Students can use another point of reflection about their own thinking process to solidify the thinking within the unit back into their mental model of other ideas — as they articulate the chain of reasoning and argument that they used.

TIP

One way to formally assess the *why* of thinking along with the *what* is to plan a conference with each group in which you talk through what they've done or are doing. This sounds very formal, but it can really just be a few minutes of conversation with them as you circle around. And it's nice to have some level of ritual around the conference. Make sure that all the students in the group are engaged and paying attention; you don't want to be talking to one student while another is still building the project.

Note that this conferencing is different from a class discussion. The group isn't sharing their process with everyone, they're sharing their process with their teacher. You are in a mentorship role, and in this exchange, your modeling of how to think through the reasoning process is more important than your takeaway about their thinking. You can ask them the sorts of questions that they should hopefully be learning to ask of themselves.

I cover the idea of getting assessment from students in the section "Trust the Experts: Students Evaluating Students" later in this chapter, and then also return to it in Chapter 12.

The Soft Skills: Assessing Collaboration and Employability Skills

Far more difficult to assess than raw academic skills are the employability skills and skills related to group work within the classroom. You should identify these soft skills as part of the learning objectives when you initially design the lesson and curriculum so that you have a clear vision of the specific employability skills you worked into the lesson and the sorts of evidence you can use to evaluate them.

Depending on how grading is handled in your situation, you might want to break out a distinct rubric specifically for the employability skills portion of the project. That rubric may not even result in a grade for the student, but you can offer them feedback anyway and let them know how they are doing on that element of their classroom behavior.

Balancing teamwork and individual accomplishment

Within a STEM project, you can find opportunities for each student to have evidence that they can look at and feel accomplished. Depending on how you define roles within your lesson, one student may be in charge of gathering and distributing the materials, another may coordinate the design, and another may give the final presentation to the class.

When looking at how to assess the soft skills, you want to jump between considering group and individual levels. Some groups may have had difficulty collaborating, which required a lot of intervention to get them working together. In this case — because you probably had a lot of interactions with the group — you may well have a sense of which people were trying to get things done and which were leaning into their drama. Each student's effort to work within a difficult group should definitely count for something in these cases.

For groups that were getting along without much need for intervention, though, you might actually realize that you don't have much information about their group dynamics. This situation could be a sign of great teamwork, but it could also be a sign that one dominant personality took charge, and the others just went along with their direction.

For these situations, documentation and assessments along the way can be helpful. If you look at worksheets, exit tickets, journals, and other forms of student feedback, and get a sense that many members of the group weren't particularly engaged, then that can give you a sense of how to evaluate the group dynamics.

Looking toward future career choices

As you find ways to provide feedback on the soft skills, giving students a context for understanding their strengths and weaknesses is important. Different careers require people with different talents. And almost every industry has a role for people with all sorts of talents.

For example, when people think of computer programming, they think of an individual person writing code, but the industry needs much more than that. They need program managers and project managers to coordinate teams. Software companies typically have sales and marketing staff that give presentations on the company's products, including those who attend major industry conferences or exhibitions and spend days talking to people non-stop about what their company is producing and how they can work together to achieve their goals.

Kids don't know that this range of careers exists. They typically know about jobs of being a teacher, a doctor, and a bit about the careers that their parents have. They might also have some ideas about a handful of jobs they see in television shows or movies.

REMEMBER

One major goal of exploring STEM projects in school is for students to get a taste of the sort of work they like doing, so they can look ahead and sort that out in the future. The goal isn't to pigeonhole them into a specific career, but to let them know the vast array of options that are available.

Trust the Experts: Students Evaluating Students

A wide variety of learning objectives exist in STEM lessons, and their scope can easily become overwhelming when you try to keep up with all of them during every stage of the lesson.

A key part of STEM lessons is collaborative work, including discussions with group partners. The first round of feedback students should receive on most ideas is from the other members of their class, and you (as the teacher) should provide feedback only after at least one round of internal classmate feedback occurs. In fact, throughout the entire lesson, you can find ways to formalize peer feedback that can minimize your need to directly respond to each student.

Exploiting peer feedback is particularly useful in identifying the soft skills that the students are using. If you've assigned students to specific roles, you can ask questions related to how team members performed the individual roles. Obviously, you have the final say in how to interpret this feedback, but remember that group dynamics may not always be how they appear from the outside. If a student seemed to be doing well — but everyone in their group is saying that they were a nightmare to work with — the feedback gives you (at least) a good hint that maybe you need to be a little more alert to the dynamics around that student in future projects.

In addition to getting feedback from other students, you can also solicit self-evaluations from the students. For example, have the students identify one good thing they contributed to the group and one thing they can work on to improve on for the next project. Then, have students identify these two points for each of the other members of their group. You can formalize this response within a survey or worksheet of some kind, or you can have it be something they write about during their reflection within their science notebook.

TIP

If your students maintain a continuing science journal between projects and they record their self-evaluation information in the journal, you can also flip back to previous entries. If the student identified something to work on in a previous entry — and you can see that they're now doing better at that skill — then take the opportunity to recognize and encourage that growth.

I offer more ideas about giving students a greater role in the classroom, including in setting and evaluating their own paths, in Chapter 12.

Chapter **12**

Taking STEM to the Next Level

Teachers and schools embrace STEM at different levels. Some build an entire educational program centered on STEM, while others treat STEM as an elective to supplement the core math and science curricula. Whatever level of integration you and your schools choose, you can always reach for deeper engagement.

In this chapter, I explore some ways to provide more opportunities for engaging students with STEM. I help you find ways that you can really let students' interests take center stage in planning, implementing, and promoting the STEM program. I also discuss how elements of play can enhance the learning experience. And I present ways that you can use STEM outside of the classroom, including structures that promote additional STEM opportunities.

Letting Student Inquiry Lead the Way

One major goal of STEM education — particularly in a project-based learning (PBL) context — is to create a student-centered classroom. Because most teachers spend a lot of time dealing with the difficulties of unmotivated students, getting students to take agency and ownership of their learning saves teachers a lot of headaches.

In Chapter 9, I cover some techniques for centering student inquiry within a classroom and within a given lesson. The assumption in that chapter is that students' questions would mostly be related to the lesson. You introduce an investigation, collect student questions about the investigation, and then help the students to find answers to those questions.

As you build a culture of question-asking, you'll find that students who really buy into the concept won't wait for you to introduce a topic for investigation before they begin asking questions. You may find that those crazy kids, with their independent thinking, begin looking at the world and asking questions about it even without prompting! Achievement unlocked!

REMEMBER

Students have required learning objectives that teachers plan out as part of the curriculum. An ideal outcome of a student-centered classroom is that students also begin to generate their own learning objectives.

Letting go of the classroom reins

The planning burden on teachers is high under the best of circumstances, and one way to lessen that burden is to shift some of it onto the students.

The educator, author, and consultant Trevor MacKenzie described four types of student inquiry.

>> **Structured Inquiry:** The teacher leads students through the investigation of a topic.

>> **Controlled Inquiry:** Students use resources found by the teacher to answer questions on a topic chosen by the teacher.

>> **Guided Inquiry:** Students work to design a product or solution based on a topic provided by the teacher.

>> **Free Inquiry:** Students are free to choose topics for investigation and define the investigation and solutions.

You can see that the types of inquiry become progressively more student-centered as you move down the list. Structured Inquiry is still largely a *sage-on-a-stage* format, in which the teacher leads the class through the inquiry process. This approach is better than a lecture, for sure, but it still puts the teacher at the center of classroom activity. On the opposite end, Free Inquiry really sets up the teacher in that *guide-on-the-side* role, as the students define not only their approach to the problem, but also which problems they want to deal with!

Free Inquiry — in its truest form — shows up rarely in the classroom, but it is a reminder of what students can achieve, if you can figure out ways to allow it.

Establishing trust going both ways

One challenge in building a student-centered classroom is letting go of the traditional classroom hierarchy with teachers as the head of the classroom. Embracing alternative models and letting go of control in the classroom can be challenging for teachers to accept. Relinquishing control flies in the face of their experience as both a learner and a teacher.

Difficulty accepting a less controlling classroom role often represents the fact that a teacher (with some measure of good cause) doesn't have faith that students will make good learning choices if given more control. And it's almost guaranteed that some bad choices will happen. But learning from making mistakes is integral to STEM education, so students should be free to make those mistakes.

REMEMBER

A student-centered learning environment does not guarantee student success. No one thing does. Preparing students for the real world they encounter when they're out of school is inherently good. A teacher-centered learning environment prepares them for only those situations in which someone else is present to tell them exactly what to do.

Just as teachers must learn to trust the students to work out their growing control in a student-centered classroom, they must also actively work to establish trust with the students. Actively establishing an intellectually safe, inquiry-based culture in the classroom is ideal. And this culture is easiest to establish, not in a single teacher's classroom, but as the overall culture across the whole school or district.

WARNING

Establishing a culture of inquiry at scale is challenging. Start by finding like-minded allies within your school or district, particularly in leadership positions. Look for experienced teachers who see the value in the effort to redirect classroom culture because they carry respect that sometimes can be difficult for newer teachers to bring to the table.

Fostering STEM student leadership

The highest goal of centering students in the STEM process is to actively engage them in formal leadership roles. Here are a variety of ways that you can use to blend STEM together with student leadership:

>> Involve students in planning STEM lessons.

>> Plan outside-of-class STEM activities or opportunities, such as teams or after-school clubs.

>> Organizing a formal STEM mentorship program.

Most schools, particularly high schools, already have some student leadership in place, such as student councils. Using existing student leadership is the most natural way to incorporate this level of student involvement. You could petition your student council to form a STEM committee, and then put out a request for those who want to be on the committee and to help plan STEM events.

You could also investigate forming a separate STEM organization at the school, such as a chapter of the National STEM Honor Society (https://nstem.org/). This organization serves students ranging all the way from Pre-K into their college years. You encounter costs and membership requirements, but having a chapter in the organization gives students a voice in advocating for more STEM programs in the school, including being present at local events (such as school board meetings), and otherwise offering a sense of STEM community.

The Dayton Regional STEM School has a Student Ambassador group that organizes students to regularly go out into the community for panels and presentations where they show their STEM skills and talk about their experiences. These ambassadors also help recruit more students to their school in future years.

Learning Through Play

One strong motivation for STEM is that kids often find the hands-on nature engaging in a way that they do not necessarily find in more abstract forms of learning. Part of this engagement comes from the fact that the STEM projects can feel more like play than (school)work. And you can find good research to support the idea that if you can make learning more playful, then it helps with the learning process.

When students engage with the lesson material as an authentic form of play, they're intrinsically motivated to keep at the task long enough for it to pass into their long-term memory. (See Chapter 9 for more information about learning and long-term memory.)

The neuroscience research finds five key characteristics that are central to effectively transferring play into learning.

>> **Pleasure:** Positive emotional states set the psychological conditions for learning. The dopamine rush that comes cognitively with play has positive impacts on memory, attention, curiosity, creativity, and neural plasticity.

>> **Meaning:** Learners bridge the known to the unknown in a safe context, transfer knowledge and understanding, draw deep connections, and gain confidence and insight into that new understanding.

>> **Engagement:** Play involves both attention to what is happening and a response on the part of the player. Their behavior is central to the play, giving them a growing sense of agency over their learning. (See the next section for more on this benefit.)

>> **Iteration:** Repetitive rounds of an activity or thought offer new opportunities to engage with the task or information from a slightly different perspective. The learner thinks, "How can I do better this time?" within a context of play.

>> **Interaction:** While students can play in isolation, playing with others helps them bond socially, figure out the emotional states of others, regulate their own emotional states, and adapt their behavior appropriately.

The connection between play and learning is often more explicit in younger grades, but whatever age of learner you work with, you can reap benefits by thinking about ways in which you can make their learning process look more like play.

Exploring flow states and engagement

Related to these benefits of play is the psychological concept of flow as formalized by University of Chicago psychologist Mihaly Csikszentmihalyi (1934–2021). In the 1970s, Csikszentmihalyi described a *flow state*, sometimes also called being *in the zone*, as being a state of energized focus that reflects full mental absorption in what a person is doing.

In Chapter 2, I discuss research showing that boredom has one of the most powerful negative correlations with learning. The American Psychological Association defines *boredom* as "resulting from a lack of engagement with stimuli in the environment." Boredom is a mental state of complete disengagement from an activity; in a sense, it's the exact opposite of a flow state. High levels of engagement, which have a positive correlation, are also likely to come closer to a state of mental flow.

REMEMBER

When you can authentically create a learning experience that blends with a genuinely enjoyable sense of play, you unite many of these psychological benefits. You'll know that you've achieved a flow state in your classroom when you tell students that the lesson is over and they have to clean up, and you are met with frustrated students who wish to continue with the project.

Highlighting the promise and peril of gamification

Related to play, *gamification* involves taking elements of game playing and applying them to other areas with the goal of driving engagement. The big problem with gamification of learning is that instead of highlighting the intrinsic motivations (learning something new), you're creating new extrinsic motivations (playing for rewards).

The advent of smartphones has made many people aware of how a savvy designer can create an app that gives users dopamine hits when they get rewards. This trait is blatant in video games, of course, but it shows up in all manner of other apps that involve gamification, including those used in education. See the sidebar "Gaming to learn?"

GAMING TO LEARN?

Consider this example from Duolingo, a language-learning app with gaming elements in which you accumulate points, track streaks of how long you've practiced, and gain levels of achievement. I once had a streak of over 400 days, but got busy and broke it, so I now had a streak of zero days. With the recognition of how much time it would take to even hope to catch up to that 400-day streak again, I never resumed use of Duolingo with the same frequency.

It's worth noting that the streak did provide some level of motivation. It seems to have worked enough as a motivation to get me to practice Spanish for over 400 days straight, even on days where I had no desire to do so. By the time the streak broke, I was motivated more by the extrinsic motivation of the game than the intrinsic motivation of wanting to learn Spanish.

WARNING

As a teacher, you'll discover an inherent problem with supplying external rewards. Deciding to use something ongoing — such as a point system, levels, or streaks — can account for the fact that some students will advance early on. If this advancement results in a disincentive for other students (or for the advanced students because they're so far ahead), then your gamification has backfired. Plan for ways that students can always feel like they have an opportunity to catch up, so the process stays compelling for all those involved.

TIP

Prioritize building gamified learning systems that have benefits for all students. For example, if you build a system where students get points for completing tasks and it takes the same number of points to get a new level each time, the students who start out ahead will just remain ahead. However, if it takes more points to advance at higher levels, the students who are taking longer to get the points have a chance to catch up to those with early leads.

Another way that you can use a level-based system (and tie it into the earlier ideas of student leadership) is by giving higher-level students certain responsibilities in the classroom, such as managing certain tools or gaining mentorship roles with students who are having more difficulty.

Here are a few ideas of gamification that I think can work well in a STEM setting.

>> **Badges:** Create task-specific badges, awards, or titles for students who complete certain challenges, ranging from use of a hot glue gun to different levels of proficiency with digital design software. These badges can be digital, or you can even print (or 3D print) physical badges.

>> **Quests and storytelling:** Frame the learning experiences as a narrative, which works well in a problem-based setting where you're tackling real-world problems. Individual tasks within the classroom are quests (or side quests) that are part of the overall narrative.

>> **Skill-growth trees:** Define chains of related skills and track how students progress through the linked skills. Break down learning objectives into discrete skills. Tie into badges for certain benchmark skills that may unlock access to new tools or types of projects.

>> **Contests:** Turn a project into a contest. You can frame the final presentation as a pitch session in which the students explain why their solution is the best one. This method is growing as a way of handling internal design projects in corporations and universities.

WARNING

Be alert to which students the gamification motivates. Popular literacy programs award students who read many books, but instead of promoting reading among poor readers, it rewards current readers. Gamification in STEM can be highly motivating to students who are already into STEM, but not necessarily for other students. If you're putting a lot of work into a system that only motivates the already-motivated students, then you can probably find better ways to direct your energy.

Encouraging the STEM Hobbyist

Many find their passion for STEM fields outside the classroom setting. My own love of science is rooted in hours spent reading science fiction novels for fun. People go into life science disciplines due to their love of animals and nature. A well-rounded STEM program not only includes classroom experiences of STEM, but also helps support a passion for STEM outside of the school day.

REMEMBER

Access to STEM supplies and opportunities is a major consideration outside the classroom. A student with an interest in coding can cultivate that interest outside of school if they have access to a computer and a coding platform (also requiring internet access). But an economically disadvantaged student without this access is less likely to cultivate their coding ability to the same degree.

A school can support the STEM enthusiast by providing opportunities for in-school or after-school activities that expand beyond the normal classroom offerings.

Forming clubs, organizations, and teams

Clubs or other formal school organizations centered on STEM offer an excellent way to encourage students who are looking for more active ways to engage with STEM.

Some schools have chapters of the National STEM Honor Society (which I mention in the section "Fostering STEM student leadership" earlier in this chapter). Others may have a generic STEM club, but you can devise more specific clubs to build communities around specific elements of STEM. Here are a few examples:

>> Maker's Club, Engineering Club, Inventing Club, LEGO Club

>> Entrepreneur's Club

>> Cooking/Culinary Science Club, Gardening/Farming/Agriculture Club

- » Science Club, Chemistry Club, Math Club, Coding Club

- » Video Game or eSports Club

- » Robotics Club or Drones Club

These clubs all give a great opportunity to embrace the student-centered goal of STEM education. Without specific learning objectives and pacing requirements, the students' interests can guide them more fully.

The goal of these clubs is twofold:

1. Explore more deeply the subject of the club, both in terms of practical experience and factual knowledge.

2. Establish community with other students who share similar interests.

Though you don't need formal lessons for clubs, you should plan on how to connect the students more deeply with the subject to make it more than just play time. The LEGO club should introduce building and design principles. An eSports club should focus on developing video game strategies.

Another way to help students push the boundaries in their STEM areas is by promoting not just cooperative work, but also competition through STEM activities. Competitive STEM provides much of the same benefits as competitive sports, but typically with less sweating involved.

Almost any of the clubs listed could involve competitive elements. The Entrepreneur's Club could end in a pitch session during which students propose their business ideas to groups of students, teachers, school administrators, or even local business owners — like the television series *Shark Tank*. The Cooking Club could have a winter cookie bake-off.

If you want to be more formal, though, you can find competitive STEM organizations that are worth investigating as a possible new activity for your school. Here are a handful of competitive STEM organizations to look into:

- » *FIRST* Robotics Competition (www.firstinspires.org/robotics/frc)

- » *FIRST* LEGO League (www.firstinspires.org/robotics/fll)

- » VEX Robotics (www.vexrobotics.com/competition)

- » Rube Goldberg Machine Contest (www.rubegoldberg.org/rube-goldberg-contests/)

» eCybermission (www.ecybermission.com/)

» Junior Solar Sprint (https://www.usaeop.com/program/jss/)

You should check with local universities and other organizations in your area, as there may be regional competitions.

Prioritizing STEM labs and makerspaces

One way to clarify that STEM is a priority in your school is to dedicate space to it. Both teachers and students benefit from a space that reflects the STEM emphasis you want in your school. It's long been the case that schools, particularly high schools, had dedicated science labs. As STEM becomes more prevalent in other grades, many schools will find that creating spaces that are conducive to engaging in STEM activities makes sense.

Consider this: STEM projects can be annoying to teachers because of the mess, which falls into two categories:

» Trash

» Partially finished projects, including unused materials that teachers must store so that the students can resume work on the project at a later time

Having a dedicated room for STEM projects allows the supplies, the on-going projects, and any setup or mess to be more contained. It also provides an easy access point for any STEM equipment, such as 3D printers or microscopes, that the school would want multiple classes of students to use.

These spaces have an assortment of names, such as a makerspace, fabrication lab, or innovation studio. You can also give your space a more distinctive individual name. A nearby library has a basement makerspace called Ignite Studio. I have heard of a school calling theirs The Makery. The United Nations International School has dubbed their STEM lab the CoLaboratory.

TIP

To get back to the idea of student leadership in STEM, establishing and naming a STEM space is a great opportunity for building the STEM community. Have students submit names for the space and then vote on the one that they most want. (You'll want to vet submissions before they go on to the formal vote. An unfettered naming poll is what resulted in the 2016 naming of a polar scientific research ship as *Boaty McBoatface*. It might not set the right tone for a school to officially call the STEM lab "The Explosion Palace," for example.)

Promoting maker fairs and entrepreneurship

Even without a dedicated makerspace in the school, many schools have long created opportunities for students to make things. And sometimes those things turn into crafts that sell at craft fairs, often with proceeds going toward some sort of school event.

This is a great way for certain clubs, like a maker's club or a STEM club, to generate some fundraising opportunities for supplies. Schools could either form a maker's fair at the school, or partner with already-existing local events, such as a craft fair, maker's fair, or farmer's market, setting up a booth where students can sell products made during the club sessions. Students can also set up demonstrations of some of the processes and equipment they use, explaining these to people who come to the fair.

One of our local schools does a fundraiser for the high-ability classes, in which those students develop a business plan, create their products, and set up an Entrepreneur's Fair in the school cafeteria.

Some students may go beyond just artistic designs, or even an entrepreneurial business plan, and come up with an actual original invention. Having this happen really is the height of engaging with the engineering element of a STEM program.

But, after a student creates an (apparently) original invention, what are the next steps? At that point, the class can engage in an integrated STEM and social studies research project to learn a little bit about how patents work! For that, the best resource about patents in the United States is the United States Patent and Trademark Office website (www.uspto.gov/).

Encouraging school and community projects

Students often care deeply about their communities, but they also aren't under the mistaken impression that everything in those communities is perfect. One way to encourage engagement is to ground a STEM program in improving the students' school or broader community. For example,

>> Students can identify and define issues in the community and then work on proposed solutions for those issues. This practice is a great way to really foster soft skills, because these projects will often involve reaching out to

community leaders and local businesses to gain information and possibly assistance in generating a solution.

» Students can become involved in a broader community through the open science movement, which can enable them to engage with real scientists to contribute to actual ongoing research. You can find out more about where to connect with open science communities in Chapter 17.

4

Troubleshooting STEM Education

Chapter **13**

Planning the STEM Classroom

P lanning for STEM projects can take more work than more straightforward traditional lessons, even as students assume more control and agency within the learning activities.

In this chapter, I go through some steps you can take to review how to make sure you're prepared for your STEM class. I tell you about a variety of STEM resources that you'll want to have available. I discuss some considerations you'll want to make in regard to students of different ages, particularly when working with younger or older students. And I discuss how to prepare for collaboration among educators, including training STEM teachers and maintaining their expertise.

Evaluating Your STEM Resources

Teaching STEM subject areas can be resource-intensive compared to other courses. These days, you can often easily access content information for free online, but the physical nature of STEM education means that students need access to materials and tools that can cost more than what they'd need to get through a standard math or English class.

Also, the emphasis on the iterative process in STEM can further result in material costs. If a student realizes they need to go all the way back to the drawing board to get an effective final project, you want to encourage them to do so. However, many of the consumable materials used in an earlier attempt can't be reused in the final project, and so, the student needs to acquire additional materials or tools.

Physical resources

One nice thing about STEM resources is that you can often teach the fundamental concepts with pretty low-cost materials, such as cardboard and masking tape. You can find a list of the sorts of materials that are great to have on hand on the Cheat Sheet for this book at www.dummies.com.

Looking for donated resources

In addition to looking at the resources you have on hand (or laying around in an old supply closet), consider ways to crowdsource resources for the lesson activity. Here are a handful of ways to gather additional supplies for free:

>> **Ask school administrators to save cardboard boxes,** such as those from the cafeteria.

>> **Organize a supply drive for students** to bring in cereal boxes, empty paper towel rolls, and other useful materials.

>> **Reach out to local businesses** to ask for material donations.

>> **Raise money to buy any needed materials** through DonorsChoose (www.donorschoose.com) or another crowdfunding platform.

TIP

Certain projects, of course, will require more specific materials. In upper grade classes — such as more formal engineering courses — you'll want more sophisticated and precise materials. For example, if you're doing something with electrical circuitry, you'll need batteries, wires, or copper tape, and maybe other components (such as LEDs), based on the project. Still, some general resources provide great options for constructing initial prototypes before you begin using more expensive materials for the final build.

Scouring the school building for resources

You'll also want to identify the other STEM resources you have available within your building. Ask around to discover resources you didn't know were available. Previous STEM teachers often leave behind construction, robotics, and other STEM supplies. And these supplies may be unused because no other teachers know about them (or know how to use them). For example,

>> I once mentioned that one of the schools had a pair of vertical garden towers and was told that several schools had obtained them years ago. Some additional searching revealed old garden towers in the corners of various schools' supply rooms, so now several of the schools use them for seed-starting STEM projects.

>> Another school had an old fish tank, which the assistant principal has now converted into a hallway hydroponics system.

>> My school district had many unopened VEX Robotics construction kits (without robotic brains, motors, or sensors) in storage. A resourceful consultant offered the suggestion to buy building carts from a local hardware store, and now each school has a mobile building cart full of VEX Robotics building supplies. Any class in the school can wheel the cart into their room and have access to the materials for STEM projects.

TIP

As you begin asking around about existing resources, be sure to organize this information in a way you can easily track. I keep a running list of STEM resources for the whole district in a Google Sheet, so that when someone asks about a certain resource, I can tell at a glance who has it and who to contact. If you need to, you can also use check-out sheets and other tools to help organize requests and distribution.

Digital resources

Even more challenging than obtaining physical resources is getting the digital resources that you need access to in order to complete projects.

REMEMBER

Digital resources are essential for anything to do with computer science. Here are some free online programming sources that are great for getting students started with coding:

CodeHS (https://codehs.com/) — At the time of this writing, the company's business model charges to access elementary school courses, as well as to access teacher tools and professional development. However, many of the high school and middle school courses are available for free.

Code.org (www.code.org) — A nonprofit organization devoted to making computer science available to every student, Code.org has free lessons and curricula. It is the organization behind the Hour of Code (https://hourofcode.com/us) movement (see Chapter 16).

Scratch (https://scratch.mit.edu/) and Scratchjr (www.scratchjr.org/) — Developed by Mitch Resnick at the MIT Media Lab, the Scratch coding language is one of the most popular visual coding languages intended for use by children.

The more streamlined version, ScratchJr, uses simple icons for pre-reader accessibility. Since Scratch is a coding language, you will often encounter Scratch on another coding platform, or you can go straight to the source and program directly on Scratch.

TIP

Beyond coding, you also want to familiarize students with common computer applications for use in a wide range of situations. One major category of digital applications that help in a variety of situations is editing apps, which can work with sound, graphics, and video. These editing applications often require access to images, videos, or sound files. Links to some of these types of (free) files are available on this book's online Cheat Sheet at www.dummies.com.

Societal and community resources

Societal resources that come with the local community can contribute to the richness of STEM lessons. Many local businesses and professionals love the opportunity to engage with schools and students to talk about the work that they do. Local city, county, and regional agencies can be great at helping you get in contact with businesses, and many communities have foundations and chambers of commerce that help with this sort of networking as well.

TIP

Earlier in this chapter, I mention reaching out to local businesses for material donations. You should also consider what expertise they may be able to offer. Although getting a local nursery to donate seeds for a gardening project is great, getting professionals who have experience growing plants into the classroom to demonstrate planting techniques can be an even better experience.

When considering the 5E model from Chapter 9, the ideal place to include professionals in the learning process is during the Explain or Expand steps. As part of these steps, the professionals can review some initial prototypes of solutions that the kids are working on and offer constructive feedback. Also always fun — if you're doing a *pitch-session*-style conclusion to the unit — is to have actual professionals be the ones the students are pitching to.

Considering the Little Ones and the Big Ones

I try to make most of the tips in this book applicable for the majority of students. But different age ranges represent students at different developmental stages, and the emphasis of STEM lessons in those grades is important to keep in mind.

In general, here are some pointers for structuring the STEM lessons for students at various grade levels.

>> **Grades Pre-K through 2:** Explore core concepts, including basic number sense, identifying key features, and expanding vocabulary. Avoid heavy reading or writing demands. Use accessible videos, pictures, or verbal communication. And promote teamwork.

>> **Grades 3 through 6:** Encourage students to continue asking questions and apply creative thinking and problem-solving efforts toward those questions. Explore deeper connections between different concepts. Students take on stronger research roles and summarize thinking in both written and verbal formats.

>> **Grades 7 through 12:** Students can specialize in areas that they are interested in. STEM projects become more course-specific. Integrating across subject areas can be more difficult in these grades but doing so is still useful and important to plan out. And you can reasonably require more polished final products.

In the Cheat Sheet for this book (found at www.dummies.com), you can find some suggestions of resources for students of different ages. The universal design principles and resources (see Chapter 15) are also useful in planning projects that are broadly accessible to a wide range of students.

Simplifying concepts for younger students

For younger students, the key thing you want to do is expose them to as many concepts as you can and get them to begin drawing valid connections between those concepts. Younger students establish a broad mental map of the world at this age, and the more extensively you can spread out the map, the better they'll be able to anchor concepts introduced later.

Here are a couple of points to keep in mind when planning lessons for younger students:

>> **Account for the level of students' language skills.** Though you're unlikely to forget this if you work with younger students, make sure that you account for their lower level of reading and writing skills. Some tools mentioned throughout this book, like keeping a science journal, can be incredibly difficult for a student who is still having difficulty writing out individual words and letters.

TIP

You can still use tools like keeping a science journal, but encourage younger students to document their thinking in ways they find more accessible, such as with drawings, lists, diagrams, or charts. Complete sentences and paragraphs are not crucial if they're going to create a stumbling block for the young student to document their thinking. Similarly, when you're providing information to students, presenting a slide with a well-placed graphic will be much more useful than one with a series of wordy bullet points.

>> **Match material resources to students' motor skills.** The motor skills of younger students are also not as refined as those of their older counterparts, so you'll want to really take that into account when considering which materials to have available in the classroom. Young students may benefit from the DUPLO line of LEGO building blocks rather than traditional LEGOs. DUPLO LEGOs are larger and therefore easier to manipulate than the smaller LEGO pieces.

There are a variety of component sets (other than LEGOs) that can be particularly appropriate and engaging for young students. Here are just a few ideas.

>> **Makedo** (www.make.do/): They offer cutting and fastening tools for safe and precise construction with cardboard.

>> **BirdBrain Technologies** (www.birdbraintechnologies.com/): You can build a robot out of any materials. The hummingbird is a great project to start with!

>> **SparkFun Electronics** (www.sparkfun.com/): You can create a variety of wearable electronics that students can weave into clothing or other items, such as adding light and sound elements to cloth puppets. I recommend checking out the lilypad project.

As you dig deeper into the world of microcontrollers and microcomputers, (discussed in Chapter 6), you'll find more possibilities for how students of different ages can use them.

Giving more autonomy to older students

If you teach in middle school or high school, one important thing to keep in mind is that STEM lessons provide a great way for students to begin taking charge of the direction of their education. At this age, students are really at the point where they're experimenting with possible career paths, and any STEM work needs to take that into account.

In Chapter 12, I discuss the importance of giving students autonomy, and the level increases as the students get older. Offering autonomy will be easier to accomplish if students' prior STEM education establishes the culture of inquiry in the years leading up to high school. But a student-centered approach can help foster involvement with the direction of study even for a student who's always been exposed to traditional teaching styles.

TIP

Older students can work at the more open-ended extreme of the autonomy spectrum, even doing work that involves Free Inquiry (see Chapter 12). You always have constraints due to course requirements, but anything you can do to give the students a sense of control over what's happening in the classroom can make for a good learning experience.

Preparing STEM Educational Teams

Implementing STEM lessons that are challenging and stimulate learning is a daunting task for teachers; it requires support and preparation to properly implement the approach. Teachers need to clearly understand what their goals are and why STEM is important, particularly since the associated lessons take the most precious commodity out of their day: time.

Emphasizing the STEM approach

One grumble I hear consistently from teachers is that their teacher education program in college did not prepare them for teaching STEM lessons. Teacher education in college focuses on developing nice, neat lessons and then delivering those lessons with fidelity. As such, teachers of all levels of experience often find themselves unprepared to teach STEM lessons, which require a more open-ended plan for students to guide how the project is resolved. In many cases, this approach flies in the face of what they're expected to do in every other aspect of their day, where a primary teacher responsibility is carefully orchestrating all of the student activities.

REMEMBER

Whether you are a fellow teacher, a coach, or an administrator, you must address the expectations for lesson delivery explicitly. Teachers have a lot to do, and if STEM is going to be a priority in your school, they need to know that. If the STEM approach is just tacked onto a list alongside all their other priorities, then it will be one of the easiest things for them to skip over.

This lack of priority is particularly true of elementary school computer science. Many teachers don't even realize that their state has computer science standards across the K-12 grades that teachers are expected to deliver to students. Even if they are aware of these standards, many elementary school teachers don't feel prepared to teach them.

Communicating STEM expectations

When communicating the STEM (potentially new) expectations to teachers, you should convey the benefits of STEM, which I introduce in Part 1 and discussed throughout the book. Here are three important aspects of STEM education to keep in mind.

REMEMBER

>> **Experience not mastery:** STEM is not high stakes in the traditional sense that students aren't generally tested at the end of the year to determine whether they have mastered the concepts. The key to STEM education is to give students experience and mentally engage them with the content, not to reach a defined level of mastery.

>> **Improvement over perfection:** For both the students and the teachers, the goal of the STEM approach is that each attempt at a project or solution will be an improvement over the last attempt. No one is expecting perfection right out of the gate.

>> **Encouraged collaboration:** Planning and discussing STEM lessons and activities among teachers is extremely helpful. Just as STEM projects require teamwork among the students, they may also require teamwork among the teachers. For example, if one teacher feels more comfortable with a certain type of project or equipment, perhaps the classes could rotate to allow that teacher to present the project to all of the students.

The teaching of STEM evolves constantly. Teachers can experience difficulty with staying up to speed on all the innovations, including new resource options. Having teachers attend conferences — where they can meet with other teachers who are using STEM projects and tools in their classroom and get hands-on practice with the them — is extremely useful.

Sending teachers to conferences

TIP

Conferences can be expensive, particularly those involving travel and hotel stays. These conferences are always looking for volunteers and often offer teachers reduced (possibly free) membership in exchange for staffing the event for a period of hours.

Many conferences are put on at the national, regional, and state level by the major educational professional organizations:

>> National Science Teaching Association (www.nsta.org/)

>> Computer Science Teachers Association (https://csteachers.org/)

>> National Council of Teachers of Mathematics (www.nctm.org/)

These conferences are great experiences for teachers, providing them with a perspective on some of the most engaging work that is happening in schools across the country or in their region. For teachers who are looking to be STEM leaders within their schools, having this broader perspective can be particularly important.

Chapter **14**

STEM at Home (and Homeschool)

The phrase, "learning begins at home," is just as true for STEM as for anything else. Just as homes that have books tend to produce high-performing students, home environments that support STEM are going to produce learners who feel more comfortable exploring STEM concepts. You don't have to be a computer programmer to raise a programmer, but very few students excel in a subject when they're told at home (explicitly or implicitly) that it's a waste of their time. If you're reading this book, I assume you don't fall into that category.

In this chapter, I focus on creating opportunities for learners within your home. I discuss creating truly personalized learning goals, which is a benefit that parents certainly have over classroom teachers who must work at a larger scale. Along with identifying goals, I review ways to expand STEM opportunities beyond just completing STEM lessons. And I discuss some great STEM-themed games that you can play with the whole family.

Personalizing Learning Goals

Each learner is different and requires different, relevant goals. A major benefit related to STEM at home is that you presumably have fewer unique learners to account for than a school, or even an individual teacher. You can focus on individual strengths, weaknesses, and interests to hone learning objectives that are extremely well-tailored to a student's unique personality.

Targeting unique goals for a learner

In the next section, I discuss ways to build lessons around your specific child's interests, but in this section, I talk about considering the actual goals. Does your student have a particular interest in digital art? Comic book superheroes? Drones? You could build out specific learning goals related to any of these areas and help your student develop a deeper appreciation for something they love — while also engaging with STEM.

REMEMBER

Teachers must create learning goals for groups of students, and they make those decisions based on how to best get the information to a class full of students, in accord with legislated academic standard requirements.

Throughout this chapter, I return to an example of a specific learning goal: a learner who has become fascinated with the idea of colonizing Mars. A teacher could certainly recognize this as a worthy goal for building lessons around, but having such a child in your home provides you with opportunities that a teacher in a classroom full of students might not be able to explore.

TIP

Become familiar with the STEM-related content expected at your learner's age. See Part 2 of this book for many of the national standards. You can look up state standards on your state government's education website. At the minimum, you want the student to become proficient with their grade-level standards, to keep them up to speed with other students their own age.

Exploring depth as well as breadth

If you're a parent reading this, there is a good chance that you have a child who is very engaged with STEM or one you *want* to be very engaged with STEM. Your instinct might be to move them ahead to higher-grade learning objectives when they've met their on-grade objectives. Before doing that, though, consider whether a deeper exploration of the grade-level concepts might be a better approach. Doing so may give you the opportunity to integrate those concepts across disciplines.

Here are a handful of examples:

>> An algebra-proficient learner begins exploring ways that they can use those algebra concepts to analyze grade-appropriate data, deepening math connections with other subject areas.

>> A strong computer science learner uses coding to simulate other on-grade content areas, like physical or biological models.

>> A biological-savvy learner begins considering more ways in which energy moves through an ecosystem.

Why would you do this? What is the problem with just pushing forward and getting the learner on to new, higher-grade content?

A deeper level of understanding and connection is inherently beneficial to the student. As I discuss in Chapter 9, you want to lay the groundwork for the learner to develop a more complete mental map of concepts and how they connect. This practice establishes deeper learning and motivates them to find ways to transfer learning from one area into other areas.

The standards outlined in Part 2 of this book include not only grade-specific content knowledge, but also a variety of standards related to practices, process skills, and crosscutting concepts. If a student is doing well at grade-level content skills, this gives them the flexibility to really explore these other elements of the standards to expand their understanding.

REMEMBER

Setting goals that explore content deeper instead of jumping to higher-level content is also a benefit if your student is currently covering related content in school (or at some point returns to school). Being too far ahead of other students in content could lead to boredom and disengagement.

Expanding Beyond Just Study Time

With your learning goals in mind, you should consider the best way to engage your student. Just like having learners read for fun at home (beyond reading assignments for school) is a good thing, having students engage in STEM tasks that aren't directly tied into their daily schoolwork is also good.

TIP

You will want to find ways to enrich your student's experience that resonate with their interests. Here are some ideas to get you started:

>> Build biology lessons centered on their favorite animals.

>> Study STEM concepts and how they relate to careers they're interested in.

>> Design STEM projects around their favorite books, television series, or movies.

REMEMBER

If you are a homeschool parent, of course, you should incorporate any of these ideas along with the more general tips about formulating a 5E lesson from Chapter 9.

Consider the example of a learner who has a specific interest in learning everything they can about Mars (because they want to colonize it). Depending on the age of the learner, the following might be great options on how to expand their STEM thinking toward their learning goal:

>> Read books, such as the classic *The Martian Chronicles*, *The Martian*, or Kim Stanley Robinson's The Mars Trilogy (*Red Mars*, *Green Mars*, and *Blue Mars*).

>> Discuss environmental and physical differences between Mars and Earth, and how these differences would affect things like movement across the surface.

>> Calculate the time it would take to get to Mars by moving at various speeds.

>> Write a short story set on Mars, with an effort to maintain as much scientific accuracy as possible.

>> Study engineering needs of spaceships, or a self-contained colony structure on Mars.

>> Consider ways that you could build a greenhouse to grow plants on Mars.

DIGGING DEEPER INTO HOMESCHOOLING

TIP

It takes a village to raise a child. If you're a homeschool parent, then you'll lack the community, resources, and support that a school has, and it's important to find ways to reach out so that the entire educational burden doesn't fall entirely on you.

• Many digital resources can help, such as those through Khan Academy (www.khanacademy.org). They don't currently offer full science courses prior to middle school, so another option is to pay for a homeschool curriculum platform, which would usually include video lessons, possibly of science experiments. Or, of course, you can use the tips from earlier in this book to develop your own STEM curriculum.

• You should also try to find other homeschool communities, both online and local, that you can work with to pool resources. Individual states often have homeschooling associations that you can join, as well as informal online collaborations through Facebook groups and other social media sites.

You can find invaluable resources for homeschooling in *Homeschooling For Dummies* and on the Cheat Sheet of that book, which is available on www.dummies.com.

TIP

Again, the goal here is to get the learner thinking about how ideas in seemingly different areas (for example, literature, biology, space travel, and habitat engineering) connect to each other. Perhaps the learner can question the claims in science fiction stories and identify outdated elements that don't seem scientifically accurate today. Even if they don't have the information and need to figure something out or do additional research, being able to quantify the unknown information is itself an achievement. This practice also gives them a new goal of other investigations they can perform. (This would be one of the "side quests" that you could explore if you're applying the gamification ideas from Chapter 12.)

Bonding over STEM Game Nights

Family game nights are a great way to incorporate STEM education for children of all ages in a way that is social, competitive, and fun. The concept has become so popular in recent years that the process of using games to teach a variety of skills has even gained a name: *gameschooling*.

Although a game that has an explicit STEM theme is the easiest type to leverage for STEM education, you can bring STEM concepts into play in a number of games, including

>> **Probability:** This obvious concept shows up in any game that involves randomness or the rolling of dice.

>> **Physics concepts:** These concepts can come up in games that involve collisions or other physical interactions. You can even use a game like Jenga (a tower-deconstruction game) as a tie-in to concepts of gravity, friction, and balance.

Many games can get players to begin asking questions about the STEM concepts, perhaps during the Engage or Explore phases of a STEM unit. See Chapter 9.

Optimizing the gameschooling process

REMEMBER

Because a home environment isn't bound by the same time constraints as a school classroom, one benefit of that flexibility is that you can take the time to play some longer and more complex games with learners. I maintain a list of STEM-related games at https://eurekagame.com/stem-games, if you are looking for ideas.

In Chapter 12, I discuss the science related to learning through play, and that certainly applies here. Some additional benefits of playing STEM-focused games include

>> **Learning across ages.** Many of these games create an opportunity for learners of different ages to come together to explore the topic.

>> **Explaining the process.** Don't just have players silently carry out their turns, but make it an expectation that they describe what is happening in the game.

>> **Exploring abstraction and simulation.** Several of these games describe an elaborate physical or technological process but abstract it down into a handful of simple concepts. Observing abstraction in games may help students create simulations of their own.

>> **Reading and vocabulary.** Many of these games use STEM-based vocabulary to describe game concepts, which means learners can begin familiarizing themselves with these terms. As part of explaining their process, students should read the name of the cards and use the terminology in describing their actions.

Examining the Terraforming Mars game

TIP

Consider one popular space exploration game, *Terraforming Mars* (created by FryxGames) — a perfect choice for the hypothetical Mars-obsessed student! In this award-winning game, the players work to make the planet Mars habitable to human life. This process involves increasing the viability of three global parameters on the planet: temperature, oxygen, and ocean. You can do many different things in the game to help improve these three global parameters, and you accumulate points throughout the game based on what you accomplish. When the temperature and oxygen levels are high enough, and you have enough oceans, the game ends and you score your final points to determine the winner because you've made Mars habitable.

Terraforming Mars is designed for one to five players aged 12 or older. Games run about 90 minutes to 2 hours. It's likely too much to work easily into a classroom setting but is better suited to playing at home. The cards and game board have numerous icons that indicate exactly which type of space or resource the player is using, but the actions also appear as text on the card. The bottom of the card also has *flavor text*, which narratively describes what is happening with the card. In other words, each individual playing card has multiple means by which a player can interact with it (highlighting a principle from universal design, as discussed in Chapter 15).

The mix of icons and text means that you can easily include both younger and older players in this game. They can read the name of the card, describe any requirements, and then describe what happens as they adjust their resources on their game board. For example, you might hear the following

> "There are six oceans, so I can play Kelp Farming, which costs 17 credits. I get two plants right now. I produce two more credits each turn, and three more plants."

You could ask the player to read the flavor text at the bottom of the card. Also, ask the player whether they know what kelp is and what animals (if any) eat kelp.

The ultimate goal is not for players to learn (let alone memorize and retain) any specific facts, but to make more connections between the events in the game and their broader mental knowledge map — connecting life in oceans to planetary exploration on Mars, for example.

TIP

Often the first few times you're playing a game like this with younger players, playing with their cards face up makes sense. I also tend to play with my cards face up when introducing young people to games, and then talk through my reasoning on my various card choices, to model the behavior I want from the other players.

WARNING

When mixing players of different ages, particularly siblings, you always have the possibility of a clash of personalities. You want to make this play a learning experience, so make sure that everyone is on the same page about the goal, which is to have fun. When playing with different ages, avoid games where bluffing or otherwise misleading another person is a major component, or where a younger player revealing their cards to ask a question puts them at a major disadvantage.

Chapter **15**

STEM for All

While innovative STEM programs have always existed, in the past educators often designated them as enrichment activities and sometimes even *gated* them so that they were accessible to only the highest-performing students. We all live in a world driven by STEM innovations. Gone are the days when you could believe that only students on track to programming or research careers need strong STEM backgrounds. Research shows that STEM education is important for all students.

In this chapter, I touch on some issues related to access, equity, and inclusion for all students in STEM education. I discuss some of the key concepts related to equity and access. And I also offer an extremely brief discussion about the known equity issues within STEM.

These ideas related to equality, access, and inclusion are sensitive and important issues. Although I have devoted my career to serving diverse student populations fairly, my background is in science and mathematics rather than as a specialist in how to engage any specific population. When considering specific populations of students that you work with, I encourage you to collaborate with experts in that population.

Being a Voice for the Underrepresented

When working to make sure that STEM education reaches everyone, you may need to have difficult conversations. If these conversations were easy, then STEM education that's accessible to everyone would already be taking place everywhere.

Unfortunately, that isn't happening. And it isn't happening, in part, because those conversations are uncomfortable. When educators avoid these difficult conversations, STEM programs are all too often implemented without explicit plans to make sure they're accessible to everyone. The result is that STEM is often treated as a de facto *enrichment program*, in which the students who are already well served get access to this great new thing. And often, the underserved student populations just come along for the ride. Hopefully, the underserved students can thrive in this new methodology (and they often do), but those administering the methodology don't make explicit plans to reach them.

I was once involved with a high school that released a promotional video of their STEM program. The video interviewed a community partner from a local non-profit, the school's assistant principal, two STEM teachers, and two STEM students. In addition to these brief interviews and testimonials, the video contained a lot of B-roll footage from classrooms. The footage from the classrooms showed the full diversity of the school's STEM program, but in the interviews, everyone except the community partner was a white male.

This school was in a diverse community with a STEM program that represented that diversity. Many STEM classes had strong female students. The resulting video, with no student minority or female voices, didn't reflect the population of the STEM program, despite there being a plethora of students available who could have been recruited to provide that voice.

The lack of minority and female student voices in the final video made it absolutely clear that no one consciously made sure that those voices were included, or they would have been. I don't mean to suggest that anyone involved in the video consciously sought to exclude those voices, but they obviously didn't consciously act to include them, either (or else they would have been in the video).

How does something like that happen? When you're looking for volunteers, you're generally happy to get any. In this case, they likely asked for volunteers in their STEM classes, and maybe the only two volunteers were both white male students. Because they were happy to have two volunteers, the educators likely passed them along to the video company doing the interviews, and didn't think about the potential bias in the video's representation.

Not consciously thinking about inclusivity related to STEM programs is precisely the problem, though. Even with a fair process managed by well-intentioned people, it is possible to end up with a biased result. Be the person who speaks up for inclusion; it can be uncomfortable, but it's worth doing.

Surveying Traditional STEM Barriers

Access to STEM education has a troubled history in terms of inclusion. Academic institutions have long implemented a variety of economic and social gatekeeping functions that limited certain people from gaining access to STEM careers.

Appendix D ("All Standards, All Students") of the NGSS focuses on accessibility and presents case studies about different inclusion issues, focused on seven groups of particular interest:

>> Economically disadvantaged students

>> Students from minority racial/ethnic groups

>> Students with disabilities

>> Students with limited English proficiency

>> Girls

>> Students in alternative education programs

>> Gifted and talented students

These groups of students have different historical barriers when it comes to STEM, although some may be correlated. Students with limited English proficiency might also be part of a racial/ethnic minority or be economically disadvantaged — and half of them will be girls. So those students get hit with several inclusion issues at the same time.

When you plan a STEM lesson, activity, or program, take the time to consider these inclusion concerns. Here are some key questions you should ask:

>> Is there an explicit monetary cost for the student's family?

>> Is there an intrinsic cost for the student's family (such as transportation, time, equipment, supplies, and so on)?

>> Is recruitment only reaching certain groups of students?

> » Are materials provided in all necessary languages to reach students?

> » Is the space physically accessible to students with disabilities?

REMEMBER

At some point, providing each STEM experience in a way that is accessible to each student may be impossible. But as you pay attention to this situation, you may notice certain groups of students being consistently excluded. As soon as you notice that exclusion, you must be sure that you're taking steps to correct it.

Incorporating Universal Design and Personalized Instruction

Universal design is a design principle that says a designer should make products, environments, and services as accessible as they can to the broadest range of people.

The concept of universal design comes from architecture, with the recognition that buildings and equipment weren't always accessible for all individuals. My mother, for example, has difficulty climbing the three steps from my driveway into my house when she visits. This and other accessibility issues in architecture led to the understanding that you should consider the needs of all users from the very initial steps of planning and designing your building. That same principle has expanded out into other areas, including education.

In other words, when initially designing your lesson (see Chapter 9), you need to consider what you can do to make sure all students can access it.

Instilling universal design in lessons

REMEMBER

Universal Design for Learning (UDL) focuses on providing multiple means for the student to interact with the material. Here are three principles of emphasis in UDL.

> » **Representation:** Students have multiple means of identifying the *what* at the core of the learning experience, through a mix of printed materials, demonstrations, lectures, videos, models, discussions, or other means.

> » **Action and expression:** Students have multiple ways to organize and express what they know back to their classmates and to the teacher.

> » **Engagement:** Students have multiple ways of engaging with and exploring the content of the lesson.

TIP

The student-centered approach to learning — as outlined in the 5E instructional model (see Chapter 9) — goes a long way toward providing a learning experience that is consistent with these three principles. You can dig much deeper into the UDL principles, and related guidelines for each principle, at `https://udlguidelines.cast.org/`.

Adjusting lessons when needed

Despite your best efforts at using UDL, you may not be able to make everything about a particular lesson accessible to every student. When this happens, you may have to offer certain adjustments for some students to fully engage with the material. Adjustments come in two varieties: accommodation and modification.

REMEMBER

An *accommodation* is an adjustment made to remove learning barriers. These adjustments are about guaranteeing that all students have access to the content. In contrast, a *modification* is an adjustment made to what a child is taught or expected to do. These adjustments are about giving students different objectives for them to achieve in the curriculum.

To offer a clear (and hopefully, relatively uncontroversial) example, consider the following potential lesson adjustments for a hearing-impaired student.

>> **Accommodation:** If a STEM lesson assignment involves watching a video about different types of environmental biomes and then writing a reflection essay on it, a hearing-impaired student in the class will need closed captioning as an accommodation to access the words from the video. But otherwise, the student can participate in the assigned task, and so won't need any modification.

>> **Modification:** If the STEM lesson involved studying harmonics and creating a musical instrument that could play different pitches, that *might* be a case in which the hearing-impaired student couldn't just do the same task like everyone else. That student's work related to sound waves and harmonics might need to be modified and therefore different from what the other students do.

WARNING

A student's Individualized Educational Plan (IEP) — or certain other types of plans for students with special educational needs — would guide the specific decision for how to adjust lessons based on that student's specific needs. Students with designated disabilities as established in IEPs have legal rights related to the instruction they receive, and you should be sure that the accommodations or modifications you provide align with the plan.

Regardless of what adjustment you might decide on for an individual student in the hypothetical harmonics example, note that the course of action you *shouldn't* take is to disregard how to best present the subject in the context of this child's needs. An immediate, no-adjustment solution — for example, placing the hearing-impaired student into a group with other students and assuming that they'll work around the lesson's difficulties — probably isn't the best course of action.

BUILDING ADJUSTMENTS

One common feature of a STEM project is that it involves the task of building an object. This is one place where certain physical disabilities might result in a challenge. Here are a variety of adjustments that can prove useful:

- A teacher or aid assists with the build, under the guidance of the disabled student or students.

- A teacher or aid prepares the building stages outside of class time, when the student is not present, and class time focuses on testing the builds rather than completing them.

- The student is part of a team where other students complete the building steps, but the student who's unable to build has a clear and distinct part of the project, such as giving the presentation to the class about their design process.

Consider the child's learning goals and specifics of their IEP in this case, and have discussions as needed with the child and their family about how they'd best like to approach the task.

5

The Part of Tens

Discover ten STEM lessons that you can easily provide for students with minimal prep.

Look into ten free or low-cost STEM resources that every teacher should be able to leverage in their classroom.

Chapter **16**

Ten STEM Lessons with Minimal Prep

Although building deep STEM lessons that connect diverse content areas in a real-world context is fantastic, sometimes you just need a quick activity to work into your lessons and class schedule.

In this chapter, I provide ten quick ideas that you can easily introduce to students and have them complete without a ton of prep time.

Providing Free Build Time

A great way for kids to become familiar with the STEM supplies you have available is to give them free build time. They can use anything, from building sets like Lincoln Logs, Erector Sets, LEGOs, and VEX build to just a collection of cardboard and other craft supplies. (Check out the *Teaching STEM For Dummies* Cheat Sheet at www.dummies.com for a list of materials.)

The idea of this *free building* activity is that the students decide what they want to build, with the only real constraint being the time and materials available. And free building can be especially good for a rainy or snowy day as an indoor recess activity. To really spice it up, add a presentation component, where students get to show off and explain their construction.

Accessing an Hour of Code

Hour of Code is a movement to make sure that as many students as possible have access to introductory computer science lessons. The goal is to give students a one-hour coding activity sometime during Computer Science Education Week, which falls in the first half of December. However, December can be a hectic month in schools, so fortunately you can plan the Hour of Code activity for any time of the year that fits better with a teacher's and school's schedule. You can find out more, and get access to free resources, on the Hour of Code website (https://hourofcode.com/us).

Designing Storage Solutions

You can enlist kids to consider ways to help with the storage of classroom materials. In this design challenge, kids are working with geometry and space constraints. You can have students physically or digitally draw designs or build models, even out of materials as simple as index cards or cardboard and tape. For a real challenge, students could create 3D printing designs for storage bins to go inside of a board game box to hold and organize the game pieces.

Making a Parachute

One of the simplest functional design projects, even appropriate in early grades, has students building a parachute to slow the fall of an object. You can make this project into a competition, where each team drops similar objects (with their parachutes attached) and the team with the longest fall time is the winner. Students can explore the properties of the best and worst parachutes to draw conclusions that will inform a second iteration of the design. This activity is a great example for students of the repetitive efforts involved in design challenges.

Setting Up a Tallest Tower Competition

For a quick and easy competitive activity, have students try to build the tallest tower to show off their engineering skills. You can do this challenge with any building materials you have available, but some classic, simple options include playing cards, index cards, craft sticks, straws, and scraps of cardboard — along with tape or glue to attach them together. (Another classic variant uses toothpicks and marshmallows.) Of course, you can also have a tallest tower challenge that uses building sets like LEGO.

Designing a Contraption

Start by showing students a video of a Rube Goldberg machine; you can get this from the Rube Goldberg competition or the "This Too Shall Pass" music video from the band OK Go. Then give the students a task — such as feeding a pet or turning off a light — and have them draw (but not actually build) a design using a series of at least four steps that are required to trigger and complete the task.

REMEMBER

You might want to give students a maximum number of steps as well, to keep the more precocious students from spiraling out of control and taking forever to finish their designs. Designing a contraption is a creative way to get the students thinking in an engineering mindset, but without the practical restriction of making the idea work in the real world.

Making Oobleck

With 1 cup of cornstarch and 3/4 cup of water, and maybe a dash of food coloring, you can make the bouncy *non-Newtonian fluid* (one that changes viscosity to behave like a solid when you apply force to it) known as *oobleck*. (If this sounds familiar, that's because it's named after a mysterious object that falls from the sky in a Dr. Seuss book.) Slowly mix the cornstarch and water, adding more of either (water or cornstarch) as needed to get the consistency right. Students should be able to squeeze the oobleck into a ball in their hand, and then as soon as they release the pressure, the solid ball will begin to turn into a fluid again. This activity involves a fun, hands-on chemistry experiment in material science that shows how different decisions result in slightly different outcomes.

Building a Catapult

With pretty much any building materials, students can construct a catapult to throw objects a given distance. Rubber bands or bungee cords are particularly useful to provide the elasticity needed to fire the catapult. You can make this a contest for distance thrown, and at higher grades, you could require students not only to fire their projectile but also to calculate the launch velocity from the catapult, touching not only on the engineering design of the catapult but also explicitly connecting it to mathematics and the underlying physical science principles of projectile motion.

Conducting a Remote Control Race

While the educational benefit of constructing robots and drones comes mostly from learning code, the constructions also frequently come with remote control options. Engaging these options means that you can use the robots (or drones) for a quick race while the students control them manually. Plan to set up brackets and have a mini tournament. The STEM skills involved include expanding engineering and technological proficiency, as well as growing intuitions related to motion, speed, and momentum.

Making an Egg Drop Challenge

The egg drop challenge is a classic culminating STEM project, in which the goal is to have students build a container for a raw egg that will allow the egg to survive a drop from a predetermined height unbroken. You can use many different material types for this, although it's highly desirable to include some sort of padding, like cotton balls or foam, among the options. This challenge uses engineering and design skills, and explores the physics of impacts and collisions.

Chapter **17**

Ten Key Resources for Every STEM Teacher

Teaching STEM is a resource-intensive process, and some of the resources you may cost money. But by writing extra grants or figuring out how to smooth-talk your district's finance folks, you can get started with STEM by using free (or relatively inexpensive) resources.

In this chapter, you discover a variety of resources that every STEM teacher can access at no or low cost.

Finding Online Interactive Simulations

You don't always have the equipment or space to do experimental tests of every scientific idea, but can carry out many experiments through online simulations (some of which are free).

University of Colorado Boulder's PhET Interactive Simulations for Science and Math (https://phet.colorado.edu/) is one of the best simulation resources. PhET originally stood for physics educational technology, although these days the university has moved beyond physics and now includes many science areas such as biology, Earth and space, chemistry, and mathematics concepts like natural selection and statistics.

TIP

Check whether your curriculum has simulations available. Penda Learning leverages the PhET simulations for their curriculum, while OpenSciEd has created their own simulations. You can also search online with some keywords plus the phrase "interactive simulation" to see whether you can find something to help with a specific subject.

Accessing Coding Platforms

Because computer science is such a key element of STEM education, having access to a quality coding platform for your students is important. A growing push in education is to make sure that all kids are exposed to computer science — starting in kindergarten. Teachers often have more advanced resources for middle and high school students, but the following resources provide great options for elementary students and teachers:

>> **CodeHS** (https://codehs.com/). At the time of this writing, the company's business model charges users to access elementary courses, as well as to access teacher tools and professional development. Many of the high school and middle school courses, however, are available for free.

>> **Code.org** (www.code.org/). This nonprofit is devoted to making computer science available to every student. They are the organization behind the Hour of Code (https://hourofcode.com/us) movement (see Chapter 16).

>> **Scratch** (https://scratch.mit.edu/) and **ScratchJr** (www.scratchjr.org/). The Scratch coding language is one of the most popular visual coding languages intended for use by children. An even more streamlined version, ScratchJr, uses simple icons accessible to pre-readers.

Using Government Websites

Many state and federal agencies have amazing educational outreach efforts. In addition to specific educational resources, many government websites offer scientific, technical, and statistical information that can provide a valuable resource when investigating a phenomenon — such as using the Department of Energy website to study forms of electricity production. Here are a handful of federal government websites with a more express emphasis on educational resources:

- » NASA's Space To Learn (http://stem.nasa.gov/)

- » NOAA Education (www.noaa.gov/education)

- » National Science Foundation (https://new.nsf.gov/)

- » EPA's Learning and Teaching about the Environment (www.epa.gov/students)

- » National Weather Service (www.weather.gov/education/)

- » Department of Defense STEM (https://www.dodstem.us/)

REMEMBER

Federal government websites also draw useful career connections, by outlining the work done in the industries associated with their mission. These connections sometimes include virtual visits with professionals in the industry. You can find similar resources, including local experts, through state departments and agencies.

Using Open Education Resources

One location for many of pre-existing lesson plans and resources is Open Educational Resources (OER) Commons (https://oercommons.org/), specifically their National Science Digital Library hub (https://oercommons.org/hubs/NSDL).

The OER Commons website enables you to search for resources within specific content areas that focus on Applied Science, Mathematics, Life Science, or Physical Science. The lessons you find there may not provide a full lesson following the 5E model (see Chapter 9), but they may provide a foundation for one of the phases. For example, you may find a lab that you can use for the Engage or Explore portion of the lesson or an assessment that can serve as the basis of the Evaluate phase.

Working with "Trash" STEM Building Supplies

While it's great to have the latest state-of-the-art gadgets, part of the benefit of STEM is that you don't actually need all of that stuff. Performing feats of engineering and design with simple materials that are commonly available is a way of tapping into students' creativity, as well as teaching them to work within a set of tight constraints. I offer examples of these sorts of supplies in the Teaching STEM For Dummies Cheat Sheet on www.dummies.com.

TIP

If you really want to lean into building with cardboard, you might also invest in a Makedo set of tools and fasteners. These allow you to cut, score, fold, and combine carboard together quickly and efficiently. You can find these gadgets at www.make.do/, and use them as a way of getting the most bang out of your cardboard-building buck.

Discovering University, Nonprofit, and Corporate Websites

Similar to governmental agencies, many universities and nonprofit websites provide a wealth of information related to their missions. For-profit corporations may sometimes also have useful information, but you need to take care in those situations (since any information on their websites is presumably there to serve the mission of making money).

Expressly educational nonprofits, like Khan Academy (www.khanacademy.org/), have a variety of videos that you can use for the Engage portion of a lesson or for students to use during the Explore step.

Using the Calculator Application

At one time, a major debate raged over whether students should even be allowed to have access to a calculator within a math class. That debate is over, largely by circumstance, and now the discussion is how to get students access to calculators in the most equitable way possible.

While some students or families might still spend money for a fancy calculator, the growing solution for this is the Desmos graphing calculator (www.desmos.com/), an open-access calculator that is the center of a free suite of math tools from Desmos Studios.

Finding Digital Editing Suites and Resources

As students do more work with technology, such as creating animations, video games, or slide decks, they need access to visual and audio resources to support this work. Part of the computer science standards outlined in Chapter 5 includes students becoming familiar with the legal responsibilities around using intellectual property found online — including making sure that they have legal authorization to use it in their creations.

A school that has a broadcasting class or a course in digital design likely has access to software licenses specifically for students taking those classes, but students more broadly may experience additional limitations on what resources they can use.

Fortunately, a number of free resources are available for various forms of sound, graphic, and video editing.

>> **HitFilm** (https://fxhome.com/) — video editing. Free version, but requires downloading.

>> **DaVinci Resolve 19** (www.blackmagicdesign.com/products/davinci resolve) — video editing. Free version, but requires downloading.

>> **Canva** (www.canva.com/) — image editing, with free educational plan.

>> **Pixlr** (https://pixlr.com/) — image editing, with free educational plan.

TIP

To make editing jobs easier for students, you should maintain a repository of graphic and audio files that they can access and know that they're able to use without violating copyright protections. Students can, of course, always create their own files.

Here are a handful of websites that are also useful for gathering these resources:

>> Freebies from Creative Fabrica (www.creativefabrica.com/freebies/)

>> Open Clipart (https://openclipart.org/)

>> Freesound (https://freesound.org/)

Locating Tinkercad and 3D Printing Websites

Tinkercad (www.tinkercad.com/) is a great resource for anyone who is teaching with 3D printers. It not only has 3D rendering software that you can use to design objects for printing, but also has a variety of simulators built into it, including the ability to simulate electric circuits (and a micro: bit) and a code block platform.

Other websites, such as PrintLab (https://weareprintlab.com/), provide training and certification for someone who needs to get up to speed on 3D printing. Check out Thingiverse (www.thingiverse.com/) to download files to print.

Looking for Citizen Science Communities and Resources

When looking for ways to engage students with science, one approach is to connect the science work done in the classroom with authentic research being done in the world through the citizen science movement.

You can find a government repository collecting these sites together at CitizenScience.gov, as well as individual sites — like Zooniverse.org and SciStarter.org — that aggregate citizen science opportunities.

Index

feedback, 202–203, 224–225

Feynman, Richard, 64

field journal, 226

FIRST LEGO League, 240

FIRST Robotics Competition, 241

5E model, 191–195

flipped classroom, 196

flow states, 237–238

flowcharts, 115

flows, in science, 96–97

food web, 91

forces, 67–69, 130

formal requirements, 211–212

formative assessment, as feedback, 224–225

formats, for coding, 118

fossils, 79

founders, of STEM education, 37

fractions, 54

A Framework for K-12 Science Education: Practices, Crosscutting Concepts, and Core Ideas, 41

free building activity, 273–274

free inquiry, 234, 235

Freebies from Creative Fabrica, 281

Freesound, 281

Fries-Gaither, Jessica (author), 227

Fröbel, Friedrich, 37

fuel, energy and, 75

function, in science, 97

functional office technologies, 103

G

Gagarin, Yuri, 37

game nights, 261–263

gameschooling, optimizing, 261–262

gamification, 31–32, 238–240

gaps, 212–213

Gary, Justin, 144

Generative AI, 121

genetic variation, 77

geological changes, 81

geological time, 81

geosphere, 83

giant nuclear furnace, 82

gifted, 99

Gilbert, Alfred Carlton, 37

goals, academic, 206–207

Goodwin, Bryan (author), 185

government websites, 278–279

grade level skills, 222–224

grammar check, 171–172

Grammarly, 171

The Grand Design (Mlodinow and Hawking), 91

gravity, 68, 81

group feedback, soliciting, 198–199

group project, 12

growth and development, 74

guided inquiry, 234

guide-on-the-side role, 235

guiding question boards, 197–198

H

habitats, 85

Hagy, Jessica, 25

hands and minds, engaging, 28–31

hard skills, 225–230

hardware, 110–111

Hattie, John, 29, 30, 188

Hawking, Stephen (author), 91

heat models, 84

heredity, 76–77

high ability, 99

high-quality STEM units, 214

high-stakes testing, 38

hinge point, 29

HitFilm, 281

hobbyists, 240–244

home/homeschool

about, 257

depth compared with breadth, 258–259

expanding beyond study time, 259–261

game nights, 261–263

personalizing learning goals, 257–259

uniqueness of goals, 258

homeostasis, 75

Homeschooling For Dummies (Kaufeld), 260

Hour of Code, 274

humanity, 84–86

hydrosphere, 83

hypothesis, 93, 166–167

I

icons, explained, 3–4

ILEARN assessment, 52

immediate memory, 182

impacts of computing, 107–108

implementation, 24

in the zone, 237–238

inclined planes, 132

incorporating day-to-day technology, 118–119

Indiana Academic Standards (IAS), 52

Individualized Educational Plan (IEP), 269

informal requirements, 211–212

information and communication, 103

information transfer, 71

information-gathering, 94

innovation, centering with invention, 126–132

input force, 131

inquiry-based learning, as a key principle of STEM education, 23–24

Instructional Design For Dummies (Land), 184

Integrated STEM, 10

intensity, for projects, 187

interaction, as a characteristic for learning through play, 237

interactive notebooks, 227

interconnected systems, 84

Internet, 105–106, 120–121

Invent to Learn: Making, Tinkering, and Engineering in the Classroom (Martinez and Stager), 186–187

invention, centering with innovation, 126–132

investigating, in engineering design process, 134

Investigation routine, 196

investigations, planning, 91–92

investment, increasing in education, 39–41

invisible force laws, 68

invisible forces, 68

Is Math Real?: How Simple Questions Lead Us to Mathematics' Deepest Truth (Cheng), 161

iterations
about, 202–203
as a characteristic for learning through play, 237
curriculum, 214–215
as a key principle of STEM education, 27
in STEM projects, 142–143

J

journals, 227

The Joy of X: A Guided Tour of Math, from One to Infinity (Strogatz), 161

Junior Solar Sprint, 241

K

K-12 Computer Science Framework, 55

Kahoot!, 109

Kaufeld, Jennifer (author), 260

Kennedy, John F., 37

Khan Academy, 260, 280

kinetic energy, 130

knowledge
levels of, 220–222
practical, 228–229

L

lab notebook, 226

Land, Susan M. (author), 184

landforms, changing, 83

Large Language Models (LLMs), 121

learning
determining outcomes, 208–209
evidence of, 209
levels of, 220–222
matching evidence to objectives, 223–224
mistakes as cornerstones of, 24
natural, 28
personalizing goals for, 257–259
through play, 31–32, 236–240
visible, 29

Learning and Teaching about the Environment, 279

Learning Evaluation and Assessment Readiness Network (ILEARN) Science assessment, 218

Learning That Sticks: A Brain-Based Model for K-12 Instructional Design and Delivery (Goodwin), 185

Leslie, Lauren (researcher), 168

lessons
about, 181–182
adjusting, 269–270
collaboration and, 203–204
connection of concepts, 184
deep learning, 188–189
developing, 209–210
ensuring time for student feedback, iterations, and reflection, 202–203
5E model, 191–195
flipped classrooms, 196
guiding question boards, 197–198
including direct instruction, 200
methods for teaching, 189–197
with minimal prep, 273–276
modifying published, 186

OpenSciEd instructional model, 195–197
Predict-Observe-Explain (POE) model, 190–191
probing background knowledge, 200–202
refining STEM project ideas, 186–188
repeated exposure, 183–184
six-phase learning model, 184–185
soliciting group feedback, 198–199
starting points for, 185–186
student roles and, 203–204
surface learning, 188–189
transfer learning, 188–189
transitioning input into long-term memory, 182–183

levers, 132

life, structure of, 73–75

life cycles, 74

life sciences, disciplinary core ideas (DCIs), 47–48

Life systems, 84

light patterns, 81

light properties, of objects, 71

light reflections, 71

light waves, 71

literacy, digital and technological, 34

living things, 72–75

logic, 160–161

long-term memory, transitioning input into, 182–183

loop, 114

M

magnetic attraction, 68

magnetism, 68

Makedo, 252, 280

maker fairs, promoting, 243

Maker Movement, 10

makerspaces, prioritizing, 242

The Makery, 242

About the Author

Andrew Zimmerman Jones earned a bachelor's degree in physics from Wabash College, followed up with a master's degree in mathematics education from Purdue University and a certificate in applied game design from Central Michigan University. Since he started teaching mathematics in Detroit Public Schools in 1999, his educational career has spanned the non-profit, private, and public sectors, with experience in math and science assessment, curriculum, and textbook design, as well as policy and implementation. He also served in the Indiana Department of Education for five years.

Jones was the Physics Guide at About.com for a decade, is the author of *String Theory For Dummies, Second Edition* and *Quantum Physics For Dummies, Third Edition*, and has been published on science topics in a variety of sources such as NPR, TED-Ed, and The Avengers and Philosophy. He currently serves as the STEM Coordinator for Anderson Community School Corporation in central Indiana, overseeing the district-wide implementation, training, and support of their STEM program in nine public schools, ranging from kindergarten through graduation. Andrew is also a robotics team coach, certified makerspace manager, husband, and father.

Dedication

To my parents, Don Jones and Nancy Zimmerman, for passing on their passion of educating the next generation to me.

Author's Acknowledgments

As always, thanks to my wonderful family for their patience as I have written and edited this book. My lovely wife, Amber, as always, encouraged me to follow up on the idea of my book proposal, and I'm always appreciative of her love and support. Thanks also to my sons, Elijah and Gideon, for putting up with my prolonged absences as I was trying to put my thinking down on the page.

This book would not be possible without the collaboration and work of the team of editors that helped bring it together, starting with Elizabeth Stilwell who accepted the proposal and put together a great team. Leah Michael and Marylouise Wiack, as always, did an exceptional job of going over every inch of this manuscript to identify places where text could be smoothed out or ideas could be clarified. This work was truly a collaboration.

The input of our technical editor, Megan Burnett, was also valuable throughout. Megan's years of experience in STEM helped to inform the book and provided reassurance that I was on the right track (or guidance when I wasn't).

Finally, I'd like to acknowledge the many teachers, mentors, researchers, authors, colleagues, and students over the years who have helped me develop a strong understanding of the interconnected nature of learning. This book draws on a wealth of personal experience and published research. It would not be possible without all those doing the work every day to improve education, in particular STEM education.

Publisher's Acknowledgments

Associate Editor: Elizabeth Stilwell

Project Manager: Leah Michael

Copy Editor: Marylouise Wiack

Technical Editor: Megan Burnett

Production Editor: Tamilmani Varadharaj

Cover Image: © Tara Moore/Getty Images